# Noncitizen Power

## Agency and the Politics of Migration

Tendayi Bloom

BLOOMSBURY ACADEMIC

LONDON • NEW YORK • OXFORD • NEW DELHI • SYDNEY

BLOOMSBURY ACADEMIC
Bloomsbury Publishing Plc
50 Bedford Square, London, WC1B 3DP, UK
1385 Broadway, New York, NY 10018, USA
29 Earlsfort Terrace, Dublin 2, Ireland

BLOOMSBURY, BLOOMSBURY ACADEMIC and the Diana logo are trademarks
of Bloomsbury Publishing Plc

First published in Great Britain 2023

A catalogue record for this book is available from the British Library.

A catalog record for this book is available from the Library of Congress.

ISBN: HB: 978-0-7556-0018-2
PB: 978-0-7556-0019-9
ePDF: 978-0-7556-0020-5
eBook: 978-0-7556-0021-2

Typeset by Deanta Global Publishing Services, Chennai, India
Printed and bound in Great Britain

To find out more about our authors and books visit www.bloomsbury.com and
sign up for our newsletters.

# Contents

# Acknowledgements

I owe a debt of gratitude to so many people for making this book possible. Primarily, there are those who gave their time to be interviewed, both named and anonymous; and those who spoke to me informally, welcomed me into meetings and other events, shared documents, and provided logistical help. This includes those who have taught me about global migration governance and those who have explained what it is like to live despite existing political and legal structures. A Leverhulme Trust Research Fellowship in 2018/19 enabled me to carry out empirical research, and I benefitted from a period as a visiting researcher at the Graduate Institute in Geneva in early 2019.

I am grateful to those who read and offered comments and suggestions on various parts of the book: Rothna Begum, Gerry Bloom, Sarah Bufkin, Alice Corr, May Darwich, Ekaterina E, Giuditta Fontana, Charlotte Galpin, Gervase Hood, Mandeep Kaur, Andrew Kauffmann, Lindsey Kingston, Andrew Knops, Mehdi Lazrak, Elaine Lebon-McGregor, Jess Melvin, Iulia Mirzac, Narissa Ramsundar, Richard Shorten, Silaja Suntharalingam, Katie Tonkiss, and Susan Williams; and to the anonymous reviewer for their incisive feedback. I also thank those to whom I presented ideas from this project at conferences and workshops and students in classes at both Management Center Innsbruck and the University of Birmingham. Their questions and comments have been invaluable. The book is certainly much better for the input of others and remaining errors are my own. The period over which I produced this book has been challenging in unexpected ways. That I have been able to complete it is thanks to the support and generosity of people who I thank privately and deeply. It has made it to publication thanks to the faith and patience of Tomasz Hoskins, Atifa Jiwa and Nayiri Kendir of Bloomsbury, and thanks to the attention to detail of their production team, including Sophie Campbell and Sharmila Mary.

In writing this book, as in all my work, I hope to honour those who have gone before me, who knew the reality of excesses of noncitizenship and who did all they could to protect me from it. Their memory continues to bring blessing. I also acknowledge those who are today forced to live and to act politically despite the international political and legal systems that organize our world. I hope I can contribute in some small way to a better future.

# Preface

It is October 2013, the second day of the second UN High-level Dialogue on International Migration and Development. In New York, the UN temporary General Assembly room is gradually filling. In front, representatives of Member States, agencies and organizations are filtering in. They take laptops from bags, adjust interpretation earpieces and leaf through the papers they picked up as they entered. Behind, the press set up their cameras. Lights flicker on in interpretation booths. Either side of me sit representatives of NGOs, UN agencies and spillover from the seats in front. Across the road and in the streets, more members of Trades Unions, Religious Groups and Migrant Associations – those who had been part of a civil society gathering the previous evening – are presumably beginning to assemble.

Meanwhile, somewhere in the Mediterranean Sea, the mid-afternoon sun sits above the wreckage of a boat that caught fire the day before. Reports suggest it had been packed with people travelling to Europe. Beneath the strip lighting and the media booth, sitting behind several hundred diplomats, it's hard to imagine the horror; impossible, in fact. The President of the UN General Assembly goes to the podium. He is projected on LCD screens around the room. There is a hush. He welcomes us. He mentions the previous day's discussions. Then he reminds us of that boat, the fire and the people. In the back of the room, there is murmured approval. The President asks us to observe two minutes' silence to honour them. It seems appropriate. We stand. Representatives of the world's leaders lower their heads. The room is silent, for about thirty seconds.

Throughout the day, representatives of States read out pre-prepared statements. Many of those sitting near me are frustrated. They shift in their seats. They speak under their breath. There is a slogan: 'Nothing About Us Without Us'. It gained particular traction a couple of years earlier among those mobilizing around the Domestic Workers Convention at the International Labour Organization. In this room, where most of us – from the highest diplomat down to an academic like myself – have moved to a new country at least once in our lives, migrants are spoken about in the third person. Mind you, few of us have any experience of what it is to migrate in fear, to leave family behind knowing it may be forever and to lack the documents that are needed to prove we are human. In this room, where most of us are migrants, few of us experience the world as noncitizens.

\* \* \*

In December 2018, in a purpose-built complex in the desert just outside Marrakech, another UN podium is projected on LCD screens. There are screens in the Plenary Room for the primary representatives of States, UN Agencies, International Organizations and others. There is also a screen hanging over the coffee machines in the cafeteria across the walkway. This is for those of us able to enter the complex but with no ticket for the main event. Before the intergovernmental conference starts, the gavel is struck for the adoption of the 'Global Compact for Safe, Orderly and Regular Migration'. In the cafeteria, it's difficult to hear what is being said above the clatter. We find out that the Compact has been adopted from someone watching the live stream on their laptop and listening through headphones. The cafeteria staff continue their work. After the plenary is over, the doors are opened so the rest of us within the complex can enter. In huge temporary buildings, the meetings continue. Meanwhile, as before, others congregate beyond the gates.

Some countries had already withdrawn from the process towards the Global Compact for Migration before the meetings in Marrakech began. They haven't sent representatives. And while the remaining State representatives meet here in Morocco, new anti-migration, anti-multilateralism protests erupt across the seas. Placards denounce the Swiss Ambassador to the UN as a traitor. The Belgian government is shaken; about a week after Marrakech, the Prime Minister would resign. Protestors in Canada, New Zealand and France block highways and disrupt cities. Some in Marrakech worry the Global Compact for Migration process might collapse. Speeches have been hurriedly rewritten. They emphasize the importance of sovereignty and make it clear that a commitment to the rights of migrants doesn't mean a right to migrate. Outside of North America, Europe and Australia, though, there is much wider State support for the Global Compact for Migration.

The day after the Compact was adopted, on the roof of a *riad* in the old city of Marrakech, perched under a cotton awning, a group of women from around the world, identifying themselves as part of migrant civil society, comment on the Global Compact for Migration. Their reflections are broadcast to their networks around the world via Facebook Live. Many of them had been involved, whether inside the buildings or on the streets, at the High-level Dialogue in New York in 2013 discussed earlier. They seem like old friends. Among their number are individuals who have played key roles in the global mobilization of migrant civil society in the context of the UN-level discussions. Some of them were invited formally to speak at the State-led meetings. Some of them were unable to gain access to the meetings at all. Those following via Facebook Live are even further removed from the UN discussions and even closer to the realities under discussion. These women and their networks provide a starting point for understanding noncitizen power in the international system.

# Introduction

## Why noncitizen power?

'Noncitizenship', as used here, is not the absence of citizenship. Instead, it functions *alongside* citizenship. It is a real, substantial, and indeed powerful, relationship in its own right. When people write 'non-citizen', with a hyphen, they are usually referring to someone whose political reality is framed as an absence: as a lack of citizenship. The emphasis is on what is missing rather than what is present. In this way, it is easier to overlook a person's interests, their politics and their agency. When I write 'noncitizen', without a hyphen, I refer to another type of relationship. In this book, I focus on noncitizen relationships with respect to the multistate system and examine how they function. This is understood in conjunction with the noncitizen relationships people may have with individual States. I have developed the discussion of State-level noncitizenship and noncitizenism elsewhere,[1] but here, the State level is relevant only insofar as it relates to the multistate system. The effect of noncitizenship in relation to the multistate system and the potential role of noncitizen power within it can be seen particularly clearly through analysing global migration governance. As such, this will form the background of this book, but it will not be the limit of it. Not all migrants experience noncitizenship strongly through their migration, and many of those who experience noncitizenship strongly are not migrants.

This book takes a noncitizenist approach. That is, it sets out to start from the perspectives of people insofar as they must live out their lives and politics *despite* the institutions that govern them. It examines the extent to which such individuals can have power in the international system and looks at what happens when they do. It suggests that noncitizen power is crucial to resolving some of our world's apparently most intractable challenges, demanding significant rethinking of how governance structures function. 'Noncitizen power', then, is the power of people insofar as, having to live their lives despite the structures that organize our world, they have access to understandings of those structures which are not available to others. This is made particularly crucial because there are some structures and mechanisms that may otherwise be invisible to those who experience the world mostly as citizens. The power of noncitizens is often framed as anomalous or threatening: in need of control. This book argues that in fact

(1) to acknowledge noncitizen power is to acknowledge the contribution of experts and to benefit from more accurate knowledge about reality. It is also (2) to acknowledge that for a governance decision to have legitimacy, it must be at least defensible to those most affected by it.

This book looks in particular at how noncitizenship functions when migration governance is discussed at the United Nations and at the extent to which noncitizen power is able to impact those discussions. It was people crossing borders they had been told not to cross that created the impetus to produce a Global Compact for Migration, but those irregular border crossers were barely consulted in the process to create the Compact. This needs to be seen in context.

When governments talk about 'migration control', what they're talking about usually isn't really controlling migration per se. It's about controlling who should be included in the community of those presumed to have agency over their own mobility. Some people move about the world easily, without noticing migration controls. Other people don't even leave their homes and are affected by them. Moreover, the same tools that control who should have agency also often control whose voices are heard in discussions about migration governance. This risks reinforcing the status quo. Some people have fought back against this in different ways and from different positions. This book introduces some of them and examines their role in bringing noncitizen power to bear on discussions of migration governance. Insofar as people live out their lives *thanks to* or *beyond* migration governance structures, they may not even notice them. This means that insofar as people live *despite* them, they bring unique and crucial insights and analyses. Noncitizen power is, therefore, an important mechanism in developing more evidence-based and equitable global structures. Yet it is currently often blocked from the governance discussions where it is most needed, dependent upon others to be heard.

This can be seen in the context of the Global Compact for Migration, the first globally negotiated document of its kind, which UN Member States adopted in 2018. The process to create the Global Compact was launched because, following economic crises and civil wars in countries around the world, larger numbers of people moved across borders they had been told not to cross and States' effort to stop the increased movement gave rise to suffering and loss of life. This was photographed and filmed by journalists and the moral outrage, as well as security concerns, that arose helped to drive the decision to take global cooperation towards a more joined-up and humane migration infrastructure seriously. Those people whose movement had initiated this process were not, for the most part, present within meeting rooms as the Compact was drafted and negotiated. However, there were some ways in which noncitizen insights were brought into discussions. This included (1) formal representation, (2) bridging by people who engaged both in formal discussions and social movements and (3) engagement through claiming both noncitizenship and liminal citizenship. This was made possible because of the work of many people in different positions as well as the input of some large organizations who opted to support such participation. This involved a vast and complex array of actors contributing in diverse important ways. It is not possible to portray this complexity here. Instead, this book picks out some actors whose work helps to indicate some core dynamics of what took place.

This book draws upon a decade of observation of global migration governance discussions and civil society engagement in them. It has benefitted from interviews with people engaging in a variety of ways as well as with those unable or unwilling to engage. Some interviewees allowed me to use their names where I thought this would be helpful. Others remain anonymous. All the interviewees, including those which are not directly quoted, have informed my thinking in important ways. Most interviews and informal discussions were conducted in English, but some were in French or Spanish. Alongside formal interviews and informal discussions, insight is also derived from policy documents, statements, and observations of the activities surrounding the key meetings under discussion. This examination of the Global Compact for Migration process is also located within a wider discussion of noncitizenship, how it functions on the global level, and what it means for the evidence base, the legitimacy, and the sustainability of governance, particularly with regard to migration. It became clear that those who wanted to bring noncitizen perspectives into meetings in various ways were required to do this within an institutional landscape not built for this purpose. Though there were tensions between people engaging in different ways in these processes, in this book I suggest that participants from a range of positions have played crucial roles in creating a political process that was new in both form and content. In this book, I examine this process through a noncitizenist lens.

The UN's commitment to cooperation for peace, prosperity and justice makes our contemporary world possible. Coming about after brutal wars, the States that created the UN aimed to prevent a repeat of the appalling institutionalized violence of the first half of the twentieth century.[2] But its parameters were negotiated by the representatives of the leaders of States and of Empires, on behalf of their citizens. The UN's founding document, its *Charter*, opens with the words: 'We the peoples.'[3] It assumes that we, the world's people, are divided into 'peoples' and that all of us will be represented at the 'Parliament of Man' through our recognized political memberships of

Nation States.[4] Citizenship, which is bestowed by States (or some other status, which is also bestowed by States), is still the only recognized relationship for an individual within that system.[5] The place of noncitizens within this – for people insofar as they must live out their life and perform their politics *despite* this institutional structure – is not easily understood. It makes people's experiences of the world as noncitizens seem anomalous. It can also make such individuals seem either powerless or threatening and sometimes, inconsistently, both. This book argues that perpetuating this error in key institutions, even inadvertently, has serious and observable ramifications for the system as a whole and for people functioning within it. Recognition and normalization of noncitizen power is essential to securing a stable and sustainable future for all.

Our world is blighted with messy, severe, often insidious, inequalities. These are based on a mix of accidents of birth and arbitrary allocations of status. A person born in one place to certain parents may never encounter the barriers that someone born elsewhere, or to other parents, must overcome at every turn.[6] The bizarre implications of this inequality are clearest at its extremes. Consider the context of migration. Those born in the most stable and wealthiest countries, to parents with the most social and other resources, may have the least need to change country. And yet, they can board budget airplanes and cross borders with cursory document checks. For a similar journey, someone born in an unstable and/or poor country, to disadvantaged parents, may be prevented from moving at all or have to raise huge funds in order to do so. Many people, unable to enjoy peace, prosperity and security within the international system, must not only live out their lives *despite* it but also challenge the system despite the system itself. Their perspective is, both symbolically and in reality, absent from how that system has been built. In fact, they are often simultaneously invisible to the global system while bearing its heaviest burdens.

This book argues that precisely these perspectives are needed when global governance is discussed, created and critiqued. This is because people with experience of noncitizenship are both experts with respect to that system and key stakeholders within it. Yet existing structures make it particularly difficult for such perspectives to be represented. Allowing endemic exclusion from the international system to persist is detrimental to everyone, including those who live mostly as comfortable citizens. In this book, I'll use the language of 'epistemic injustice' to help to explain the layered way in which this functions.[7] I'll show how in fact noncitizen power has entered into discussions of migration governance, with benefits for sustainability and coherence, but that it has done this *despite* the surrounding structures.

The experience of 'noncitizenship' in relation to the international system gives individuals a unique insight into how our world works. Leaving those particularly affected by noncitizenship out of the conversation about global governance does not only risk silencing specific voices. It also makes it possible to overlook their existence and so remain ignorant of key aspects of reality. A citizenist focus which ignores noncitizenship leads to policy frameworks that are designed on the basis of incorrect facts about the world as well as overlooking the needs, interests, and insights of some subsection of humanity. This book looks at the positive role of noncitizen power in finding new ways to frame discussion of migration. It also interrogates how migration governance infrastructure creates barriers to the inclusion of noncitizen perspectives in the discussion of migration and the implications of this for how those discussions are able to proceed, irrespective of the intentions of organizers. Noncitizenism starts from the idea that all people should be presumed to be agentive and potential interlocutors. This isn't so much about sympathy for, or empathy with, noncitizens. It is rather about deference to, and solidarity with, those who have expertise-by-experience.

For a while now, the inclusion of global civil society, largely in the form of NGOs, has been seen by those involved in global governance processes as a mechanism for achieving greater democratic accountability in the international system and to bring otherwise hidden voices into key discussions.[8] In the context of global migration governance, the engagement of civil society goes well beyond NGOs. A complex array of civil society organizations (CSOs) and non-governmental organizations (NGOs) and others have been active since the 1990s. They make up a complex civil society landscape at this level. This book considers the ways and extent to which this facilitates the inclusion of noncitizen expertise. In September 2016, representatives of UN Member States unanimously declared that a new approach to human mobility was needed. They agreed to negotiate the first-ever global agreement on how migration should be governed: a 'Global Compact for Safe, Orderly and Regular Migration'. This would be negotiated alongside a separate compact on refugees. Global migrant civil society networks and networks of networks mobilized to engage in the process.

In February 2018, a first draft of the Global Compact for Migration, intended as a roadmap for organizing global migration governance in the years ahead, was released. For many of those who had been part of the drafting, it felt like the dawn of a new era. Others were less positive. The draft document was then negotiated by State representatives in New York, edits were made, and the final version was adopted in December 2018, at an intergovernmental conference in Marrakech and confirmed at the General Assembly in New York that same month. It had the support of the overwhelming majority of

UN Member States. Throughout this process, migrant rights activists and members of movements fought to be heard. They did this within negotiating rooms and outside the gates. Others didn't find out about the Compact until the process to create it was well underway or else not at all. During the State negotiations, representatives of those movements, along with NGOs, religious organizations, trades unions and academics, as well as UN agencies watched as commitments were weakened and ambitions reduced. However, many still celebrated a document which explicitly tempered sovereignty with human rights and which addressed several issue areas that had not been addressed in this way before. They had been part of the process to create this document to an extent not seen previously, and yet their participation was constrained.

Towards the end of the process, a new constituency found out about the Compact. This was made up of people opposed to multilateralism, globalization and international migration. Protestors from this constituency took to the streets, mostly in wealthy cities, around the world, and they took to the internet to criticize the Global Compact and the principles of multilateralism on which it stood. Governments which had seen the Compact as a way to respond to, and to contain, people crossing borders now also had to respond to marchers on the streets of their capitals, demanding harsher barriers to human mobility and withdrawal from global discussions of migration.

About a year after the Compact was adopted, the emergence of Covid-19 provided a new lens for considering migration governance. The most privileged people, who could move easily about the world, were spreading a disease that would go on to have severe effects – both directly and indirectly – for some of the poorest. The value of noncitizen power is made ever clearer by experiences of Covid-19. Over this time, the governance of mobility has been evolving, but although the pandemic may seem unprecedented in living memory, the evolution of migration governance in this context has largely continued along traditional lines. Outdated tropes that frame who should be able to make decisions about their own mobility have been both unsettled and entrenched. In the first year of the pandemic, commentators already began to speak of two mobility crises: (1) a 'crisis of immobility', leading to efforts at reopening global migration routes;[9] and (2) a 'crisis of mobility', as measures associated with infection control forced people to move in new ways.[10] However, underlying each of these is a crisis that doesn't really relate to mobility per se but to agency. Crucial to people's experiences of mobility has, for centuries, been their status or relationship with respect to the international system.

Iris Marion Young's 2011 posthumously published book, *Responsibility for Justice*, ends with the following exhortation:

Those who are beneficiaries of racialized structures with unjust outcomes [. . .] can properly be called to a special moral and political responsibility to recognize our privilege, to acknowledge its continuities with historical injustice, and to act on an obligation to work on transforming the institutions that offer this privilege, even if this means worsening one's own conditions and opportunities compared to what they would have been.[11]

This book draws attention to those structures that one way or another require some people to live out their lives *despite* an international system that benefits others. In starting from the perspective of those who experience the international system in this way the noncitizenist lens is required in order to develop a clearer picture of how the world functions. Having this more accurate picture will help in the development of a world where more people are able to pursue their well-being mutually, promoting broader access to cooperation for peace, prosperity and justice.

# 1

# Noncitizenism is the new '-ism'

There are a variety of '-isms'. Some describe systems of prejudice, which focus on some aspect of a person, like 'racism', 'sexism' or 'citizenism' (the last of these will be explained later). Then there are those that express political movements like 'liberalism', 'conservatism', or 'feminism'. Feminism, in its various iterations, has focused on how particular characteristics such as gender and sex affect how people are positioned in structures of power, domination, and recognition. Noncitizenism starts with the political relationship itself.[1] There are, then, diverse dimensions to noncitizen politics. The logic of noncitizenism can help to demonstrate solidarity between them, even when they seem divergent.

Noncitizenship, as understood here, is not the absence of citizenship. Whereas the hyphenated term 'non-citizenship' emphasizes a lack of, or opposite to, citizenship, this is not the case for the unhyphenated term 'noncitizenship'. Indeed, one person may experience both citizenship and noncitizenship with respect to the multistate system. In this book, I focus on noncitizenship in relation to the multistate system and discuss noncitizenship in relation to States only insofar as it relates to this international noncitizenship.[2] A person is in a noncitizen relationship with the multistate system insofar as they must live out their life *despite* that system. This does not necessarily make that person abject or dependent, but it does mean that their relationship includes a struggle over some component of their ability to act as they see fit, that is, over their 'agency'.

This chapter introduces three political actors whose politics cannot easily be understood through the language of citizenship alone. These individuals are experiencing noncitizenship in different ways. They each draw on their unique insights from the perspective of noncitizenship in developing their politics. These examples illustrate some ways in which noncitizen power functions. I suggest that these individuals wield it as a positive force and that this uncovers reasons for centring noncitizen power, and so promoting noncitizenism, in progressive politics.

There need not be any *intentional* effort to obscure noncitizen perspectives for them to be obscured.[3] Most people who participate in the formal processes of making, analysing and publically critiquing policy experience those institutions mostly as citizens. They, like me, are little confronted by the constraints it creates. This helps the citizenist perspective to dominate and noncitizen insights to be obscured.[4] Those whose own understanding of the world is privileged may not recognize that there are realities that they do not encounter (this will be developed further in the discussion of 'epistemic injustice' in subsequent chapters).[5] Key to addressing this will be to ensure that people who are experiencing the international system mostly as noncitizens are able to be part of framing and describing that system. It also requires that those with a mostly citizen experience consciously try to adopt a noncitizenist lens and defer to noncitizen expertise. One aspect of this will be to try to understand impacts of noncitizenship on the function of a person's agency.

## Ghillar Michael Anderson

On 26 January 1972, a small group of activists raised an umbrella on the lawn outside the Parliament of Australia building in Canberra. They called this a 'Tent Embassy'.[6] Among them was Michael Anderson, who also uses the name Ghillar. The day before, then Australian Prime Minister William ('Billy') McMahon had announced that Aboriginal land would be *leased* to Aboriginal people. On hearing this, Anderson reflects that it 'turned my stomach upside down'.[7] And so, the small group, along with a newspaper photographer, borrowed money from the communist party to rent a car to drive from Sydney to Canberra to set up the Embassy.[8] As shown in Figure 1.1 the Embassy was initially formed under a beach umbrella. The symbolism of the Embassy was multi-layered. Crucially, as Gary Foley, who joined the protest soon after it had started, observed: the 'government had declared us aliens in our own land [. . .] we needed an Embassy just like all the other aliens'.[9] That is, they were not acting *qua citizens* but rather arguing that if they are not going to be treated as full citizens, then they needed to have the rights held by members of other non-Australian nations. It was a protest for land, but also for agency, for Aboriginal people to have 'both land and the ability to determine their own futures'.[10]

On first glance, this could seem to be a claiming of 'non-citizenship' with respect to Australia. But it is more than this and particularly so when considered beyond the State level. It also draws attention to a reality in which First Nations people have been forced to live out their lives *despite* the Australian State, in a special relationship with it, and with the agreement of the international system. As Anderson says of the initial Tent Embassy, 'we

**Figure 1.1** Left to right, Billy Craigie, Bert Williams, Michael Anderson, and Tony Coorey founding the Tent Embassy outside Parliament House, Canberra, Australia, 27 January 1972, Mitchell Library, State Library of New South Wales, SEARCH Foundation. Creative Commons Attribution 4.0.

had a very clear line as to what it is we were after: land rights, civil liberties and civil rights'.[11] It wasn't exactly about citizenship and it wasn't exactly about non-citizenship. In this way, I suggest, it can usefully be described as noncitizenist.

Today, Anderson plays a leadership role as Convenor of the Sovereign Union, a union of First Nations in Australia seeking sovereignty. The Sovereign Union doesn't claim to speak for all First Nations people in Australia but rather argues that each of the many national groups should be able to govern and represent themselves. When I first contacted him about this book project, he referred me to the Sovereign Union website. On that site, in 2019 Anderson explained: '[w]e are Sovereign Peoples, always was, always will be. We are NOT Australians. We are who we are. Let them never forget that this is the case.'[12] He describes the policies of the Australian State as a continued process of colonization and elimination of Aboriginal peoples. He frames his struggle for the rights of individuals not as a struggle for citizen rights but rather as a struggle against enforced citizenship: against Australian 'assimilationism'. However, this struggle takes place within a territory that is governed by Australia. It is not possible to live there without some relationship with the State.

The politics of the Tent Embassy, then, directly challenges citizenism. Anderson, like the other founders of the Tent Embassy, *is* a citizen of Australia, but he also experiences noncitizenship in relation to Australia and in relation to the multistate system. Only five years before the Tent Embassy was set up, a referendum had been held in Australia in 1967, which finally determined that Indigenous Australians like Anderson should be added to the Australian census. As Linda Burney, the first Indigenous woman elected to the Australian Parliament, observed in her maiden speech in 2016: 'I was born at a time when the Australian government knew how many sheep there were but not how many Aboriginal people.'[13] Anderson, like Burney, demonstrates the complexity of this relationship.

In setting up their Embassy, Anderson and his fellow campaigners were also asserting that the relationship between Aboriginal peoples and Australia is an *international* one. However, while Anderson and others engage with the UN, for example, and use International Treaties to support their claims, they also argue that the international system is not designed to promote their struggles. It is built upon a logic that recognizes the sovereignty of Australia and not of the many other nations living on the same lands. In this way, I suggest, they also function as noncitizens in relation to that international system. This is illustrated provocatively through the work of another activist, Burnum Burnum.[14] Describing himself as influenced by his own experience in Mission Homes, Burnum Burnum was involved in establishing the Tent Embassy and in campaigning for Aboriginal rights,[15] both as an activist and as an official.[16] On 'Australia Day' 1988 (the day when many Australians celebrate European settlement in Sydney), to try to illustrate the way in which international politics was still interpreted through a colonial gaze, Burnum Burnum 'parodied the arrival of the British fleet at Botany Bay by planting an Aboriginal flag on the white cliffs of Dover and claiming sovereignty over Britain. Beads and trinkets were given to a bemused passer-by who turned out to be an Australian tourist.'[17] In Figure 1.2, Burnum Burnum holds the flag in front of the cliffs. Another account describes his planting a flag in Trafalgar Square in London and making a now-famous declaration, claiming Great Britain for 'the Aboriginal Crown of Australia – and telling the natives that we're bringing them good manners and refinement', and offering the opportunity for the more advanced British people to learn the language of the Pitjantjajara.[18]

Burnum Burnum was demonstrating the absurdity of the idea that anyone could 'discover' the land on which someone else was living and simply claim it for themselves. Yet the colonial logics that appeared to legitimize the 'discovery' and violent settlement of Australia persist. They influence how people today relate to the international system.[19] They mean both that First Nations in Australia continue to lack full sovereignty and that the UK's

**Figure 1.2** Burnum Burnum plants Aboriginal flag in the sand beneath the white cliffs of Dover, UK, Invasion Day / Australia Day, 26 January 1988. PA Images / Alamy Stock Photo.

sovereignty was not toppled by its discovery in 1988 by Burnum Burnum. Like the Tent Embassy, this highlights how international structures make certain norms unquestionable, while certain sorts of politics remain unthinkable. A noncitizenist approach is needed in order to see these structures in a different light. Acts like those of Burnum Burnum and Michael Anderson are important in this. Noncitizenism as seen here involves a political movement for recognition of those who must live, act politically, and flourish *despite* the arrangement of States that currently exists. Noncitizenism recognizes a politics that is often obscured or overlooked and which is mostly silenced by a dominant citizenist focus.

## Masud Rana

One of the most famous fictional heroes in Bengali literature is Masud Rana, Agent MR-9, who features in hundreds of novels in a series launched in 1966 by author Kazi Anwar Hussain.[20] He has been described as Bangladesh's answer to James Bond.[21] Each novel reportedly opens in the same way:[22]

An untameable daredevil spy of Bangladesh Counter Intelligence. On secret missions he travels the globe. Varied is his life. Mysterious

**Figure 1.3** Masud Rana showering in spring water, Cameron Highlands, Malaysia. Drik Picture Library Limited. Image by Shahidul Alam, 2017.

and strange are his movements. His heart, a beautiful mix of gentle and tough. Single. He attracts, but refuses to get snared. Wherever he encounters injustice, oppression, and wrong, he fights back. Every step he takes is shadowed by danger, fear, and the risk of death. Come, let us acquaint ourselves with this daring, always hip young man. In a flash, he will lift us out of the monotony of a mundane life to an awesome world of our dreams. You are invited. Thank you.

In 2015 in the Cameron Highlands of Malaysia, photographer Shahidul Alam met someone identifying himself as Masud Rana. He was an irregular immigrant from Bogra (also known as Bogura) in Northern Bangladesh.[23] Alam told me that he has no reason to think 'Masud Rana' is a pseudonym. Either way, the implied linkage between a fearless secret agent and an irregular migrant is interesting. It perhaps echoes the framing of migration as epic and as part of a long heritage of seafaring that has been traced by Joya Chatterji through generations of published narratives of Bangladeshi emigrants.[24]

Alam's photograph of Rana, which appears here as Figure 1.3, is part of a project which uses photography to map and record the experiences of Bangladeshi migrant workers around the world. Alam first realized the power of images for social activism while he was himself a Bangladeshi living overseas, pursuing doctoral studies in London, UK. He has gone on to use photography to advocate for rights for Bangladeshis both at home and overseas as part of what he calls a 'battle for social justice'.[25] The Bangladeshi diaspora is one of the largest globally, with estimates ranging from 1.2 million to 7.1 million members,[26] spread mainly across the Middle East, Europe, Asia, North America and Australia. Rana is just one of many individuals, including engineers, entrepreneurs, factory workers and agricultural labourers that Alam has photographed.[27] We will return to Alam in Chapter 7. Here, the discussion's focus is Rana and his colleagues in the Cameron Highlands.

In 2019, Bangladesh was the fastest-growing economy in the Asia-Pacific region, having more than halved poverty in twenty-five years.[28] A report from HSBC predicted that Bangladesh would move from being the forty-second largest economy in 2018 to the twenty-sixth in 2030.[29] And yet Bangladesh still continues to contend with the impact of centuries of colonization, decolonization and conflict, as well as bearing disproportionate effects of climate change.[30]

When India was partitioned by the British in 1947, causing huge displacement and unrest, Bangladesh was part of Pakistan. It gained full independence from Pakistan in 1971 after a bitter war,[31] the year before Michael Ghillar Anderson and his colleagues were setting up the Tent Embassy in Canberra in Australia. Meanwhile, Bangladesh's geography makes it particularly susceptible to the effects of climate change. This includes the risk of flooding in coastal regions resulting from both increased rainfall and rising sea levels and drought in its north-western and south-western agricultural areas.[32] More frequent cyclones and other adverse weather events, with increased water salinity, affect crops, and weather changes affect the incidence of infectious disease and access to water.[33] A significant number of Bangladeshis have already been displaced internally as a result of climate change, many of whom are believed to be at risk of further displacement as climatic conditions continue to shift.[34]

Bangladesh has been undergoing meteoric economic growth in recent years. This is associated with other improvements, like an increase in life expectancy (from 58.2 in 1990 to 72.6 in 2019) for example. Yet life expectancy in Bangladesh is still comparatively low, and in 2020, the UNDP ranked Bangladesh 133 out of 189 countries in terms of 'human development'.[35]

In 2021, Bangladeshi passports remained near the bottom of the Global Passport Index, which ranks passports according to the ease of travel of their holders. At the time of writing, a Bangladeshi passport requires a pre-entry visa before moving to any of 157 countries.[36] To travel, Masud Rana in Figure 1.3 would have had to prove he had particular skills or bank balance or else find ways around the international institutional structures that seek to exclude him. In some ways, then, he would have had to act like his namesake, the 'untameable daredevil spy'. Before he even left home, Rana was in a relationship with international political structures that were not designed for his benefit. The history of colonization from abroad and the international community's failure to act on climate change have an impact on life in Bangladesh, while the global governance of migration makes it difficult for Rana to access international community's benefits elsewhere. The international system of States is not designed to help him. Instead, he must live out his life *despite* it.

Shahidul Alam explains that a *dalal*, or manpower agent, likely arranged for Rana to travel to Malaysia, where he was working on a plantation in the Cameron Highlands.[37] One 2009 study found that 53 per cent of Bangladeshi migrant workers have used a *dalal*[38] through a relationship which is mostly informal and so difficult to trace if things go wrong.[39] From what he told Alam, Rana recognizes that he is living within a system of domination and that the way the political structures are framed makes him more vulnerable to others, impairing a key dimension of his agency. Alam notes of Rana and his colleagues that they are

> Too poor to go home, they did all the work locals would not touch, and stayed hoping to recover the money they had paid the *dalal*, the police, and the many other parasites that lived off migrant workers. 'There is only one law here', said Masud. 'The word of the owner.'[40]

They must pay the police to leave them alone. They are undocumented and so particularly vulnerable to others. Glorene Das, whom we will meet in Chapter 3, based in Malaysia, has written about the conditions for workers like Rana. She observes that because workers are generally paid on a piece rate, rather than through a fixed wage, their pay is widely variable. In addition, she writes, they are often dependent on the employer for living and working conditions.[41] In Malaysia, it is reported that about 30 per cent of the workforce is composed of migrant workers, though the exact number is unknown.[42] As in Das's observations, such individuals can find themselves presumed excludable. A report in 2019 identified that, like elsewhere, migrant workers in Malaysia experience problems of workplace safety, fees for contracts, non-payment of wages and difficulties pursuing redress for crimes suffered.[43] Others have highlighted raids on homes and workplaces,[44] arrests and brutality in detention, followed by release without charge.

Rana and his colleagues are not the only 'foreigners' in the Cameron Highlands. The region is known for tourism. Many migrant workers also work in tourism, welcoming other visitors. The tourists have a different relationship with the international system, a different relationship with the Malaysian State and a different experience of the Highlands. Many obtain visas with ease at airports and move smoothly about the country. They don't need to approach a *dalal* or pay off the police. They don't experience the noncitizenship of Rana. The different ways in which these groups of foreigners relate to Malaysia and the international system are affected by history. Today's major tea plantations in the Highlands were established by British settlers using Sri Lankan and Indian, as well as local, workers to clear the forests.[45] British tourists who travel to the region today obtain visas at the airport. A writer for the travel series *Lonely Planet* suggests that tourists should visit plantation houses, eat strawberries and stop for 'English Afternoon Tea'.[46] But the colonial past is not only apparent in an afternoon tea taken on a veranda. The implications of that system are pervasive, as will be picked up explicitly in Chapter 2.

Masud Rana's noncitizenship in relation to the international system developed long before he moved. Climate change driven by emissions from elsewhere and historic global structures arising from colonialism and decolonization meant that he already experienced a noncitizen relationship with the international system while he was at home in Bangladesh. It was this international noncitizenship that meant that if he wanted to move, it would be *despite* the international system. It is also this which forces him to live as a noncitizen in Malaysia, while others enjoy quasi-citizenship. Like his namesake, it seems that Rana too tries to push back against injustice and faces 'danger, fear, and the risk of death' as he does so.

## Ekaterina E

Ekaterina E is part of a unique mobilization of Americans without citizenship of any State, persons described as 'stateless'.[47] When I asked E if there was an image she'd like me to use to represent her, she suggested two images by stateless artist Mawa Rannahr. The first of these, Figure 1.4, shows the great weight of papers and the lack of them on a stateless person's life.

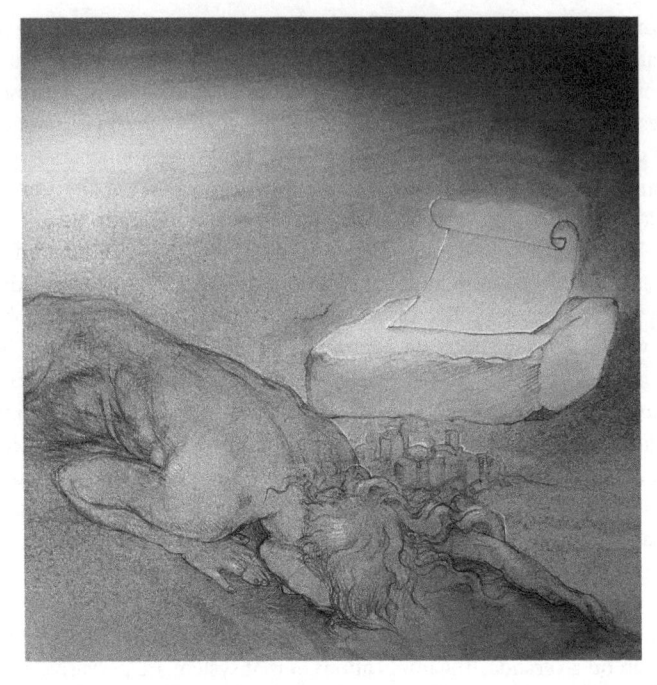

**Figure 1.4** 'The Weight of Paper', Mawa Rannahr, pencil on paper. This is the first of two images that Ekaterina E selected from work by stateless artist Mawa Rannahr to illustrate this section.

Without citizenship of any State, a person may in turn struggle to access the international system of rights, security and prosperity. But, as E and her colleagues demonstrate, stateless persons should not be seen as abject. Instead, insofar as a person without any recognized citizenship is able to use their agency, they must do it *despite* the State and *despite* the system of States. Michael Anderson, mentioned earlier, was demanding the recognition of noncitizenship in Australia, where formally he held citizenship. As a citizen of Bangladesh, Masud Rana had limited rights to travel and limited rights once in Malaysia. The situation for Ekaterina E and her colleagues is different, but she herself also identifies important solidarities.[48]

The situation of statelessness is widely misunderstood.[49] E explains that not only does she face the challenges arising from statelessness, but she also faces the meta-challenge that there is 'a near total lack of public awareness around the issue [of statelessness] not only among the legal and advocacy circles, but in the immigrant community itself'.[50] That is, there is not only a blindness about statelessness but an unawareness that there is even something to be blind about.[51] As a result, E argues, stateless persons are left 'invisible, voiceless, and completely unprotected, and at the same time unable to leave to seek protections elsewhere in the world'.[52] And yet, E and her colleagues have found a voice through creating an advocacy organization founded and led by stateless persons in the United States. They have called it United Stateless.[53]

E became stateless for reasons beyond her control. She made what she and her family thought was a temporary journey. The USSR had fallen in 1991 and in 1994 the young E left for a visit in the United States, travelling on her Soviet passport.[54] While she was away, the landscape of citizenship in the territory she had left changed dramatically. By the time she tried to register for the new citizenship, it was too late. Her passport had become meaningless. Decades later, she still lives in the United States, without citizenship of any country and without any route to obtain one. Without a citizenship, she cannot have her own bank account or social security number. She cannot work regularly and she cannot travel internationally.[55] Writing in 2020, she observed,

> I, for example, have been separated from my family for over 26 years, and am unable to even deport myself due to the fact that no country considers me its citizen, including the country of my birth.[56]

Elsewhere, she explains that when she learnt that her father was dying, 'I made the heart-wrenching decision to deport myself to be by his side. I was denied deportation'.[57] She is in a relationship with the State where she lives, but it is neither primarily one of citizenship nor of a mere absence of citizenship. I suggest that we could describe her overriding relationship with the United States and with the multistate system as one of noncitizenship.

E experiences the international system intensely and politically. E explains that she and others in United Stateless fight for both a route to citizenship of the United States, their home country, and recognition of stateless persons within the international system as people with rights and contributions to make.[58] The power of this is apparent in one of their first actions. E explains that she and her colleagues learnt that UNHCR listed the number of stateless persons in the United States as '0'. This was absurd. In response, they launched the campaign: #WeAreNotZero. Their pressure led to change. The official number of stateless persons in the United States was altered from '0' to '–'. That is, there was an acknowledgement that the number was unknown. This then led to efforts to map the realities of statelessness in the United States. Members of United Stateless have worked with the US government, UNHCR and academics to try to address this gap in knowledge.[59] As a result, in 2020, it was estimated that 218,000 US residents were 'potentially stateless' or 'potentially at risk of statelessness'.[60]

This change was possible because the unique expertise-by-experience of members of United Stateless meant they could see realities that were invisible to others. It was made possible by their noncitizen power. This is not only to the benefit of people who share these experiences. Correcting US and UNHCR data on statelessness may provide some recognition for stateless persons, but it also helps everyone to have a more accurate understanding of reality. Noncitizen power is borne of a deeper knowledge of international political structures. Insofar as people relate to States and to the international system as citizens, they may not even notice the political structures that hold it together. It is insofar as a person relates as a noncitizen that they encounter those structures. This makes it crucial to see those experiencing noncitizenship not only as agentive and as rights-holders but also as interlocutors and as experts.

In Figure 1.5, the second of the two images that E had suggested for this section, Rannahr – and E, through her choice of it – illustrate how the many

**Figure 1.5** 'The Guardian', Mawa Rannahr, gouache on paper. This is the second of the two images that Ekaterina E selected to illustrate this section of this chapter.

empowered noncitizen narratives presented through this chapter – and through this book – align. The artist explains:

> This image was inspired by a trip I took to North Dakota with a caravan to deliver supplies during the NDPL Oil drilling protest in 2017 [. . .]. I travelled to North Dakota and witnessed the greatest gathering of North American First Nations people since the Wounded Knee. We brought food, salmon, cedar branches, clothing, medical supplies and at our camp hosted a dinner for about 1000 people. [. . .]. The experience changed me forever.[61]

This illustrates a noncitizenship which is not simply about a lack or an absence. Rannahr and E describe instead a unique power among those who must live their lives, perform their politics and flourish *despite* the political and legal structures that organize our world. Moreover, Rannahr and E show the importance of noncitizen power in shining a light on realities invisible to others and contributing to more effective and more just – and so more sustainable – governance at all levels.

## Citizenist and noncitizenist lenses, and the risk of banal citizenism

This book doesn't set out to say much about citizenship. There is plenty said and written elsewhere. But it does need to say something about citizen*ism*. When the world is seen through what I call a 'citizenist lens', formally recognized State citizenship (including quasi-citizenships, e.g. in the form of visas) looks like the only way of understanding how people relate politically to States or the multistate system. This can be explicit and intentional, but there is also a more pervasive form, what we could call a 'banal citizenism', underlying much of contemporary politics and theorizing about politics, not actively promoted, but rather 'as a quiet and underlying truth'.[62] It is thanks to this citizenism that insofar as a person's relationship to international structures isn't citizen-like, that person is framed as not being in any relationship at all. Such a person can be made peripheral or anomalous. Their interactions with political systems are difficult to describe in the language of citizenship, making it easier to see them only as victims of, or threats to, the world of citizens or as apolitical others in relation to the 'real world' of citizenship and States. A noncitizenist lens can help.

Paulo Gerbaudo presents 'citizenism' as an emerging form of contemporary populism, where movements coalesce around the claims of their members *qua* citizens.[63] He observes contemporary political protest movements in which protestors carry national flags and make claims based on their entitlements as citizens. For him, rather than wanting to dismantle the international system, members of such movements want to make incremental change that keeps the system as it is. For example, they may want power and wealth to be more fairly distributed within the existing system. In Gerbaudo's citizenism, the citizen, 'outraged at being deprived of citizenship', is claiming power from elites in the name of a truer democracy – and doing so *qua* citizen.[64]

On the left, this can be framed in two main ways. On the one hand, this has been seen as a radical claiming of direct democracy.[65] On the other hand, it has been described as a social democratic move to sanitize capitalism, to invite people to become 'partners in their own domination'.[66] Either way, it involves an uncritical presumption of the underlying rightness of citizenship. This is not neutral. Manuel Delgado critiques citizenist politics on the left as allowing itself to be co-opted in the service of 'sustaining the capitalist system'[67] and failing to interrogate the domination, exclusion, racism and boundary-creation at its heart.[68]

On the right, and particularly explicitly in the United States, 'citizenism' has also been used to frame a challenge to elites; in this case a challenge to some forms of elite libertarianism.[69] That is, as one key proponent who has been influential on the direction of right-wing politics in the United States over the past decade or so, Steve Sailer, writes: '[c]itizenism calls upon Americans to favor the welfare, even at some cost to ourselves, of our current fellow citizens over that of foreigners and internal factions'.[70] Sailer defends this citizenist move as a move beyond racialized politics to a focus on current citizens. However, in practice, he seems to employ citizenism in defence of prioritizing some current citizens over others on the basis of race.[71] Citizenism on the right, as on the left, allows citizenship to be treated as a natural category, obscuring the structural prejudice which might affect a person's access to or experience of that status.

Citizenism isn't only found at the fringes. There is a more pervasive form of citizenism, 'banal citizenism', and being more pervasive, it is also more insidious. Whether on the left or on the right, the central risk of citizenisms is that they fail to interrogate citizenship itself, instead deferring to whichever institutional elites set its conditions and prescriptions. This makes it difficult to conceive of any alternative politics – and all the more so because 'citizenship' can seem like a neutral legal category. Banal citizenism is apparent when 'the citizens' is assumed to refer to everyone, when 'citizen' is conflated with 'good person' or even with 'person'.[72] Banal citizenism is also in play when citizenship is presumed to be the only type of political relationship a person can have.[73] I am taking the language of the 'banal' here from Michael Billig's 'banal nationalism', the nationalism of the forgotten flag in the corner of a room or 'we' in a newspaper article.[74] However, this citizenism could also be seen as one of the 'banal mechanisms', which Alasia Nuti identifies as producing and reproducing structural injustice.[75] Indeed, for Nuti, these are rooted in history and, as will be presented particularly in Chapter 2, so is banal citizenism.

This banal form of citizenism can be difficult to see because it is so pervasive. As Philippe Muray has put it, our epoque is 'stitched together' by citizenship.[76] It is like a collective religion. In a 1998 episode of the BBC documentary 'Louis Theroux's Weird Weekends',[77] a member of a radical Christian group observes: 'Christianity is not religion'. Theroux asks, 'What is it then?'. The speaker explains: 'It's reality'. The same might be said by someone invested in banal citizenism. They may not see this as ideology. Through a banal citizenist lens the world of citizenship just is how things are. Some scholars try to address problems by stretching citizenship. They reclaim the politics of citizenship by also including claimed citizenships which do not defer to the State. However, the use of the language of 'citizenship' in this context risks obscuring something central to the politics of those we have met in this chapter: that there are forms of politics that must be realized *despite* the State and *despite* the international system.

The cases of Michael Ghillar Anderson, Masud Rana and Ekaterina E demonstrate the complex and diverse ways in which this noncitizenship is experienced and claimed. They also show the importance of historical contexts in producing the structures with which these individuals must contend. Michael Ghillar Anderson's political relationships only make sense in the context of settler colonialism. Ekaterina E's situation arises from the history of the Soviet Union and its dismantling. Masud Rana's relationships with Bangladesh and Malaysia cannot be understood without the backdrop of colonization, decolonization and the effects of climate change. A noncitizenist perspective must, then, include historical contexts. A noncitizenist lens forces us to see the history that made and continues to make contemporary political institutions from the perspective of those who were, and are, forced to relate to them in one way or another as noncitizens. This is not about looking at history for its own sake but using history to understand the structures within which we all live out our lives today.[78]

There is another layer to this. As mentioned by E, those who bear the heaviest weight of noncitizenship may also do this in a context of meta-blindness. That is, they must try to explain their situation to people who not only do not understand but also do not realize that there is something that they do not understand. This makes the active adoption of a noncitizenist approach particularly important, but also more challenging, for those who experience the world mostly as citizens. Whereas noncitizens may be repeatedly forced to adopt a citizenist lens, for example, asking for rights or recognition from within the citizenist gaze, '[i]s this what they think we deserve?',[79] citizens must actively opt to try to cultivate a noncitizenist lens. This includes what philosopher Kelly Staples has described as a form of 'respect' in recognition.[80] Whereas a citizenist lens starts from the citizen relationship, a noncitizenist lens starts instead from the noncitizen relationship. That is, it begins by considering what the institutional structures of States and of the international system mean to those who experience them as noncitizens. It considers the extent to which people must live their lives *despite* these institutions.

Not everyone experiences the international system strongly. Some people may live out their lives neither *thanks to* nor *despite* a particular State or the system of States. Think of yourself. Open an atlas at random or close your eyes and put your finger on a spinning globe. Are you aware of the State on which you land in your daily life? Does that State affect you? Must you live *despite* it or do you live *thanks to* it? If you do not experience it either way, this does not mean that there is no relationship, but it does mean that the relationship is not particularly relevant to the discussion in this book. Think of the international structures of trade, rights and mobility. Do you encounter these in your everyday life? Not everyone does notice the impact of the international system directly. But insofar as you must live out your life *despite* such structures, you can be understood to be in a noncitizen relationship with the international system. Noncitizenship, like citizenship, describes a substantive relationship between an individual and a State and between an individual and the international system, albeit in a different form.

Noncitizenism depends upon some basic commitments. First, it holds that all of our political reality, no matter how local or how global, is made up, at root, of people. A State can be separated into constituencies; a family can be considered in terms of its members; but if you try to divide an individual human you will not find any more basic political actor. The second noncitizenist commitment is that those individual humans do not need to be given permission to act politically and that they may have political relationships even with the institutions that seek to deny them – perhaps even particularly so. Third, noncitizenism holds that noncitizens (i.e. those that must live and act politically *despite* States or the multistate system) are an important and fundamental part of that system and that the perspectives of people insofar as they experience noncitizenship are crucial if a more just and more evidence-based version of that system is to be established.

Noncitizenism does not deny citizenship, nor that citizens may have special relationships with each other and with their State. It just says that this is not all there is. Noncitizenism moves beyond citizenship also to recognize political relationships that people have with States and the multistate system whether those States or that system like it or not.

# 'Migrant' is a slippery term

**migrant** / *ˈmaigrent/* adj. *& n.* – adj. *that migrates.* – n. *a migrant person or animal, esp. a bird.*
**migrate** /*maiˈgreit/* v.intr. 1 *(of people) move from one place of abode to another, esp. in a different country.* 2 *(of a bird or fish) change its area of habitation with the seasons.* 3 *move under natural forces.*[1]

Most of us probably have a sense of what we mean by 'migrant'. It may be broadly in line with the aforementioned *Oxford English Dictionary* definition. But the word's meaning is harder to pin down than it at first seems. This chapter introduces a range of people, each of whom has been referred to as 'migrant', and explores what this means to them and how this contributes to developing a lens of noncitizenism. It also examines how the meanings of 'migrant' are intertwined with those of 'sovereignty', another shaky term. It transpires that while both 'migrant' and 'sovereignty' seem fixed, in fact neither term is stable. Contemporary geopolitics, as well as the contemporary results of shared global histories, affect how both terms are used and understood today. This chapter draws on the language of noncitizenship and the discussion of its implications for mobility from Chapter 1.

It becomes apparent that being identified as a 'migrant' is not so much about moving across borders as about membership – membership of State societies on the one hand and membership of the international system of mobility on the other. First, when the label 'migrant' is attached to someone, whether or not they have moved, it can seem to justify their exclusion from the society in which they live. The 'migrant' label can put a person into a noncitizen relationship even with the State of which they are a citizen. The presumption that there is a generally shared understanding of 'migrant' that doesn't need stating can hide what is happening in such cases. It means that policies justified as being about managing international movement can in fact end up being used to control societal membership. Once a person is defined as a migrant, it is common for them to be subjected to policies curbing their agency in the place where they live. Second, insofar as the 'migrant' label is applied to people migrating, its effects aren't evenly felt. The examples presented in this chapter indicate that there is a relationship between individuals' access to international systems of migration and States' access to sovereignty. This chapter opens by showing this through two examples which are tightly bound up with contemporary implications of British colonial histories. These examples trouble both the label of 'migrant' and the nature of 'sovereignty'.

## 'I don't *feel* British. I *am* British.'[2] : How Paulette Wilson was labelled as a 'migrant' without going anywhere

Six years after Jamaican independence from the UK, while there was still free movement between Jamaica and the UK, in 1968, a ten-year old, Paulette, left her home in Jamaica. She travelled 7,000 kilometres alone to settle on another island. As Jamaica was part of the Commonwealth, she had the right to permanent residence upon arrival in the UK and made her new home there. She grew up there. She became a mother and then grandmother.[3] She had first settled in Wolverhampton in a region known as 'the Midlands' just as, also in Wolverhampton, far-right politician Enoch Powell was writing his vitriolic 'Rivers of Blood' speech, warning that non-White immigration to the UK would destroy British society. Powell was stoking a xenophobia that was already strong in the country,[4] but he was also forcing the framing of economic and social concerns through the lens of immigration and race.[5] Free movement to the UK from other Commonwealth countries was discontinued.[6] By 1973, anyone wanting to travel from Jamaica to the UK needed a visa.[7] From 1973, a hard international border was effectively drawn behind the then teenage Paulette, separating Jamaica, her birthplace, from the UK, where she would live most of her life, as yet unaware of how these changes would affect her.[8]

By all accounts, Paulette Wilson, who is pictured in Figure 2.1, lived a pretty normal life. She'd not had to think about her status and she didn't think to secure the citizenship documents to which she was entitled. Then, in the 2000s, a series of new 'migration control' measures were introduced in the UK.[9] Commonly now referred to as 'Hostile Environment' policies, they required people to prove their eligibility for accessing an increasing number of rights. In 2015, Wilson started to receive letters from the UK Home Office telling her she was an illegal immigrant.[10] She panicked. She recalled: 'I felt like I didn't exist.'[11] She couldn't understand what was happening. She was asked to go regularly to a Home Office reporting centre. She did this while trying to gather proof of her half-century in the UK – her entire adult life. In 2017,

**Figure 2.1** Paulette Wilson. Photograph by Alicia Canter, 2018.

before she had everything together, she was seized. Paulette Wilson, a British citizen without documentation, was declared to be an illegal immigrant in her home country and taken into detention, with a view to removal.[12]

Wilson fought back. Reportedly, she and her daughter had first tried to meet the Home Office's demands – supplying all the evidence they could for Wilson's right to be in the UK. No one would listen. It seemed to them that no evidence would be sufficient.[13] Once Wilson had been redefined as an illegal immigrant her words were assumed false. She suddenly had to live *despite* the political and legal structures of her home country. Others had tried to raise the alarm,[14] but it was the publication of Wilson's own presentation of her reality that set the wheels in motion for public recognition of what became known as the 'Windrush Scandal' and eventually for change.

Wilson's decision to speak to a journalist was political. She demanded that others hear and acknowledge that government policies had given rise to utterly unjust effects. Until then, '[m]ost assumed they alone had been caught up in a bureaucratic tangle.'[15] Wilson's work eventually helped to show that there were many people affected and that the problem was structural. Once Wilson's story was published, others started to go public too. Alerted to the issue, academics started to research the structural conditions in more depth. It transpired that up to 57,000 people might be affected,[16] though to those unaffected, these structures were invisible. Guy Hewitt, a Barbadian British Priest, and Kevin Isaac, the High Commissioner for St Kitts and Nevis in the

UK, describe the vital role of those like Wilson: 'an audacity of courage [. . . and . . .] incredible bravery of those whose lives and livelihoods were injured in this crisis but who bravely came forward, after suffering in silence, to carry the burden and become the face of the Windrush Generation'.[17]

Eventually, things shifted. Members of the international community started to support the cause of Wilson and others. In 2018, the Heads of Government of twelve Caribbean countries who were in London for a meeting made a formal request to meet with the then Prime Minister Theresa May.[18] Their request was initially rejected, but then May was forced to meet them. She was forced to apologize. The new Home Secretary was forced to resign. An unknown number of people had lost jobs, were denied healthcare and were forced into debt; some had even decided to flee their homes in the UK to avoid the threats of removal. The power of Wilson and others means that the structures that produced this have been made visible and shown to be indefensible. Wilson herself died in 2020 at age sixty-four.[19] The struggle continues after her.[20]

Scholar Nicholas De Genova has observed that '[i]f there were no borders, there would be no migrants – only mobility'.[21] However, in Wilson's case, it becomes apparent that borders are more important than mobility and that borders can be folded around someone irrespective of movement. De Genova shows how borders and status produce illegal migration, but here the border also produces status without the person having to do anything at all.[22] This case is not unique. Often, measures framed as migration controls do not only affect people migrating. Such policies can even make people who have never migrated into 'migrants'.[23] Consider States across global regions in which members of some minoritized group are denied citizenship recognition, including in their country of birth, leaving them 'stateless'. This includes for example Haitian Dominicans in the Dominican Republic, Russian speakers in Estonia, Shona people in Kenya, members of the Bidoon community in Kuwait, and Rohingya in Myanmar.[24] Treated as illegal immigrants, in their home society, individuals might be prevented from working regularly, owning property, taking out mobile phone contracts, receiving social security or seeking redress for crimes committed against them. In many countries, people who have never migrated are even at risk of immigration detention.[25] As in the case of Paulette Wilson, who was detained in the UK, migration controls can effectively expel people from their home societies.[26] This means that decisions about how migration controls are organized can dictate who can be considered an 'insider' and who an 'outsider' of a society that they call home – whether or not they are migrating or have migrated.

This suggests that even when migration controls *do* affect people migrating, those controls may not be affecting those individuals *insofar as* they are migrating. While several millions of people are migrating at any one time, not all of them are affected by so-called 'migration controls' in the same ways. Some people can move freely, like the tourists visiting Malaysia's Cameron Highlands mentioned in Chapter 1. Others, like Masud Rana and his colleagues, also in the Cameron Highlands, must struggle and even take significant risks in order to make similar journeys. Migration controls are not, then, so much about movement but about who is considered to be entitled to agency with respect to both movement and membership. This also affects how migration governance is discussed in international contexts like the United Nations.

Even if there might be a shared sense of what it is to 'migrate', the meaning of 'migrant' is slippery. Paulette Wilson was living her life peacefully in the small city of Wolverhampton when she was hit by so-called 'migration controls'. Despite being part of the 'migration control' infrastructure in the UK, the policies which affected her were not really directed at controlling people moving. Instead, they were directed at controlling people who were being identified as 'migrants'. There is a risk that such policies informally risk simply putting people because of race or some other arbitrary characteristic into the category of 'migrant' and so ostensibly justifying their control.[27] This can be seen in the next example, the Partition of India in 1947, an extraordinary instance of border creation, which led to one of the largest moments of mobility in human history and one of the most bloody. During this time, people weren't defined as 'migrants', but as outsiders, and forced to move as a result, with catastrophic consequences.

## Borders, migration and sovereignty: Partition

Harcharanjit Singh is an old man in Figure 2.2, but he was not long out of infancy when, over a period of months, his country was split apart. Like Paulette Wilson who we met earlier, he was living out his life while borders were drawn around him, radically changing his relationship with the international system. Also like Wilson, he *had* moved, but it wasn't that movement that led him to be defined as an outsider. In June 1947, after centuries of enforced colonial rule, Lord Mountbatten, the British Viceroy in India, declared that Indian leaders had three months to prepare for British withdrawal from the country.[28] Leaders of different regions and interest groups struggled to agree how to cooperate to manage a peaceful transition of power. Predictably with such a tight deadline in such a fraught situation agreement was not reached. There is debate about who wanted and who didn't want Partition.[29] But in the end, the British government set

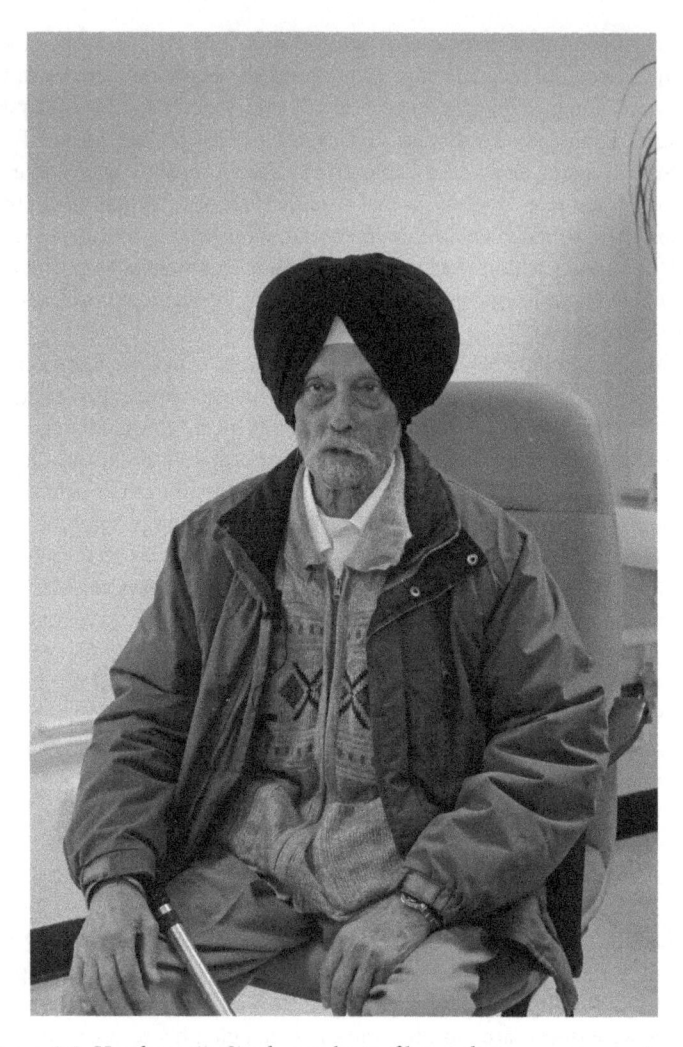

**Figure 2.2** Harcharanjit Singh speaks to film-makers commemorating 70 years since Partition in 'The Reality of Partition', image courtesy of DESIblitz.

up two boundary committees to facilitate India's Partition, with a British lawyer who had little knowledge of the region as Chair of them both. He had five weeks to draw the lines needed to create two new countries: India and Pakistan (the territories of Pakistan would be formed of two non-contiguous parts, the eastern of which would become Bangladesh in 1971). He was still drawing lines as the two countries became independent. Their respective governments would only discover the extent of their respective territories some time later.[30]

Just as people from some States have greater access to systems of mobility, governments of some States have a greater say in what happens at and to their borders. And indeed, entities have different levels of acceptance and contestation over the recognition of Statehood.[31] There is also a correlation between which people and which States are presumed agentive. The reality of Partition wouldn't be in meeting rooms or on maps. Like Harcharanjit Singh and his family, introduced earlier, of the many everyday individuals that she has interviewed in both modern-day India and modern-day Pakistan, Urvashi Butalia writes: 'it is they whose lives *are* the history of Partition.'[32] And through this example, we can see how, tied into the definition of the border and State sovereignty is the definition of the outsider, of the migrant, and the sovereignty of the individual affected.

Before Partition was on the table, the consensus is that for the most part communities across India lived together peacefully.[33] This also accords with Harcharanjit Singh's recollection. Before Partition, his family had moved to the city of Wazirabad for his father's work. He'd been an infant when they moved. Initially, the announcement of Partition is reported to have left hundreds of thousands of people 'with a sense of bewilderment.'[34] Celebrated storyteller Saadat Hasan Manto captures the confusion: 'I found it impossible to decide which of the two countries was now my homeland – India or Pakistan.'[35] Quickly, violence and riots were erupting in different parts of the country. This included Wazirabad, an important train terminus close to the new border.[36] Economist Amartya Sen recalls from his childhood experience of Partition that 'the broad human beings of January were suddenly transformed into the ruthless Hindus and fierce Muslims of July.'[37] Within months, huge numbers of people either fled their homes across the new border or were killed. Partition didn't only create a border on a map but also seemed to legitimize a much greater rupture.

Singh's family was Sikh. When, in August, Partition was effected, they found themselves living in Pakistan, despite their roots in what was now India. The family left. It is unknown how many others did the same, though estimates suggest around 12-17 million people.[38] In Singh's region, the movement was particularly intense. One study using historical census data estimates that 21 per cent of Pakistani Punjab's population left and by 1951 26 per cent was from across the border, while for Indian Punjab the numbers were 30 per cent and 16 per cent, respectively.[39] Others left the subcontinent for elsewhere in Asia, for parts of East Africa and for the UK. For those who travelled to join Asian communities in Kenya and Uganda, for example, decades later they would again be displaced by independence and new racialized citizenship regimes as Britain again hastily retreated from colonial rule, leaving those with Indian subcontinent heritage stranded.

This movement was tough. In a video produced by DESIblitz to mark seventy years since Partition, Singh's voice breaks when he describes his younger sister's hunger after they had been forced to leave their home. He survived Partition and would eventually make it to Birmingham in the UK. He was made into a noncitizen everywhere for a while, with no clear connection to any existing State and forced to live despite the system that was changing around him. He settled in the UK and made his home in Birmingham, not far from Paulette Wilson's Wolverhampton. Singh became a British citizen.

The death toll from the Partition of India was staggering. It is estimated at anything from 200,000 to 1 million people lost their lives in the violence, disruption and famine that resulted.[40] As the new States were instituting new governments and dismantling colonial systems, they also had to accommodate millions of people arriving with nothing. In this example and developing across spaces of European influence was the idea of a bounded territorial 'nation', defined by a shared race, religion and/or language among the people living within it. Control over the composition of a national group became an essential part of 'sovereignty'.[41]

The creation of binary borders like this carries high risk of producing exclusions. The partitioning line across the Punjab shows how such border-drawing not only creates domestic outsiders but can also relocate some people out of the international system entirely. This is epitomized in the story told of Ghulam Ali, who, it is said, was on a work trip on the day of Partition.[42] He had left home fully expecting to return. But he was Muslim and his work had taken him to what had overnight become Pakistan, so that he was unable to return to his home in what had become India. He had no connection to Pakistan and no route back to India. Vazira Fazila-Yacoobali Zamindar, who writes of this case, explains that Ali would spend the rest of his life on an endless cycle of being detained and deported from one State to the other, unable to prove his connection to either.[43] As with so many, Ali reportedly suddenly found himself defined by a border over which he had no control – and over which those in charge of both India and Pakistan had no control. The sovereignty of the States and the individuals involved was weak. And in Ali it created a noncitizen relationship also with respect to the international system.

That there is a relationship between sovereignty and migration is commonly expressed, and it is seen in the text of the Global Compact for Migration. On the one hand, there is a debate about the extent to which State self-determination can justify border controls.[44] On the other hand, some scholars start from whether self-determination really needs exclusionary territorial borders.[45] There is another thread, examining whether existing border regimes reflect the 'structural presence of the unjust history'.[46] Some have argued that this intertwined past and resulting shared culture creates obligations on the former colonizer to admit those from former colonies to their territories.[47]

In practice, different countries and different groups of people have access to different sorts of sovereignty. For some States, not least, those who participated in the Peace of Westphalia, multi-dimensional sovereignty has long been presumed. For others, the fight for international legal recognition and domestic sovereignty continues. Whereas western European movements for popular self-determination largely emphasized sovereignty of the people against mostly internal elite interests (such as domestic monarchies), movements for sovereignty in countries colonized by them also emphasized the need to be freed from *foreign* (mostly, but not exclusively, European) domination, against which some are still struggling.[48] People who come from countries with the least control over their affairs often also have least permission to move globally. People who come from countries which maintain significant controls over their own affairs and over their borders often have the most freedom to move elsewhere.

The current constellation of States and the dominant ways in which they are understood can seem like the only way of understanding the world. European colonization of earlier centuries brought populations not only under the rule of specific rulers but also forced them to function within a particular logic of States and nations,[49] which persists today among States with unequal power, unequal rights and unequal protection from each other.[50] The presumption that this is the only way to organize global society has been described as an epistemic 'coloniality'.[51] Novelist Ngũgĩ wa Thiong'o has observed: '[i]mperialism is total: it has economic political, military, cultural and psychological consequences for the people of the world today'.[52] This means that some forms of truth and some experiences are less likely to be taken into account by dominant and dominating ways of thinking and doing. When States come together to discuss migration governance, then, they come with different options regarding sovereignty and different experiences of the connection between migration and sovereignty. This also has implications for individual human sovereignty and so also for migration.

## Sovereignty and mobility: An unknown migrant

Sitting in the port area of the Catalan city of Barcelona, near an area known as Barceloneta, in 2014, I came across a statement written in permanent

**Figure 2.3** A note on a flagstone, Barcelona Port Area, photograph taken by the author.

marker on the flagstones. Pictured in Figure 2.3, it read: 'If money across borderline so do we!'. I was sitting in an area frequented by groups of new migrants, the breeze coming in from the sea. The note, as I understood it, referred to the idea that while money can often move freely around the world, people cannot.[53] From the statement, it seems likely that the person who wrote it is an expert by experience on the global system of borders and how it functions. This Unknown Migrant may well have experienced those borders intensely, but as we will see in the following chapters, they are not invited to the meeting rooms where migration governance is discussed. They are likely not writing books and articles about the global system of borders. Instead, this Unknown Migrant left these words in permanent marker for someone sitting by the sea to read and to interact with.

Scholar Barry Hindess would agree that unlike people, money appears to move easily around the world. He has described 'a tension or even a contradiction in an international regime which, on one hand, promotes the free movement of goods, services, and financial instruments (especially those produced within the OECD or by multinational corporations) while severely restricting the movement of many, but not all, people'.[54] Others have argued that rather than a contradiction, the irregularization of some people's migration and the consequent 'dismantling of rights and political agency' may actually be part of free-functioning globalized economy.[55] Perhaps what is relevant here is not whether it is people or money that is moving, but rather *which* people and *whose* money it is that is moving. The question is more about who should benefit from and who should shoulder the burden of the international system. The smooth movement of some money and the costs of moving other money also are not really about mobility but rather about agency.[56] Perhaps, then, we could understand the comment from the Unknown Migrant as not only referring to money but also to *those who have or control money*.

A recent global study on migration policy changes over the past century shows a move towards less restrictive policies overall, alongside increased selection – that is, the global trend has been towards the freer movement for some, but with harsher selection of who should enjoy that freer movement.[57] This is reflected, for example, in the huge boom in budget airlines. For an increasing number of people in an increasing number of countries, it has become normal to travel long distances for work or vacations. This phenomenon of cheaper and easier travel has occurred alongside the implications for those blocked by selective visa and other systems and those who must move irregularly if they are to move at all.

For some, visa regimes have become increasingly restrictive.[58] According to the Global Passport Index 2019 iteration, the strongest passports allow entry without pre-entry visa to around 90 per cent of countries. Mauritania, the strongest African passport in the 2019 rankings, would allow travel to 70 per cent of countries without a pre-entry visa. The weakest passports, from Sudan, Yemen, Somalia, Pakistan and Syria, would need pre-entry visas for travel to most other countries. In addition, not all visa applications are treated equally. Measures like the Global Passport Index, the European Visa Database[59] or the Visa Network Data,[60] while helpful, are unable to show this discrepancy. However, some targeted research uncovers, for example, that, in 2019, African passport holders were more than twice as likely to be denied a visa to the UK in comparison with holders of other passports.[61] This research also identified enormous barriers imposed on applicants, including fees, documentation and in some cases even requiring travel to third countries in order to submit applications.[62] This had implications, for example, for collaborations on Covid response as will be developed in the following section[63] and led an Ethiopian government advisor to observe that this highlights a further inequality, since African visa applicants to the UK 'are often charged much higher fees than British visitors pay to enter African countries'.[64]

If poorer, less stable countries have weaker passports, then citizens of these countries may be both more likely to struggle to enjoy peace, stability, and prosperity if they stay at home and struggle to travel elsewhere. Countries with weaker passports have also experienced generations of colonization, war, international interference and now also the results of climate change. As a result, people holding these passports, like Masud Rana from Bangladesh, who we met in Chapter 1, may have particular need to move internationally while also being particularly excluded from international systems of mobility. This suggests that the perceived need to control migration relates not to numbers or capacity[65] but to a mismatch between who has an interest in moving and who those with power think should be able to move – who should be entitled to that sort of agency.[66] The visa process provides a mechanism for States to sort people at border posts.[67] Those who need to show visas are presumed unwanted (or untrustworthy) unless they can prove otherwise. I don't know who wrote the message on the flagstone in Barceloneta. But the way the international systems of migration work means that it was likely written by someone who had significant interest in migrating, but was denied access to the world of increasing international mobility. As I will show, the person who wrote that note may have travelled from anywhere from Bangladesh to Zimbabwe and is much less likely to have travelled from Britain or New Zealand.

For obvious reasons, there isn't reliable data about irregular migration, but there is estimated data, for example, on deaths along irregular migration routes. Travellers from Africa and the Middle East to Europe make up a small proportion of the world's migrant population, but they represent a large proportion of those reported to die while migrating.[68] In 2015, of the estimated more than 1 million people moving to Europe irregularly (which included those moving to seek asylum), most came from Syria, various parts of sub-Saharan Africa and South Asia. It is unsurprising that the world's irregular migrant population is made up of those who simultaneously both have the greatest need to move[69] and are most likely to lack access to regular travel.

The United Nations Development Programme produces an annual ranking of countries according to their level of 'human development'.[70] Although there are conceptual problems with this ranking, it can be useful. The ranking is determined by measures like literacy, infant mortality and life expectancy. Countries are then organized into four categories: very high, high, medium and low human development.[71] On average, in 2019, citizens of countries identified as having 'very high' human development could enter 149 countries without a pre-entry visa. For citizens of countries with 'high' development, it was 100, for 'medium' it was 72 and for 'low' it was only 58. For the most part, the citizens of countries where UN peacekeeping missions are located also struggle to access international mobility. They need to apply for a pre-entry visa to travel to most other countries.

The realities encountered so far in this book show that there is a crisis in our global system and that this manifests particularly in the governance of migration. Those who are unable to access the world of peace, security and prosperity where they are, are also least able to migrate through regular channels.[72] Their particular need to migrate may be created by those very structures of power that prevent them from moving. When political leaders speak euphemistically of 'irregular', 'undocumented' or 'illegal' migrants, the aforementioned factors affect who they are talking about. This is directly produced by global structures of power, control, discrimination and inequality. If people migrate irregularly, then, rather than wanton rule breakers, they are often people for whom the rules are impossible. This makes the decision to travel irregularly look more like civil disobedience than criminality.[73] This will be developed in Chapter 7.

## Unhelpful tropes and the restriction of agency in the context of Covid-19

The tropes that frame who should be able to make decisions about their own mobility have been both unsettled and entrenched by policy responses to the emergence of Covid-19. In early 2020, Covid-19 spread particularly in wealthy countries and was attributed to those identified as migrants,[74] or outsiders,[75] and people of Chinese origin in particular;[76] to those working in vital so-called 'dirty' employment such as care and cleaning;[77] and to those framed as somehow 'unclean'.[78] Covid-19 gave rise to both forced mobility and forced immobility, and underlying this was a question of agency.

Although initial responses to Covid-19 were varied, they can often be traced to local systems of prejudice. Even in countries where the disease had demonstrably not been brought from China, Chinese communities were targeted. This was reinforced by the labelling of it as a 'Chinese virus'.[79] In 2020, one commentator observed, 'what is interesting is that all the initial cases of the virus in sub-Saharan Africa have been linked to European travel rather than China. Yet there is no equivalent anti-European feeling'.[80] Other reports suggest that in some Black-majority countries, Covid-19 was instead initially framed by some as precisely a White person's disease[81] and as a disease of the rich (and rich foreigners in particular).[82] Meanwhile, in some countries with historic discrimination against Black minorities, Black people were targeted. When there were still few recorded cases of Covid-19 on the African continent, and Italy was becoming a major infection centre, Italian politician Matteo Salvini warned that migration from Africa would bring the disease to the country.[83] There are reports of Black residents being particularly targeted with Covid-19 measures in the Chinese city of Guangzhou.[84]

From February 2020 onwards, most countries began to implement some form of border closures and travel restrictions.[85] These were often driven by existing tropes rather than the demands of public health. Several governments initially focused on further restricting the mobility of those whose mobility was already restricted: foreigners, including those seeking asylum. Restrictions on the entry, including screening, of a country's own citizens, often took much longer to come into effect. In March 2020, UNHCR and IOM reported temporarily suspending all refugee resettlement.[86] UNHCR reports that of the 167 countries with full or partial border closure by mid-April 2020, 57 made no exception for access to asylum.[87] And yet, initially, the virus was largely spread by people travelling home rather than going abroad.[88] It largely travelled on cruise ships and airplanes rather than in dinghies or by foot. It was spread by the world's wealthy and middle class returning from university study, business meetings or foreign holidays. After circulating among the rich, it spread among the poor and those most at risk: those working in frontline professions, those with untreated or underlying health conditions and those without access to healthcare or sanitary conditions.[89] Ironically, in those early stages at least, Covid-19 was spread by people moving freely[90] and went on to produce particularly disastrous effects for those least able and so least likely to travel: people who are poorer, older and with a lower standard of general health and those with the most 'limited ability to control their surroundings'.[91]

Italy, Germany, the United Kingdom and the United States were severely hit by Covid-19 early on. They also sit around the top of the Global Passport Index. These countries have mutually beneficial visa waiver agreements or free movement policies. They also have tight controls of entry for those outside the club. Their strong migration controls and repressive policies of detention, deportation and destitution did not protect them from the virus. Those controls only affected people who, at least initially, were least likely to carry it. The countries at the top of the Global Passport Index that managed to suppress the spread of the virus were those that quickly introduced measures managing all entries, including of their own citizens. As the virus took hold in one country after another, internal controls on foreigners put those individuals at increased risk, making it harder for them to protect themselves and others.[92] By April 2020, three in four countries, home to 91 per cent of the global population, had put in place partial or complete border closures; one in two human beings was reportedly in some form of lockdown.[93]

As Covid-19 initially disproportionately affected wealthier countries with large migrant worker populations, mass return migration began. While in some countries, measures were imposed to minimize the possibility of returning migrants bringing Covid-19, in others, there were no such measures.[94] Meanwhile, migrants, including those who had been in-country since before the pandemic, were targeted and scapegoated. In Australia, the Prime Minister told all migrants to go home but many were unable to do so. Many migrants were stranded around the world by the grounding of flights while at the same time put into ever more precarious situations by job losses and the difficulty of meeting visa conditions (e.g. working hours, incomes and expiration dates).[95] This was taking place within a logic of security – mobility for some and immobility for others – that was largely unchanged from before Covid-19. As foreigners were framed as virus-carrying, there was more impetus to remove them, including from countries with high infection rates to countries with lower infection rates. The unequal ways in which people were seen not as individuals with agency but as representatives of tropes had severe impacts on the spread of Covid-19.

Globally, populations identified as migrants who had neither left nor entered at any point from the beginning of the pandemic (so that they were no more or less likely to carry the virus than their neighbours) were subjected to abuse. Once migrants and migration were framed as the problem, this then seemed to legitimize the targeting of anyone identified as such. Discourse relating to migration governance can be muddled at the best of times. This was exacerbated by the imprecise linking of mobility and the spread of the virus. This is seen, for example, in a now-famous statement by Hungarian Prime Minister Viktor Orban: '[w]e are fighting a two-front war, one front is called migration, and the other one belongs to the corona virus, there is a logical connection between the two, as both spread with movement'.[96] Orban blamed the first outbreaks of Covid-19 in Hungary on Iranian students (though there was no evidence that they had brought the virus) and used this to close transit zones along the border with Serbia (though this would block the movement of asylum seekers rather than foreign students).[97]

Covid-19 emerged in a world of unprecedented free movement for some, and those populations continued to enjoy the greatest agency. I was speaking to Ekaterina E, who we met in Chapter 1, on WhatsApp as the Covid-19 pandemic was emerging and country after country was going into lockdown. She remarked on the shock expressed by people who hold powerful passports who were now suddenly unable to move. She explained that for people without citizenship of any country, enforced immobility is part of normal life. She said in some ways it was like watching wider society reacting to becoming stateless. However, there is a difference between having your choices limited by a system designed to protect you and having your choices limited by a system that is designed to protect someone else from you. What's at stake then isn't so much mobility or immobility, but rather agency and interests.

Assuming that some people are not agentive can have catastrophic effects, as was shown in the context of the unforeseen mass movement as a result of the Partition discussed earlier. This can also be seen in the context of Covid. On 24 March 2020, the Government of India announced a stay-at-home order in response to Covid-19. It was one of a series of such orders. On the face of it, this seemed to be a crucial way to reduce internal movement and so to address the growing infection rates in the country.[98] However, it didn't take into account the several hundred million internal migrants in the country who live precariously, without savings and without access to social welfare. Though citizens of India, they also experience noncitizenship in relation to the State. Staying at their homes in cities would mean that they'd have no way to work and so no way to eat. So they left. The suspension of much of the national rail network meant that they travelled by foot. At the announcement of a further stay-at-home order in May 2020, for example, an estimated '104 lakh [hundred thousand] of migrant labourers moved from urban areas to rural areas of origin in about 30 days from 1 May to 31 May 2020', many reportedly dying en route.[99] This also led to an initial shift in India of Covid-19 infection predominance from urban to rural areas with a weaker health infrastructure.[100]

People who are unable to self-isolate, lack easy access to clean water and soap, are unable to seek medical treatment and cannot eat unless they work that day are much more likely to catch as well as spread an infectious disease during a pandemic. Indeed, for some of those who already struggle for access to water, food and basic healthcare, Covid-19 may not have been their primary concern. And yet, for these communities, Covid-19 might also have presented a greater risk.[101] Forcing people into such circumstances, then, not only is problematic from the perspective of that person, but also produces wider concerns. Recognizing that people act with agency from within an 'intention world'[102] that may be unknown to others is crucial to evidence-based policy making.

## Noncitizenism and the birdcage: Migration and sovereignty in the context of agency

*Consider a birdcage. If you look very closely at just one wire in the cage, you cannot see the other wires. If your conception of what is before you is determined by this myopic focus, you could look at that one wire, up and down the length of it, and be unable to see why a bird would not just fly around the wire any time it wanted to go somewhere.*

Marilyn Frye, 1983[103]

In her now-famous example of the birdcage, Marilyn Frye was illustrating the need for a feminism that understands that a person's agency may be constrained by many structural factors that interact to contain them. When looking at one or another dimension, it can be difficult to see why a person's life may be constrained. Noncitizenism also demands a step back from specificity. It requires instead a move to look at the world from the perspective of those who must live out their lives *despite* the structures that organize it. That is, it starts with this political relationship. Rather than starting with this or that dimension of exclusion or discrimination, for example, it starts with the reality of a bird unable to fly or a person whose agency is constrained (which may lead, as we have seen, to either immobility or mobility). A noncitizenist approach prioritizes expertise-by-experience of political structures. It acknowledges that an observer might not be able to see all the bars of someone else's cage until they are pointed out.

This book takes 'agency' to refer both to the ability of an individual to act consciously and intentionally and to the ability to choose and to imagine – to 'reach for meaning'[104] – in ways that are meaningful to that person. This does not necessarily mean acting rationally.[105] Rather, it allows for action taken on the basis of a messy mix of human interests, desires, hopes and fears, in the context of an individual's own understanding of the world.[106] It also does not mean acting without constraint: a person may act with agency even when only 'tragic choices' are available – that is, choices where none of the options are desirable.[107] Finally, agency does not preclude collective action: when individuals participate in such action with agency, they do it consciously and intentionally. Crucial to the idea of humans as agents is that they aren't only acted upon. They also act. Even those people who are assumed passive; whose desires, dreams and interpretations of the world are ignored; and whose options are constrained also act and do so with agency.[108]

Discussion of agency places the person acting as the *protagonist* of their actions.[109] This includes everything from the production of works of art to the desperate decisions a person makes when trying to stay afloat. This means that, as one commentator on the global governance of migration observes, even 'transnationally marginalized groups [. . .] can nonetheless strive for achieving agency as well as advocate for political and social transformation'.[110] François Crépeau, then OHCHR[111] Special Rapporteur for the Human Rights of Migrants, also adds: '[marginalised] migrants don't lack agency: they take vital decisions every day, with courage and determination: however they try to do it with discretion'.[112] That is, they must try to disguise this very human part of themselves where it is seen as threatening and illegitimate.

There are political risks associated with talking about 'agency' in the context of migration.[113] Unauthorized or irregular migrants in particular are often framed as being either decision-makers and so culpable for taking the decision to migrate without authorization, or as choiceless, and so non-agentive victims (this is also picked up in the note on the refugee definition in the next section). An all-or-nothing account of agency may risk reinforcing this. However, the potential risks associated with talking about agency are not as great as those associated with not talking about agency.[114] To say a person has agency doesn't mean that they're unfettered by social and political structures. It merely suggests that a person's agency logically precedes the arbitrary categories of status, which they must then use their agency to navigate. When a person's agency is not explicitly recognized, it becomes easier to relegate them to the realm of the faceless, of those merely acted upon. This is a problem both for the person so relegated and for a world that thereby loses their insight and expertise.

Sitting behind this discussion is a dangerous history of the denial of some people's agency. The European colonial tradition of framing those who are perceived to be racially or culturally un-European as simply reactive has been used to justify brutal things.[115] This has included the domination of people who colonizers supposed could not think for themselves. That mentality has not disappeared from the international system[116] or from discussions of migration governance. This makes it particularly important to push back explicitly against the tropes that underlie it, including the racialized ideas of who should and who should not be allowed to make decisions about their own mobility. This pushback includes framing all people as equally able to have agency, and so seeing all people as potential interlocutors, as individuals of whom any other human might say: 'I am inclined to negotiate' with them.[117] This is relevant to the creation, critique and re-creation of systems of global governance, including systems of global migration governance. This includes attributing agency even to those who make decisions one cannot understand or with which one does not agree. Agency may or may not involve contestation, and it need not be progressive.[118] Starting with the perspectives of people insofar as they experience the international system as noncitizens may well lead to a wide variety of conclusions.

This chapter's examination of the meanings and structures around 'migration' and 'sovereignty' provides a key step in understanding why there may be radically different experiences of the world of international mobility. Today's differentiation between who is enabled to make decisions about their own mobility and who is not isn't new.[119] Global empires have represented vast spaces of free movement for some and of forced migration or immobility for others. Jacqueline Bhabha has observed in her analysis of contemporary migration dynamics:

historically by far the largest abuse in matters of human migration was not forced exclusion or removal from national territory but, rather, the forced importation of enslaved or indentured populations. Population imports or increases were generally considered mechanisms for enhancing wealth, productivity, and power.[120]

The epitome of this idea that some people can be relocated at the will of a powerful State is found perhaps in the horror of the Transatlantic Slave Trade and its pervasive echoes today.

The trade in human beings from Atlantic west and central Africa to the Americas and the Caribbean began in the sixteenth century but was focused around the seventeenth and eighteenth centuries.[121] The mapping by project SlaveVoyages indicates that during this period, 12.5 million people were kidnapped and transported in appalling conditions into slavery, many dying en route.[122] It is difficult to digest the number of individuals, what they experienced and the cultural norms that made this seem acceptable to so many people for so long.[123] However, it is necessary to acknowledge the place of the Transatlantic Slave Trade in the global history of the governance of human mobility. Crucial to what made the slave trade possible was the idea that some people, defined as 'outsiders' to the burgeoning international system, could be treated as chattel, while others, as 'insiders', could not.[124] That is, some people could choose whether to stay put or to move, while for others this choice was not available.

For those buying slaves for the Transatlantic Trade, this definition was based on race. An already long history of scattered anti-Black prejudice in European societies escalated in step with the escalation of the slave trade and was used to 'justify' it.[125] Central to this was a perception, also cemented in law, that Black people were barbaric, uncivilized and incapable of ruling themselves.[126] These tropes were used to present people as non-agentive and to rationalize their appalling treatment. Political Scientist Patricia Ihuoma Ogu argues that there are sinister echoes of the horrors of the historic slave trade in today's experiences of sub-Saharan irregular migration to Europe.[127] For her, this can be seen in a combination of the danger of the journey, the high death rate, the appalling treatment irregular migrants receive in Europe as cheap and expendable labour, the menial jobs irregular migrants must undertake and the impossibility of return. The two cases are radically different. Not least, those who were taken into slavery were taken by physical force.[128] Yet Ogu's case for acknowledging sinister echoes of the one in the other is convincing. Underlying today's landscape of irregular migration is a system of visas and passports which frame some people as 'outsiders' to the international system of mobility, to move or stay put at the will of others.

Presumed excludable, individuals must prove their worth in order to move regularly. Unable to do this, many people move irregularly, putting them at risk of the exploitations Ogu lists, and may face forcible relocation through deportation. Deportations of those marked as irregular migrants has been described as a form of 'forced migration' and even as a crime of international law.[129] The fact that the people in both contexts are coming from similar regions is also hard to ignore. As migration theorist Joseoph Carens has observed, policies that seem abhorrent today seemed normal and necessary to many of those who benefitted from them in the past.[130]

As the examples in this chapter show, some powerful States have long-standing control over their borders and their territories. These States have restrictive visa policies both for those hoping to arrive and for citizens who are able to make easy use of international systems of mobility. On the other hand, there are some States which still face challenges in maintaining control over their borders and over what happens within their territories. Citizens of these States may also struggle to access international systems of mobility, while still others have no citizenship at all. There is a relationship between sovereignty and migration. It is one of agency and hierarchy. It is the reality of a global system in which the prosperity, peace and security of some people are seen as precious, while the prosperity, peace and security of others less so.

## 'Migrants' and 'refugees': A question of agency?

This language of 'agency' raises another important question of terminology. In political discussions of international mobility, the labels of 'migrant' (or 'economic migrant') and 'refugee' are often used as if to identify distinct categories of people, setting up those whose movement is framed as 'voluntary' against those whose movement is framed as 'forced'.[131] However, this risks creating false distinctions between people as apparently deserving or undeserving, framed as either victims or else villainous based on the idea that some move without any agency and others with a surfeit of it. While the refugee definition has been a vital way to protect some people it also risks producing what researchers Heaven Crawley and Dimintris Skleparis have called a 'categorical fetishism' and an unhelpful binary[132].

Consider the self-reflections of anthropologist Shahram Khosravi. Writing about his experience of being an 'illegal traveller' from Iran, eventually arriving in Sweden, Khosravi presents how his decision to leave home was complex. He observes that he was fleeing likely death serving in an army he did not support, but he notes that others in a similar position did not make the decision to leave.[133] In practice, many of those displaced by violence will not meet the refugee definition,[134] and many of those fleeing contexts of persecution and violence may also describe economic and other reasons for the decision to move.[135] Meanwhile, those moving primarily because of structurally produced poverty and environmental degradation or loss of land to climate change have no special international law category.[136] There is a growing tradition in scholarship which acknowledges refugee movement as a type of migration[137] and which recognizes that there may be reasons why people may move with urgency which do not meet the refugee definition.

Contemporary international law usage of 'refugee' terminology arises from efforts in the early twentieth century to coordinate the relocation and protection of displaced populations defined by ethnicity who were both lacking protection and suffering poverty.[138] At that time, their relocation as workers was seen by international actors as key, and in 1925 the International Labour Organization (ILO) became the responsible agency. This will be discussed further in Chapter 3. The global economic downturn in the 1930s changed the politics of refugee resettlement in Europe and North America. Scholar Katy Long observes that as a result: 'many of the persecuted who applied for entry to the USA were refused entry because they were also *poor*'.[139] Whereas previously poverty and the desire to work were reasons for refugee resettlement, now they were reasons against it. It was in this context that, during the Second World War, people trying to flee Nazism were blocked.[140]

By the 1930s the international community were primarily framing refugees not in terms of their poverty but in terms of their lack of protection.[141] After the war, some of those displaced across Europe were recruited to work in post-war rebuilding. This was largely coordinated by the International Refugee Organization (IRO), which itself was largely funded by the United States. This was replaced by the establishment of the Office of the United Nations High Commissioner for Refugees (UNHCR) in 1950. The 1951 Refugee Convention with its 1967 Protocol officially created the new legal category of the individual refugee. Since that time, the UNHCR has explicitly separated refugee resettlement from 'migration' and 'development' for two main reasons: (1) to ensure that people unable to work would still be given protection[142] and (2) to protect the status of refugee from anti-migrant politics. As Erika Feller, then UNHCR's Director for International Protection, observed in 2005: 'it is dangerous, and detrimental to refugee protection, to confuse the two groups, terminologically or otherwise'.[143]

However, sustaining this sharp distinction is detrimental, including for those who would seek refugee status. First, a person must usually apply for refugee status within the country in which they seek protection. This means that increased impediments to migration, including controls on irregular migration and privations for irregular migrants, make it more difficult to seek, let alone enjoy, asylum.[144] This risks removing asylum as an option from those who most need it. Second, it serves to separate out discussion of administrative matters that may affect any people moving, such as how to bring qualifications with them when they travel and the cost of remittances. Third, as will be developed in subsequent chapters, the elevation of the deserving refugee in contrast to the undeserving migrant risks seeming to justify the repression of those already bearing particularly heavy burdens of the international system who are identified as irregular or illegal migrants. That is, as scholar Tazreena Sajjid has observed: 'the idea of opportunistic decision-making [. . .] generates little sympathy when considering questions of the rights and dignity of the individual in question'.[145] However, as has been shown in this chapter, people are 'condemned to choose'.[146] As agents, at each moment, people are making decisions about what to do based on their understanding of the options available and of their interests. And noncitizen agency, seen as threatening, is often constrained. Accounts refer repeatedly to how, once a person is identified as an 'illegal migrant', their fate can be placed 'in someone else's hands'.[147]

Noncitizenship in relation to the international system involves challenges that those who live predominantly as citizens cannot imagine.[148] Someone who has refused to die at home from poverty or violence and instead has, against the odds, travelled to somewhere of greater prosperity and security, is claiming agency. And is doing so in a way that need not seem threatening. The effort to move discussion of refugees away from the discussion of 'development' makes sense. As we will see in the coming chapters, migrant rights activists have also argued that it is inappropriate to frame people only insofar as they do or do not contribute to States' development, at the expense of considering their human rights for example.

In 2016, UN Member States met in New York to discuss large movements of migrants and refugees. This meeting launched two proesses: one would produce a Global Compact for Migration, the other a Global Compact on Refugees. Some of those involved told me they were disappointed that this meeting did not take the opportunity to bring together discussions of migrants and refugees. As well as aforementioned reasons, this separation would make it practically more difficult to discuss shared policy areas (like portability of qualifications for example). The creation of two separate processes, one largely centered in New York and the other in Geneva also split the constituencies participating. Few of those I interviewed had had capacity, either themselves or in their organizations and networks, to participate in both. This book focuses on the process that produced the Global Compact for Migration, and in Chapter 3, we will meet some of those who participated in shaping it.

# Finding new ways to talk about migration

In November 1947, a few months after the order for India's Partition would create a new border and displace many thousands of people, the United Nations General Assembly (UNGA) had its second-ever meeting. A resolution passed at that meeting expressed the need for

> [i]nternational co-operation for the prevention of immigration which is likely to disturb friendly relations between nations.[1]

This framing of migration as a problem to be prevented failed to acknowledge migrants as agents. It set the tone for subsequent discussion of migration in the UN – but so did the chaos caused by events like those in the Indian subcontinent as a result of Partition, discussed in Chapter 2. Analysis of global migration governance is traditionally State-centric. When, for example, scholar Alexander Betts identifies 'a rapidly emerging "bottom-up" global migration governance framework', the relevant actors he speaks about are States.[2] In this context, this chapter shows how a diverse group of activists identifying as 'global migrant civil society', advocating for the rights of people who are not neatly folded into the world of States, have claimed space within UN discussions of migration. This would be crucial to how the Global Compact for Migration 2018 would be developed.

The expertise and interests of the people introduced in previous chapters had not been systematically sought out in the creation of the international migration infrastructure, with detrimental effects. Relegating their experiences and their insights affects what can be known about migration, producing what Miranda Fricker has called 'epistemic injustice', showing both how different dimensions of epistemic injustice intertwine and its real-world effects.[3] Discussions about epistemic injustice traditionally focus on how a person's testimony might be doubted ('testimonial injustice') or need to be framed in a language that does not acknowledge their experiences ('hermeneutical injustice'). In the context of migration governance, this is underpinned by another concern. That is, the structures that produce noncitizenship produce a situation in which those with the most direct experience and bearing the heaviest burden are not seen as potential experts and interlocutors in discussion about those structures that affect them.

As this chapter sketches, from the 1990s, a growing number of civil society actors have developed a variety of global and regional networks, which have in turn created their own processes for consultation and movement-growing. From 2011, these movements have become more joined-up and more organized. They are composed of a diverse array of labour associations, grassroots movements and community groups, and religious organizations, as well as academics and others. As this ecosystem has developed, new actors have joined, bringing their own expertise and claiming their own niches. Those participating in this occupy a range of positions within the international system, both inside the meeting rooms and outside the gates.[4] The interaction – and sometimes the tension – between these positionalities has contributed to creating a more open discussion about migration governance, despite existing structures.[5] This book now focuses on how noncitizen power functioned in the lead-up to the adoption, in 2018, of the UN Global Compact for Migration. This chapter shows how noncitizen power has depended on citizen relationships in various ways. This chapter does not try to define who counts as 'global migrant civil society', but instead defers to how people define themselves. This is examined more critically toward the end of Chapter 4.

There are many people involved in these movements in diverse and complex ways. This chapter sketches this complex reality through three key individuals, though many others could have been chosen. They help to illustrate three main ways in which noncitizen power functioned in the process towards the Global Compact for Migration:

(1) a labour representative who used a citizen position to formally represent noncitizen perspectives;

(2) a coordinator of migrant and community social movements who used a claimed citizen position to provide a bridge between discussions in social movements and discussions in formal policy spaces; and

(3) a migrant network leader who was simultaneously claiming a form of both noncitizen and liminal citizen participation.

There is a fourth way in which noncitizen power functioned:

(4) through the very many people who crossed borders they had been told not to cross.

This fourth group were crucial in initiating the process, but they had no chance of being heard within the UN policy spaces. This will be addressed directly in Chapter 5.

Considering these three figures, this chapter makes three main observations. First, waves of actors have navigated institutional structures that are not designed to include them. Second, in claiming and creating spaces in this way, these actors themselves also become seen as gatekeepers. This meant that some interviewees described on the one hand still struggling for access, while on the other hand trying to facilitate access for others. Third, some of the challenges can be usefully framed using the language of 'epistemic injustice'.

## Migrants as workers, and the power of 'being there'

A trade unionist, Gemma Adaba provides an example of the first way in which noncitizen power functioned in the Compact process. As we sat in the back of a café near the UN building in New York in 2019, Adaba explained that she came to the discussion of migrant workers' rights almost by accident. As a trade unionist, she was interested in the cause of migrant workers *because they were workers* – and they were workers who were not being treated properly *because they were migrants*.[6] Adaba has had a long involvement in the international labour movement, including serving as the International Trade Union Confederation (ITUC) representative to the UN from 2006 to 2010, as well as its predecessor, the International Confederation of Free Trade Unions (ICFTU) from 1999 to 2005. She became involved in the early discussions of migration and development in the 2000s. She remembers that Member States, used to framing migration in terms of security, were initially reticent to discuss the topic within the remit of the UN Charter's normative human rights framework. The focus of Adaba's published work and interventions since the 1990s has consistently been on the need to protect the wages and basic rights of all workers, including the right to organize, irrespective of geographic location or migration status.[7]

The preamble to the International Labour Organization (ILO) Constitution, its founding document, states that 'universal and lasting peace can be established only if it is based upon social justice'. One of the things identified as crucial to this is the 'protection of the interest of workers when employed in countries other than their own'.[8] It is in this context that the first Migration for Employment Convention was adopted in 1949.[9] Migrants were recognized as persons making positive contributions to States. On the one hand, this meant that they were seen as useful to States. On the other hand, as workers, they were seen as having both agency and rights. In her engagement in the Global Compact for Migration, working with Global Unions,[10] Adaba explained that she prioritized ensuring the Compact would include minimum standards on social protection, relating to workers' access to benefits (e.g. sickness, unemployment, old age, injury, maternity and family benefits), to enable economic and social security, while providing suggestions for how this could be implemented.[11]

Coming from this focused position, Adaba also worked with other civil society actors on issues relating specifically to labour, as we will see later. Adaba's position within the Compact process was a formally recognized one. She coordinated the policy positions of the Global Unions, which have had a long-standing history of engagement with the UN on labour policy matters as members of the UN Economic and Social Council (ECOSOC). In this way, and according to the definitions presented in Chapters 1 and 2, insofar as she participated, she did so as a 'citizen' of the multistate system. However, in the way she explained her position to me, she acted as

> an advocate for change in the condition of migrant workers who lack voice, agency and protections in the workplaces and communities where they lived out their lives.[12]

The structures of labour organizing gave her a particular legitimacy to represent this perspective. In this way, she was using a citizen position, coordinating the work of international trade unions, to formally represent people in a noncitizen relationship with the multistate system. This is the first form of noncitizen power functioning presented in this chapter.

ILO membership is composed of three constituencies: States, employers' organizations and workers' organizations.[13] Members of these different constituencies participate in discussions and have equal vote on decisions. ILO, uniquely among international organizations, was set up intentionally to avoid being a forum in which 'governments and governments alone have a voice'.[14] As presented in Chapter 2, it has been addressing the question of migrant labour since its inception in 1919[15] and has long been the primary location for discussing the rights and status of migrant workers.[16] Before the modern refugee regime and in response to the displacement of people in the wake of the Second World War, ILO took a lead in coordinating the relocation of displaced persons to countries which needed their labour.[17] When the United States objected to USSR membership of the ILO, the Provisional Intergovernmental Committee for European Migration (PICMME) was created in 1951 to support the 'orderly migration' of those displaced in Europe.[18] For scholar Vincent Chetail, PICMME was explicitly set up as a US-led organization in the context of the Cold War, with an emphasis on 'admission of immigrants as a matter of domestic jurisdiction', and a role distinct from that of ILO and UNHCR.[19] In 1989 PICMME would become the International Organization for Migration (IOM), whose role in the

Global Compact for Migration process will be discussed in Chapter 4. This history would affect how it is seen today.

The ILO has, then, long been a key actor in the coordination of global migration governance. It has also been a place for migrant labour activists to drive global discussions.[20] This is seen in the mobilization around two processes in particular: the ILO Migrant Workers Convention 1975 and the ILO Domestic Workers Convention 2011. Already in 1975, the ILO Migrant Workers Convention addressed issues like the rights of irregular migrants, temporary migration, and human trafficking.[21] It received muted reception.[22] Some found it too permissive, while others found it too restrictive.[23] There was some push (particularly from the governments of Morocco and Mexico) to move the discussion of migration into the UN. From 1974 onwards, the UN General Assembly had passed annual resolutions expressing a commitment to the human rights and dignity of migrant workers.[24] This included resolving to draft a UN Convention relating to the rights of migrant workers and their families. What became known as the UN Migrant Workers Convention was tough to negotiate and was eventually adopted over a decade and a half later, on 18 December 1990.[25] A further decade later, in 2000, this was the date chosen for the annual celebration of International Migrants Day.

The UN Migrant Workers Convention was not radically new in substance. It reiterated existing provisions and stated that universal rights also applied to migrant workers – which should already have been obvious.[26] But it was controversial. Within the UN, migration continued to be framed largely as a security issue. To come into force, a UN Convention needs to be ratified by twenty States. It took the Migrant Workers Convention an unprecedented 151 months to achieve this, far longer than any other core human rights instrument.[27] To date, no State with a high level of immigration has ratified or signed. Some States which today receive relatively high numbers of immigrants *are* signatories, but they had different migration landscapes at the time of signing. And the implications of the Convention are understood differently by different governments. Rhodora Abano of the Center for Migrant Advocacy (CMA) in the Philippines, for example, observed that while the Philippines has been a leader in promoting the rights of the Filipino diaspora, it 'has not yet become as focused or as vocal on how does our country also do our responsibility vis-à-vis foreigners coming in'.[28] Some told me that they thought that the Migrant Workers Convention is toothless. Others described it as a vital piece of international law formalizing the rights of migrants. One interviewee, who told me they had experienced difficulties as a migrant worker, said that its existence gives them hope that the international community is there for them too. In recent decades, the way migration is framed in the UN has evolved. Labour movements, including the ITUC and Adaba, have played a role in this.

While it can be tempting to talk about global discussions in terms of monolithic organizations and entities, as Adaba explained, and as I have observed, individual people involved in those organizations are key to how policy discussions unfold. Two key appointments around the turn of the millennium are examples of this.

First, in 1999, the Office of the High Commissioner for Human Rights (OHCHR) appointed the first Special Rapporteur on the Human Rights of Migrants, Gabriela Rodríguez Pizarro, the first individual in the UN assigned directly and solely to monitor the global protection of migrants' rights.[29] There would be two Special Rapporteurs during the period of the process towards the Global Compact for Migration: François Crépeau (2011–17) and Felipe González Morales (2017–). Michele Levoy, who worked with Adaba to advocate consideration of irregular migrant rights in the Compact, told me that this office was a particularly useful ally in promoting this at the highest levels. This was in no small part, Levoy explained, due to Crépeau's own academic work and writings on the rights of irregular migrants and the need for 'firewalls' separating individuals' access to rights and protections from any need to disclose migration status.[30] Firewalls are also important to Adaba, as part of ensuring labour rights and protections irrespective of status. Crépeau's appointment was interesting also because of his reflections on global discussions of 'migration management' themselves and the possibility of centring migrant rights within them.[31]

Second, in 2006, the then UN Secretary General Kofi Annan created the new post of Special Representative for Migration and Development to the Secretary General (SRSG). In 2000, Annan had announced that a 'comprehensive look' at migration in the UN was needed.[32] He commissioned a report that would examine this. What would become the 'Doyle Report' was influential on what would follow. It was part of what drove the launch of a new set of processes. The UN Department for Economic and Social Affairs (UNDESA) had surveyed Member States about the possibility of meeting to discuss migration in 1995, 1997, 1999 and 2003, and it was in 2003 that enough were in favour to begin the process of organizing the High-level Dialogue on International Migration and Development.[33] Annan created the SRSG role to try to ensure that this meeting would be productive.[34] He appointed Peter Sutherland into that role.[35]

Sutherland came from the private sector. He also had a proven record in institutional redesign and supporting Member States through changes in governance structures. It was during Sutherland's tenure as Director General of the General Agreement on Tariffs and Trade (GATT) that the weakened and controversial GATT was transformed into the new World Trade Organization (WTO), established in 1995, a move which is widely considered to have been necessary, difficult and ultimately successful.[36] As researcher Elaine McGregor-Lebon points out, this included the recognition that the 'movement of natural persons' was 'considered essential to the functioning of the business'.[37] After his appointment to the new SRSG role, Sutherland's initial focus was on finding a way for UN Member States to be willing to talk about migration. He believed that this would need to build on an already growing focus on migrants' contribution to development and to suppress efforts to frame this in terms of rights. McGregor-Lebon cites a letter Sutherland sent to Annan in which he observes:

> [e]verything I have heard from delegations suggests that we would be much better advised focusing on the economic aspects of migration while making the obligatory references to the rights issue.[38]

This indicates that there were strategic reasons for focusing on development and for avoiding substantive discussion of rights. Looking back in 2010, Sutherland would describe this bringing together of migration and development as a 'marriage', which would finally make it possible for States to talk about migration in a meaningful way.[39]

Many global migrant civil society organizers were critical of Sutherland's approach, both because of his focus on migration and development and because of his suppression of discussion of rights. Criticisms of the migration and development framing are discussed later. Here, consider the question of rights. Adaba told me:

> I distinctly remember Peter Sutherland saying that governments are not ready to talk about human rights in relation to migration. They're just not ready, so you need to give them time.[40]

This approach was problematic. While all persons, including migrants, are in theory protected by international human rights regimes,[41] in practice States often do not protect the rights of certain migrants.[42] For Adaba and others, taking this off the table was unacceptable. However, for Sutherland, it seems that this is exactly why shutting down discussion of human rights of migrants at least initially seemed strategically necessary in order to get States to talk about migration at all.[43]

Then, in 2013, Sutherland wrote: '[a] major impediment to the establishment of rights for international migrants has been the lack of advocates with powerful tools to hold governments accountable.'[44] For Adaba and other activists, this was why it had been necessary to talk about migrant rights in global migration governance discussions from the outset: to hold governments accountable. In the event, perhaps both perspectives were needed: that of Adaba and other civil society activists and that of Sutherland. The space for dialogue on migration between States and civil society that exists today was arguably made possible *both* by Sutherland's trust-building with States *and* by civil society actors' persistent challenging of this approach. Having actors coming from different positions helped to address the 'advocate's dilemma'.[45] That is, to address the challenge of promoting universal norms of human rights within debates framed around prioritization of the nation-State. In 2019, and reflecting back, Adaba told me that 'things have evolved in a remarkable way over the years'. And I think she is right. In the final negotiations of the text of the Global Compact for Migration in 2018, a number of States were not only acknowledging human rights but also openly defending the human rights of migrants regardless of status.

Adaba told me that discussion at the UN, despite its ostensible human rights framework, is affected by both who can participate and what they're allowed to say. This illustrates the policy implications of the control over narrative – and so of 'epistemic injustice', to be discussed later. It also shows the need to address – and the difficulty in addressing – what Catherine Lu has referred to as an 'unjust baseline'.[46] Adaba explained that, unconstrained by official policies or diplomatic concerns, civil society, including trade unions, plays a key role in saying what she calls 'the unsaid' and in presenting apparently impossible policy considerations as feasible. In this way, having those formally representing migrant workers globally, like herself, at the table can help State representatives to get past politically difficult discussion points. Adaba puts it simply. She says that it takes civil society actors to say 'this is a human being', where governments are nervous to come out and say that.[47]

## Migrant civil society organizations mobilize as a global network

Monami Maulik has come from grassroots migrant community organizing. She has claimed a citizen-like space in international discussions of migration governance while continuing to work with grassroots and other organizations. In this way, she illustrates the second way in which noncitizen power has entered the discussion of the Global Compact for Migration. That is, rather than acting as representative, she effectively provided a bridge between a vast and heterogeneous network of networks of civil society organizations and

**Figure 3.1** Monami Maulik, speaking at a side event of the 61st session of the Commission on the Status of Women, on integrating a gender perspective in the global compact for safe, orderly and regular migration, March 2017. Image courtesy of Monami Maulik.

formal international policy discussions. Maulik, who is pictured in Figure 3.1, had founded the community organization, Desis Rising Up and Moving (DRUM) in New York in 2000. Her work in that organization was directed at solving immediate local issues, such as those relating to detention and deportation, providing support for families and would-be youth activists and advocating for wider policy change.[48] Her global activism is bound up in this history of community activism. She was one of a number of grassroots civil society organizers who went on to claim an entitlement to space within UN policy discussions, eventually providing bridging between discussions in the social movements of which they are part and discussions within those formal policy spaces. Insofar as she engages in policy spaces, she does so as an insider, as a 'citizen' to use the language introduced earlier, but prioritizing the perspectives of those with direct and immediate experiences of noncitizenship. Crucial also to understanding Maulik's role is that, to an observer, she seemed to be simultaneously working to claim and create space for noncitizen entry and also seen by some others as an insider protecting access to that space.

When I interviewed her, Maulik was coordinating the Global Coalition on Migration ('the Coalition') follow-up on the Global Compact for Migration. Founded by Maulik and others in 2011 with funding from the MacArthur Foundation, the Coalition was a key dimension of civil society engagement in the Global Compact process. As coordinator of the Coalition during the Compact's creation, Maulik was holding together a large number of moving parts, coordinating consultation with and representation of a diverse global range of actors, mostly grassroots movements, based across global regions. She explained that for her this was an extension of the work involved in founding DRUM: as the founder of a grassroots community organization connecting with other social issue movements which are intersectional. When I spoke with her, she explained: 'a lot of the work that I've done historically is intersecting immigrant rights work with other kinds of issues affecting communities marginalised or excluded from shaping public policies'.[49] Indeed, this forming of networks and then also networks of networks of organizations and movements can be observed across civil society engagement in the migration governance discussions.

This structure made it possible for actors to engage in ways that may not otherwise have been possible, including drawing on diverse expertise, access and knowledge. For example, on the one hand, it would make it more possible to bring inputs from grassroots organizations, which would have no hope of entering the discussions formally; but on the other hand, it would enable those with access to meeting rooms to be able to draw on a much wider knowledge of what was needed on the ground. One representative of a member organization explained it this way: 'it's not only [each member] alone as an organisation, but it's more of a network strategy'.[50] That is, it enabled contribution to a much stronger global effort. It was this global effort that Maulik, to an extent, was coordinating.

This work isn't easy. For example, Maulik recalled some of the challenges involved in leading a global network of networks, each with different priorities and approaches. She says:

> We were having exchanges every day sometimes during GCM [Global Compact for Migration] negotiations because there were so many new things coming out all the time that had to be explained. And then if I explain it to the 17 networks [in] my coalition, they then have to filter that back to where they have to make their decisions from, and then feed that through to us.[51]

This was, she explained, different from the engagement of an organization with representatives or officials. As Ignacio Packer, a civil society activist who was part of creating what would become called the 'Action Committee' told me, there is no 'NGO Parliament' and there cannot be.[52] As a result, rather than the more formal processes found within trade unions, for example, Maulik and others, including Packer, describe the much messier and more complex sets of processes found among social movements to ensure fairness, voice and legitimacy. In this way, Maulik played a bridging role between the different fora.

The forming of this global network of networks needs to be understood in the context of each of its member's work on the ground. For example, in her published work, Maulik describes how, after the September 11 attacks on the World Trade Centre in New York in 2001, people started contacting DRUM's detainee helpline in greater numbers, seeking help for people who had suddenly started being arrested and detained without explanation. She explains: 'I took calls all through the night for weeks [from men in detention centres in New Jersey] who did not know where they were or why they had been brought there.'[53] In response, as part of DRUM, she worked with others to support immigrant detainees and their families to call for greater transparency. Maulik describes working in detention centres, giving public statements, working with civil liberties and legal institutions, and coming together with other community groups. She describes how DRUM was at the centre of New York-based activism to bring attention to racialized post-9/11 policies from that time until 2005.[54] It is, then, in this context of grassroots work, that she joined with others who were also involved in grassroots movements in 2006. While States were meeting for the first High-level Dialogue on International Migration and Development (HLD) at the United Nations headquarters in New York, civil society had their own meeting outside the gates. She explained that it was here that the seeds of what would become various coalitions were sewn.

Maulik's work was also taking place within a wider context of changing civil society engagement in the UN. As mentioned earlier, in the 1990s, a new landscape for talking about migration was beginning to emerge. Arguably, this was driven in part by two broader developments.

First, it was affected by intense rethinking of sovereignty and citizenship in response to events like the fall of the iron curtain and tragic genocides. In Rwanda in Spring 1994, during a period of violence lasting around 100 days, it is estimated that over half a million people were killed. Although the international community knew what was happening, there was no attempt to intervene. In 1992, following a Bosnian attempt to break away from Serbia, a systematic effort began to remove Bosnian Muslims from the territory, driving Bosniaks into camps. Although in 1993 the UN declared the situation to be under control, killings continued. In 1994, NATO carried out air strikes to try to stop the attacks. In July 1995, Srebrenica saw the largest massacre in Europe since the Second World War. The violence in these contexts led people to flee their homes, both within countries and across borders, and drove a rethinking of the nature and limits of sovereignty within the international system, as well as how to respond to new situations of displacement.

Second, a new notion of 'global civil society' was emerging in the international system,[55] as part of a strategy to democratize global decision-making.[56] Across issue areas (including migration), this global civil society came to be represented by a network of NGOs, which were mostly fairly large and headquartered in wealthy countries.[57] This new role for NGOs had already been seen at the 1994 Global Conference on Population in Cairo. Global civil society had been represented at Cairo by NGOs that were members of the UN's ECOSOC. In the field of migration, interviewees told me that already in the 1990s, some NGOs were connecting with a wider network of organizations beyond ECOSOC. The notion of 'civil society' itself in this new sphere was being hammered out.[58] One way or another, the Cairo Conference provided a focus for growing civil society mobilization around global migration governance. It also uncovered tensions within civil society that persist and will be taken up in more detail toward the end of Chapter 4.

By the end of the 1990s, global networks of migrant civil society activists had formed. They had made a start in the campaign for the Migrant Workers Convention and in the development of the Cairo Declaration. The language of 'migration management' had emerged in the UN and then of 'migration governance'.[59] Some UN Member States were pushing for there to be a world conference on migration, but they were in the minority. By the early 2000s, global migrant civil society movements were beginning to meet more regularly, primarily around UN events. They were supported in this by larger NGOs and religious organizations as well as UN entities like the OHCHR. Meanwhile, there was unprecedented growth in interest in migration across the UN system,[60] which was now increasingly being framed through the lens of 'migration and development'.[61]

In the early 2000s, global migrant civil society mobilization was growing and becoming more formalized. Migrant Forum in Asia was continuing to expand, to become one of the most organized and influential regional migrant civil society networks. In 2005, the World Social Forum for Migrations (WSFM) was set up in Brazil, a spin-off of the World Social Forum. These movements were loudly critical of the migration and development framing and of IOM. Meanwhile, as mentioned earlier, in 2006, the UN held its first High-level Dialogue on International Migration and Development. Protest meetings outside the new UN events discussing migration and development would gather alongside key meetings of UN Member States and would morph into a regular meeting, known as the People's Global Action on Migration, Development and Human Rights

(PGA). Located outside the gates of the UN while the policy discussions were taking place inside, at this point, it was noncitizen-like in its relationship to the multistate discussions.

It was also at this time that, like Monami Maulik, several of those who would play important roles in the Global Compact for Migration process became involved. Michele Levoy, for example, of the Platform for International Cooperation on Undocumented Migrants (PICUM) said that while her organization had been participating in global-level discussions about migration governance before 2006, it was in 2006 that global civil society, and PICUM within it, began to define the role that they would go on to play.[62] A key outcome of the 2006 UN High-level Dialogue was the institution of an annual Global Forum on International Migration and Development (GFMD) in which UN Member States could talk informally outside the formality of UN structures. This would force civil society networks to make a choice.

Members of civil society movements mentioned that they feared that locating discussion about migration outside the structures of the UN would produce a more repressive migration regime. This led to a split.[63] For some, it was impossible to discuss migration with States outside the UN and they refused to participate in the GFMD. For others, the GFMD represented an opportunity to engage in new ways with States and potentially drive a new way of talking about migration. Maulik explains that despite having questions about it she decided to try to engage in the GFMD. Echoing the thoughts of Adaba presented in the previous section, she recalls that 'in the initial years of the GFMD, the human rights of migrants was not a focus of discussion' but that she and others continued to advocate for change within these processes, looking for commonalities with governmental participants.[64] Colin Rajah, who we will meet in Chapter 4, agrees with Maulik. Describing trying to participate in the first GFMD, he says: 'talk about a huge challenge! It really really ended up being more ceremonial than anything'[65]. But they and their many colleagues continued to try to engage. Various civil society movements and organizations continued to meet at PGA events alongside the early State-centred GFMD and its Civil Society Days, while at the same time trying to gain access and influence into intergovernmental discussions.

Those involved told me that they regularly interrogated the impacts of their participation. For example, Maulik observed:

> there's always a conversation on whether we can actually impact human rights issues of migrants in the space rather than largely using the migration for development lens, which can be instrumentalising.[66]

Most of those I spoke to who were engaging from a civil society perspective with the UN processes discussed here mentioned this tension to a greater or lesser extent. They were trying to effect change in a flawed institutional structure. The strategy that Maulik and others adopted seems to be something like what scholars Helmut Anheier, Marlies Glasius and Mary Kaldor have referred to as an attempt to 'civilize' globalization from within,[67] by bringing in the views of those outside. It wasn't only civil society representatives that were frustrated. States and agencies shared their concerns. The Philippines had a long history of engagement with its diaspora. Mexico and Morocco, for example, had also been playing an important and visible role since the Migrant Workers Convention. Step by step, the GFMD events hosted by the Philippines in 2008 and Mexico in 2010 changed the position of migrant civil society within the GFMD.

The strategic roles of many actors, including Maulik, was crucial to this, both inside and outside the gates. One interviewee who has moved between civil society and UN agency positions mentions the 'tenacity of civil society actors' during this period:

> when the GFMD was formed, there was little to no civil society participation at all so NGOs pitched up outside of the space and protested. And then through some hard-fought victories were able to eventually have the blessing of the GFMD organisers.[68]

And at the same time, Rajah told me, those involved found that they were able to have conversations at the PGA events that were not possible elsewhere: 'these political discussions actually help us to carve out long-term strategy and to think about shifting policy and things like that'.[69] This set the scene for a more fundamental shift at the Swiss GFMD in 2011, in which the International Catholic Migration Commission (ICMC) would take a leading role. This will be examined in Chapter 4.

For Maulik the real change would come in 2016, with the New York Declaration, which would launch the process towards the Global Compact for Migration. However, this change was in no small part thanks to the work done at successive GFMDs. Stéphane Jaquemet, who became the Head of Policy for ICMC during this period, has put it in this way:

> many many would say that because the Global Forum on Migration and Development has been on during all these past years that it has been a little bit the Forum that has somehow made possible the Global Compact for Migration which has now moved to the UN.[70]

Maulik explained that to her it was the framing of the New York Declaration in 2016 that finally made it possible to begin to speak substantively about issues 'like rights of irregular migrants, or access to services, or access to justice'. For Maulik, this substantive change was made possible by the inclusion of migrant civil society in the discussions.[71]

The inclusion of those with first-hand experience of problems caused by governance structures is a thread that comes through from the beginnings of Maulik's local activist work. She explains: 'DRUM holds our people as the experts on their own lives and communities.'[72] Maulik told me that when, in 2013, over a hundred members of DRUM came together outside the UN buildings on the occasion of the second High-level Dialogue, central to DRUM's message was that they should be seen not only as part of development but also, and centrally, as humans with rights.[73] However, inclusion in policy discussions had to be mediated through those few people like herself who had managed to claim citizen-like admission to spaces within the rooms where migration was being discussed. This is the second of the three ways in which noncitizen power could enter UN discussions of migration governance presented in this chapter.

## Migrant workers as activists, and the implications of 'migration and development'

Eni Lestari Andayani, who is pictured in Figure 3.2, provides an example of the third way in which noncitizen power was brought into the Global Compact for Migration process. Lestari actively and simultaneously claimed both a noncitizenship and a liminal citizenship in relation to the international system. She explains that she didn't start out as an activist. When she was younger, she had wanted to study but had needed to work instead. When she learnt she could earn more by leaving her home in Indonesia to become a domestic worker overseas, that's what she decided to do. She has described significant mistreatment first in a training facility in Indonesia and then by her employer in Hong Kong. She reports that for months, her wage was withheld, she was denied time off and she had to share a bed with a fourteen-year-old boy of the family where she worked. When she learnt that this treatment was unlawful, she began legal proceedings and then ran away from her employer.[74] She received shelter from Bethune House Migrant Women's Refuge for migrant workers and reflects: 'I was reborn in that place.'[75] In the shelter, she met people from different countries and was astonished by how many had similar experiences.[76] Unwilling to accept this, in 2000, just as the OHCHR and the UNGA were starting to think seriously about migration, Lestari and others formed the Association of Indonesian Migrant Workers in

**Figure 3.2** Eni Lestari speaks as Chairperson of International Migrants Alliance (IMA) in the opening segment of the United Nations high-level summit on large movements of refugees and migrants, September 2016. Image courtesy of United Nations Photo Library.

Hong Kong. As she explained to me, she believed that she and others should demand to be part of discussions that affect their lives, partly because they are workers and partly because the way in which grassroots migrants are treated is, for her, a true measure of a society's values.[77]

As she became more involved in mobilization for migrant rights beyond Hong Kong, Lestari became increasingly critical of the civil society landscape that she encountered. She observed: 'many of the advocacy groups at the regional or international level are actually NGOs. They are not migrant workers [. . .]. A lot of the speaking out is on *behalf* of the migrants'.[78] To counter this, she believed:

> we really need a solid and strong international grassroots migrant refugee movement who can speak out loud [. . .] the migrants cannot hold our breath while speaking about the truth on the ground.[79]

In Lestari's framing, it's possible to see the importance of expertise-by-experience both in identifying truths about reality as presented earlier and for the emotional content this provides. That is, direct experience also affects how issues are prioritised and the urgency attributed to addressing the challenges faced as a result of existing migration governance structures.[80] In

2008, the International Migrants' Alliance (IMA) was formed and Lestari was elected as its chairperson – a role she continues to hold at the time of writing.

Back in 2000, while Lestari and her colleagues were forming the Association of Indonesian Migrant Workers and Maulik was forming DRUM, the international community was adopting Millennium Development Goals (MDGs), setting international targets for development over the following fifteen years.[81] The MDGs included aims like ending poverty and hunger, reducing infant mortality, increasing life expectancy, ensuring universal access to education and so forth. Migration wasn't addressed in the MDGs, but this new language of development soon dominated international discourses, including those relating to migration. This was the time when Peter Sutherland was being appointed and the UN started having regular meetings about migration governance.

Glorene Das, who was the treasurer of IMA when I spoke to her in 2018, explained that IMA was formed specifically of groups that rejected this framing of 'migration and development' and the international processes that arose around it. Das explained: 'we saw that the process did not really or directly involve migrants who have been affected or exploited'.[82] Like the PGA and the Coalition, IMA is made up of a network of member organizations. Some of these organizations have been able to send representatives to UN discussions about migration, while others have not. IMA, like the PGA and the Coalition, is, then, one of a number of what can be referred to as 'networks of migrant civil society networks'. Crucially, whereas members of the PGA and the Coalition decided, despite their misgivings, to participate in processes framed around migration and development, members of IMA initially did not.

Lestari told me that in 2011, around the time that civil society engagement at the GFMD was becoming more structured, she began applying to participate. She was not successful. She saw this as evidence that those who were organizing civil society spaces were not willing to represent grassroots migrant civil society perspectives.[83] Maulik, who we met earlier, also comes from grassroots activism and still functions between global governance spaces and those of grassroots movements, bridging the two. However, Maulik has also managed to access formal policy systems and claim a more formal position within them. Movement leaders who had managed to secure citizen-like access to spaces came to be seen by those such as Lestari as insiders. Given there is no 'NGO Parliament' as mentioned earlier, there is no formalized system of representation within social movements. There is always, necessarily, a jostling for voice and legitimacy.

In 2016, Lestari's positionality altered. She was invited to speak on behalf of migrant workers in the Plenary of the meeting at the UN Headquarters that would launch the New York Declaration and so also the process towards the

Global Compact for Migration. She herself had now also transitioned into the formal policy space, and she now also had to grapple with associated risks. When I met her, Lestari was still navigating this. She had been incorporated into the formal process, though only as a guest. She was not protesting at the gates, but she was also still only liminally present. In this way, she provides an example of the third of the ways, identified earlier, in which noncitizen power acts within the global migration governance discussions. That is, she simultaneously claimed a noncitizen and a liminal citizen relationship with the international system.

## Noncitizenship and epistemic injustice in UN discussions and implications for civil society engagement

The three activists presented in this chapter represent three different ways in which noncitizen power entered into the formal UN discussions that produced the Global Compact for Migration. When I spoke to them, they also framed themselves, in different ways, as challenging dominant ways of thinking and knowing about migration. That is, they were challenging what can be understood as a form of 'epistemic injustice'.[84] There is a link between epistemic injustice and the presumptions about agency introduced in Chapter 2. That is, just as States have different experiences of sovereignty, some people are presumed entitled to have greater agency over their own mobility than others. There is a correlation between these different experiences of State sovereignty and the different access to mobility of people associated with those States. Underlying both this reality and how it is framed is a banal citizenism. That is, there is an underlying privileging of the interests and perspectives of those who experience the world as citizens: as insiders to the formal political structures. The discussion in this chapter has shown the importance of a citizen-like relationship with the international system for the emergence of the perspectives of people insofar as they must live and act *despite* that system.

People were forced to frame their experiences within a language and a conceptual framework, which was not designed to include them.[85] This is seen, for example, in the need to participate in discussions of migration and development while at the same time challenging this framing. The three individuals introduced in this chapter, three of a great many others, brought otherwise excluded noncitizen perspectives to global migration discussions. As shown, these perspectives needed to be brought by representation, bridging, and other forms of space-claiming, and then packaged in ways that would resonate with a citizenist audience. Miranda Fricker describes two main types of 'epistemic injustice': 'testimonial injustice' and 'hermeneutical injustice'.[86] Testimonial injustice refers to direct prejudice relating to what a person says: perhaps the veracity of a person's testimony is questioned, or its importance minimized. This is also affected by a hermeneutical injustice. Fricker describes hermeneutical injustice as 'having some significant area of one's social experience obscured from collective understanding'.[87] This may be a result of a lack of the appropriate terminology or social context. It might be that some forms of experience are not recognized as salient.

José Medina and Emmalon Davis both add an important further dimension to this.[88] Whereas Fricker focuses on the justice implications for individuals whose credibility is presumed *limited*, Medina and Davis look at the implications for others of an excess of credibility. First, Medina refers to the wider societal implications of putting too much weight on the authority of a narrow range of experts who are unable to access the experiences of the marginalized. This, he suggests, results in an impoverished understanding of the world, and so a limited 'social imaginary'.[89] Second, Davis refers to the implications for an individual of elevating them tokenistically to stand in as a spokesperson for a particular minority group or based on some expertise they are presumed on the basis of prejudiced thinking about a minority group to have.[90] In the context of migration governance, there is another layer to this. That is, those with the most direct experience of the implications of migration policies are also, *and because of those very policies*, least able to participate in policy discussions in this area. As a result, as will be developed in Chapter 5, others are forced to stand in.

One interviewee told me that they felt it strange to be expected to 'stand in' for the whole of global migrant civil society. Some interviewees from civil society organizations who do not themselves have personal experience of difficulties associated with migration policies expressed discomfort in the role in which they found themselves. For example, some such individuals said that short timescales and structural barriers to attendance meant that they were called upon at short notice to attend events 'on behalf of civil society', when they felt that their role should instead have been to facilitate people with direct experience of the sharp side of the migration governance infrastructure to speak and to participate in discussion.

Adaba, Maulik and Lestari all argue that those with direct experience of the implications of migration policies need to be part of the conversation about how to design better systems of migration governance. To those without this experience, without the insight of such experts, the problems may be invisible and their urgency obscured. This produces what José

Medina has called 'meta-blindness', and, related, what Phillip Cole, in the context of thinking about citizenship and statelessness, has called an 'insider theory problem'.[91] That is, on the one hand, following Medina, people may both be unaware of the burdens borne as a result of migration policies and at the same time be unaware that there is anything more to know. On the other hand, following Cole, this means that the conceptual underpinning of the system is produced and reproduced by insiders to that system who are unable to see how it looks to others.

To illustrate the function of meta-blindness, Medina describes how different observers of the wrongful conviction of a Black man by an all-White jury in Harper Lee's 1960 American novel, *To Kill a Mockingbird*,[92] may have different interpretations of what happened:

> The hermeneutically disadvantaged listeners, thanks to their special sensitivity to insensitivity – their painful awareness of the prevailing blindness – could understand why certain things were not said, why others were only half-said, and why others appeared laughable or illogical even though they could very well be real. The hermeneutically privileged audience members did not have this capacity to understand (or to acknowledge that there is more to understand) readily available; and, in fact, because they were not only blind but meta-blind, because they were insensitive to their own insensitivity, they faced serious obstacles against becoming good listeners, against acquiring or developing the capacity to understand what is difficult to understand.

When Adaba describes civil society actors as playing a key role in saying 'the unsaid', or Lestari notes that 'the migrants cannot hold our breath while speaking about the truth on the ground', perhaps this can be seen as saying the things that may seem obvious to some, but which may not be visible to those Medina describes as the 'hermeneutically privileged'. This also provides another layer to understanding Maulik's description of members of DRUM as 'the experts on their own lives and communities'. That is, they not only know the details of their lives but can also see how key realities are obscured by dominant narratives. This makes it particularly important for people with these experiences to be part of policy discussion, and for those who are able to do so to facilitate their inclusion.

When Adaba declares that 'this is a person' and Maulik describes members of DRUM as humans with rights, they are demanding that the needs, interests and expertise of those with direct experience of the migration governance infrastructure are acknowledged to be both valid and important. In pushing back against testimonial injustice, they are not presenting those affected *only* as providing stories and testimonies to support decision-making others. They are instead arguing for deference to them as experts-by-experience and advocating for their participation in critiquing and developing better approaches to migration governance.

The processes described in this chapter emerged against a backdrop of presumptions about sovereignty, migration and agency. These were the 'background' conditions for the discussion and for who was presumed an appropriate interlocutor within it.[93] The underlying structures are 'citizenist': they presume citizenship, and that each person's interests can be neatly organized according to citizenship(s). The people we have met throughout this book so far demonstrate in different ways that this is not the case. In different ways, they show that there are people whose lived realities and whose politics are best understood through the lens of noncitizenship: through their need to live and to perform their politics *despite* the institutions with most power over them. And yet there is no simple mechanism for ensuring that noncitizen perspectives are included in global governance discussions. In this chapter, we met three individuals who, along with a great many others, have tried to address this. This includes the formal representation provided by Adaba, the bridging provided by Maulik and the noncitizen–citizenship provided by Lestari. In practice, then, in order for noncitizen perspectives to be taken seriously, they needed to be taken up by those with citizen-like relationships with the relevant institutions.

# Joining the conversation about migration governance

Thanks in no small part to the work of actors like those introduced in Chapter 3, coordinators of the process towards the Global Compact for Migration approached civil society representatives and invited them to join. Two large organizations, in particular, supported this, though there were several others that played key roles. One was a large international faith-based NGO, the International Catholic Migration Commission (ICMC). The other was an international organization, the International Organization for Migration (IOM). The individuals working for these organizations were institutional insiders in different ways and in different ways they helped to facilitate access to policy discussions.

This chapter explores aspects of what emerged, showing how the possibility of creating these new spaces depended upon the commitments of individuals occupying key roles within these large organizations as well as on the priorities of the organizations themselves. The way in which this unfolded affected and was affected by both who could be considered to be part of discussions about migration governance and also the sorts of narratives that could emerge. Existing structures make noncitizen power in global migration governance discussions dependent upon the decisions of institutional insiders, irrespective of whether those individuals want to have this power. This chapter ends by showing how this, and the composition of 'civil society' in this process, has affected which issues could be pursued by civil society and which could not. This in turn affected the issues brought into governmental discussions and has implications for understanding the possibility of noncitizen power in global governance. Some of the implications from Chapters 3 and 4 will then be further examined in Chapters 5 and 6.

## Leveraging insidership and implications for noncitizen power

Attending meetings of migrant civil society and speaking to those present, it is evident that religion plays a significant part in grassroots activism, whether explicitly or implicitly. Many interviewees reference religious commitment, at least in passing, and there is significant visible engagement from religious leaders. Religious organizations (overwhelmingly, but not exclusively, Christian) have also supported migrant civil society access to global migration governance discussions. While surprisingly few large human rights NGOs chose to have significant involvement in the process towards the Global Compact for Migration,[1] the International Catholic Migration Commission (ICMC) was a central player throughout. This built upon decades of work, led by its former Head of Policy, John Bingham, especially since 2011. The baton was picked up, upon Bingham's retirement, by Stéphane Jaquemet, who joined ICMC after twenty-five years working for UNCHR. This section considers the transformative work of Bingham, carried on by Jaquemet. They were vital to providing a way for forms of noncitizen power to emerge in key discussions by ensuring that people with experiences of noncitizenship could shape discourse. However, the forced reliance on a large faith-based NGO headquartered in Geneva to facilitate access also raises questions for the function of noncitizen power at the UN.

The work of ICMC is vast and global. It conducts widely cited research into migration and migration policies, including providing advice for governments.[2] Its member organizations coordinate relief work around the world. This includes supporting people migrating and people who have migrated, to enjoy greater access to the UN promise of peace, security and prosperity. The focus here is on ICMC's work in the area of global migration governance discussions, but this takes place against the broader backdrop. ICMC has an established place as one of a large number of key NGOs within the international system. Led by its Heads of Policy, it has set out to leverage the capacity and voice that this provides in the context of global migration governance discussions. This is not an official role. And it has included both speaking themselves and supporting people with direct experience of the migration infrastructure to be part of global policy discussions. While the UN had long had no dedicated agency on migration to facilitate coordination among Member States, in some senses ICMC had come to serve that role informally for civil society, particularly since 2011, enabling a radical shift in the way in which civil society has been able to engage in global migration governance discussions. Indeed, as this section shows, ICMC also played a key role in supporting the inclusion of some networks and movements mentioned in Chapter 3.

ICMC had already been an important player, but this was cemented with the Global Forum on International Migration and Development

(GFMD) in 2011. Chapter 3 introduced the GFMD, a regular meeting for UN Member States held outside the UN since 2007. Hosted by a different country each year, to begin with it was up to each host government to engage a local organization and secure local funding to ensure some form of civil society participation.[3] Initially, this was cursory. The role of civil society became more substantive, for example, when, in Mexico's GFMD in 2010, for the first time specific provision was made for a three-hour window in which civil society and Member States would come together.[4] In Switzerland in 2011, everything changed. The Swiss Chair approached ICMC not only to support civil society engagement in 2011 but to provide an ongoing hub for the coordination of civil society engagement moving forward. John Bingham, then the organization's Head of Policy, pictured in Figure 4.1, told me that ICMC put conditions on taking up this role. Not least among these conditions was that they 'receive support from other leading civil society organizations engaged in GFMD activity'.[5] In this way, a permanent Civil Society Coordinating Office was established within ICMC in 2011, centred in Geneva.

This was the same year that the Global Coalition for Migration mentioned in Chapter 3 was launched, with funding from the MacArthur Foundation. Together, these two developments changed the way in which civil society was able to engage. Having ICMC as a permanent GFMD hub meant that civil society would no longer be dependent upon each host

**Figure 4.1** John K. Bingham, ICMC Head of Policy, speaking at the 13th Coordination Meeting on International Migration in New York, February 2015. Photo credit: UN Web TV, with thanks to ICMC.

State to negotiate anew with funders and local civil society organizers. Unlike Governments, from 2011 civil society had a permanent GFMD centre for discussing migration governance at the global level and was able to begin to create institutional memory. However, it also fixed the centre for civil society GFMD coordination within a large faith-based organization and one based in Geneva. Several of those who were present through this time observed that the changes in 2011 created greater unity and a greater possibility of collective action among people who had previously been disparate and had struggled independently to find footholds in governance discussions. This was not only about access but also about capacity. This change at the GFMD was crucial to enabling those participating as part of global civil society to develop a stronger collective capacity and competence in setting agendas and drafting documents, which would go on to have a direct impact on how the Global Compact for Migration process would unfold in 2016–18.

This institutional memory and coordination also helped to support States. Research commissioned in 2012 by the US-based funder the MacArthur Foundation on civil society engagement found: 'Numerous stakeholders noted that, while the previous arrangement had "done its job", the transfer to the ICMC was one of the most positive changes they had seen in the CSD [Civil Society Days of the GFMD]'.[6] As mentioned in Chapter 3, the SRSG Peter Sutherland had advised civil society actors involved in the 2006 High-level Dialogue to avoid talking about human rights. However, over time the language of rights emerged in the GFMDs, and there were new opportunities for civil society actors and governments to begin to encounter each other's concerns, discover shared aims and look for ways to move forward.[7] In the Second High-level Dialogue in 2013, language of human rights had become mainstreamed, even if it maybe seemed rhetorical rather than substantive. The agenda was also more open. Global civil society representatives including members of the networks of networks mentioned in Chapter 3 spoke in the plenary and were allowed into meeting rooms. They were also challenging the ways in which they could be integrated into the process. Rather than agreeing to sit in remote rooms with video screens, many civil society observers went directly to the rooms where the discussions were taking place, helping to create new imaginaries of those spaces. They were assisted in this by Bingham of ICMC.

One observable example of the substantive impact of this greater role for global civil society is the influence of the so-called '5-year 8-point plan of action'[8] by the ICMC and the Global Coalition on Migration. Framed around the themes of the four 'roundtables' of the High-level Dialogue, it provided concrete proposals for collaboration relating to 'development issues', 'the rights of migrants', 'partnerships' and 'labour mobility'. Produced through a series of global civil society gatherings, it provided an organizing logic for civil society engagement in the 2013 High-level Dialogue. The plan of action has been described as a 'key achievement' in the promotion of a human rights-centred approach to migration[9] and as an important step in civil society actors' work as 'norm entrepreneurs', directly influencing policy norms.[10]

In 2014 Bingham explained that this had emerged from a recognition among civil society activists that they were always 'too much at the cliff', being responsive to State-led discussions rather than driving their own long-term strategies for change.[11] The aim, he said, was to begin working *with* States rather than *responding to* them. He observed of the 5-year 8-point plan that it 'gives this idea of a unified agenda, of a multiyear approach, of a tone and commitment to collaboration with governments on a set of issues'.[12] This helped to build trust and confidence in civil society among UN agencies and some Member States. That their agenda-setting was seen as helpful rather than threatening can also be seen in the fact that the 5-year 8-point action plan aligned remarkably closely with the official government outputs of the 2013 High-level Dialogue.[13]

ICMC occupies an unusual place within international governance structures. Examining this challenges the idea that there is a clear distinction between 'civil society' and the intergovernmental system. ICMC was launched after the Second World War, in 1951, at the request of the then Pope Pius XII as an 'umbrella' for national Catholic organizations around the world working on migration.[14] James Norris, who had been involved in ICMC's creation, writing in the 1950s, recalled that '[w]hen the termination of the IRO [International Refugee Organization] came into sight, it became obvious that the activities of private agencies would have to be greatly expanded to complement the work of governments'.[15] The ICMC was created to contribute to filling this gap. It was, then, at the heart of the global governance system from the outset, representing, as Norris put it, 'Catholic interests at international governmental and non-governmental meetings'.[16] This affects how its engagement should be analysed. Several interviewees mentioned that, for example, the commitments of faith-based organisations in their networks had constrained how topics like sex, gender, and reproductive health could be discussed, though none mentioned this specifically in the context of ICMC. This is presented in the final section of this chapter.

The role of ICMC is made more complex by its relationship to the Holy See, operating from the Vatican, which, though not a Member State, is a Permanent Observer to the UN General Assembly.[17] In 2014, Peter Sutherland who was still the Special Representative to the Secretary General also joined the civil society space, becoming president of ICMC until 2017 when he stepped down due to ill health.[18] The role of ICMC, then, is complex. It is an explicitly religious organisation which sits between the non-governmental and the governmental parts of the global system. At interview, both Bingham and Jaquemet acknowledged ICMC's insider position and told me that their focus was to leverage this to ensure civil society in all its diversity could be included in discussions. Indeed, Jaquemet, who is pictured in Figure 4.2, told me that for him the difference between civil society and the intergovernmental UN is not so clear-cut as it might first appear: 'I believe that whether we work for the UN or for civil society, and indeed if we believe in what we are doing, we are mainly working for people.'[19] This relationship between civil society and other constituencies will be examined more closely in the final section of this chapter. ICMC has played a significant role in creating ways for members of civil society movements to participate in global migration governance discussions. Had the Head of Policy at ICMC at such a crucial moment been different, it seems unlikely that the global

**Figure 4.2** Stéphane Jaquemet, ICMC Head of Policy, at an informal multi-stakeholder hearing held ahead of the International Migration Review Forum (to assess progress on the Global Compact for Migration) in New York in May 2022. Photo credit: UN Web TV, with thanks to ICMC.

migration governance discussions would have unfolded in the way they have done.

In taking up the responsibility of trying to facilitate civil society access to the GFMD, ICMC inadvertently also became a gatekeeper for that access. From when ICMC became the secretariat for civil society engagement in the GFMDs in 2011, the organization has also coordinated the selection of agendas and participants. Both Jaquemet and Bingham developed mechanisms to try to facilitate fairness. When I asked him in December 2018 how this worked, Jaquemet told me that it was challenging. Giving the example of the then upcoming GFMD, he explained that invitations to apply were sent to all of those on ICMC's database, comprising 'several thousands of NGOs, civil society organisations, trade unions, and networks, and each of the networks represents several civil society organisations'.[20] He told me that in 2018, they received 1,200 applications, which had to be whittled down to less than 300 participants for reasons of capacity. Mechanisms were in place for representation by region and by thematic focus. Then there were efforts to ensure that among the representatives there would be 'gender equality, that you have youth representation, etc etc'.[21] To do this, three people in each region and each thematic area were asked to make selections independently. The results of this would then be compiled. This large task was undertaken because those in leadership positions believed it was necessary. If Bingham and then Jaquemet had thought differently about legitimacy, there would likely have been a different composition of civil society at the GFMD.

There is, then, a tension in the structures that have made the emergence of global migrant civil society participation in governance discussions dependent on ICMC in this way. It is problematic that the structures within which global policy discussion occur make global noncitizen interests in migration governance dependent on existing institutional insiders like ICMC deciding to prioritize them. This is not to diminish the importance of the role ICMC has played but to trouble the structures that have made it necessary – a troubling which will be further developed in this chapter's final section. Led by their Heads of Policy, ICMC recognized their insidership and initially used their institutional position to speak at and to bring key speakers into meetings. They then used their resources and location in Geneva to provide a coordination hub for those activities. They also supported a broader move towards greater cohesion. The work of Sutherland, set out in Chapter 3, is often credited with making the Global Compact for Migration possible. However, it is unlikely that the process would have unfolded as it did in 2016–18 without the work that had been done by ICMC, particularly since 2011.

## Insider–outsidership and implications for noncitizen power

Colin Rajah, pictured in Figure 4.3, has played what could be called an insider–outsider role as a civil society liaison for the International Organization for Migration (IOM) during the process towards the Global Compact for Migration. Like Maulik, Rajah started out in grassroots migrant community activism and went on to claim space in international discussions of migration, including as a founding leader of the Global Coalition on Migration before Maulik took the role described in Chapter 3. During the process towards the Global Compact for Migration, Rajah was employed by IOM, a Geneva-based international organization that had become a 'related organization' of the UN in 2016.[22] There were several key entities involved in organizing the Global Compact for Migration Process. The Office of the Secretary General of the UN played a key coordinating role, with IOM also involved in coordination, including facilitating wider consultations. Other international organizations, including those mentioned in Chapter 3, played key roles. This section focuses in on the work of IOM's Civil Society Liaison Officer in this context. Rajah's own trajectory presents an interesting next step in what has been described particularly by scholar Stefan Rother as an 'inside–outside' approach to engagement,[23] by which migrant civil society organizations simultaneously try to engage from within the UN system and organize outside it.[24]

The IOM has simultaneously been part of facilitating civil society entry to policy discussions and often had a contentious relationship with global migrant civil society. Central to the former, arguably, has been the work of Michele Klein Solomon, in her position as Permanent Observer of IOM to the UN in New York from 2010, whose importance had been emphasized by interviewees in 2014[25] and reiterated by Rajah, who, in 2018, described Klein Solomon as an 'IOM champion for civil society'.[26] This approach was also apparent in others from IOM, like Azrah Karim Rajput who told me that 'we felt it was very important for the GCM to really hear what civil society was thinking'. To Rajah, his role within IOM would be important for two reasons: to help manage the large increase in civil society voices that he hoped would emerge within the Global Compact for Migration process and 'to help civil society meaningfully engage in as many ways as possible'.[27] Indeed, the novel approach to civil society engagement that was adopted in the Global Compact process did provide new and impressive ways for civil society to participate. However, this was also affected by ongoing structural challenges that will be addressed later.

**Figure 4.3** Colin Rajah facilitating a civil society panel during a stakeholder hearing of the Global Compact for Migration consultations, at the UN's Palais Nations in Geneva, 2017. Image credit: Colin Rajah.

Central to civil society actors' concerns about IOM is that the Organization is seen to function outside the UN Charter's commitment to rights. Indeed, IOM's constitution does not explicitly include a commitment to protect migrants and their human rights.[28] Critics argue that this impacts IOM's institutional structure,[29] and so also its work on the ground, such as collaboration with States to effect policies of removal and deportation. Consequently, there was widespread disappointment among civil society representatives when IOM became a related agency of the UN in 2016 and would play a key role in coordinating the process towards the Global Compact for Migration. Some decided to turn away from the process entirely in response. Others looked for ways to work with IOM. When I asked Rajput, an IOM official who was heavily involved in work towards the Compact, what she thought of this, Rajput responded: 'It's fair enough [. . .]. That's their right.' She went on: 'I mean the smarter thing would be just to engage with us and tell us how we can do better.'[30] However, some interviewees told me that they believed trying to work with IOM would not be productive, even if there was a discussion of rights and inclusion. Their reasons are also found in the literature. This included 'implementation on the field of sometimes severe migration control measures on behalf of so-called destination countries',[31] and a tension in the protection and aid for vulnerable migrants provided by IOM for example through 'voluntary return programmes'.[32] Rajput acknowledged that there could sometimes be a disconnect between IOM's country teams and the office at the UN.

The way in which IOM functions on the ground has been described as something akin to a 'private contractor' for Member States, implementing projects on behalf of contracting governments.[33] This has implications for its international role. As legal scholar Jan Klabbers puts it, for example, 'voluntary returns' programmes cannot only involve one State. As such, he observes, IOM 'in fact both influences and aims to influence the policies and practices of its member states to a considerable extent'.[34] Meanwhile, there are concerns about the funding of IOM, whose main source of revenue is 'voluntary earmarked contributions', with 90.5 per cent of the budget made up largely of payment for projects.[35] Critics say that this makes IOM's role slippery, as it 'strategically synthesizes the language of international rights and humanitarianism and equally prevalent discourses of national security' to make it look like a supranational agency while in practice acting for individual States and for certain individual States in particular.[36] However, all international organizations are dependent, albeit in different ways, upon the expectations and interests of Member States[37] – and they are all, including IOM, also subject to international laws including those protecting human rights.[38] As Michele Klein Solomon and Suzanne Sheldon, two IOM officials engaging in the UN, observe: '[w]hile most States [. . .] want (and need) to cooperate on migration challenges, they do not necessarily welcome limitations to this bedrock principle of national sovereignty'.[39] IOM navigates a variety of roles at a variety of levels, with significant influence on discourse. Its vast size and scope (with 175 Member States at the time of writing and almost 14,000 staff)[40] makes it more difficult to hold the organization to account. These debates became more pressing as IOM assumed a key role in the Global Compact for Migration process.

Most of those I spoke to felt that the UN needed a lead agency for working on migration. Indeed, it is extraordinary that a policy area as important as migration has no such agency. If a lead agency on migration were to be chosen from among existing agencies, analyst Kathleen Newland was not alone when in 2010 she presented UNHCR or ILO as the most likely candidates, identifying challenges to IOM taking this role, including those mentioned earlier.[41] Other scholars identify 'at least four entitles with mandates related to migration: the United Nations High Commissioner for Refugees (UNHCR); the United Nations Relief and Works Agency for Palestine Refugees (UNRWA); the International Labour Organization (ILO);

and the International Organization for Migration'.[42] There *had* reportedly been talk of the GFMD itself becoming a norm-setting organization.[43] Since its 2016 conversion into being a 'related organization' of the UN, the IOM comms team has reframed IOM as the 'UN Migration Agency'. However, this identification is challenged.[44] Some saw IOM's leading role in the process towards the Global Compact for Migration as a move towards centring itself in UN migration discussions.[45] As such, rejection of IOM as the UN migration agency contributed to hesitation among some civil society organizers to join IOM's work in relation to the Compact. The decision to locate the secretariat for the new UN Migration Network – a network of agencies working on migration, replacing the Global Migration Group (GMG) – within IOM is interesting. It could be seen as a move to make IOM's role for the UN akin to ICMC's role for civil society.

Rajput explained IOM's strategy regarding the inclusion of civil society in the Global Compact for Migration: 'we just decided early on that we thought it was important to give civil society space and to facilitate their engagement'. In order to achieve this, IOM needed both to secure funding and to improve communication with civil society. They sought funding from States and from groups of States, and they appointed Rajah as a 'Civil Society Liaison Officer'. Rajput observed of Rajah that 'he had this privileged insight into civil society'.[46] Some civil society actors told me that they felt this effectively co-opted Rajah to provide symbolic legitimacy to the work of IOM. But those who were involved directly – both from civil society and from IOM – described trying to provide a more inclusive space, though doing so within the parameters of a global system that is already skewed against the participation of some groups of people. To Rajah, addressing the structural problems would be key but difficult. Each time I've interviewed him, he has been reflective about the nature of his role. Given the fractured relationship that some parts of global migrant civil society had with IOM, Rajah's role was going to be challenging. In 2018, when I asked him what he thought about the fact that some accused him of being co-opted by the organization, he told me that it's something about which he also worries.

Explaining how she and her team sourced funding for civil society participation, Rajput described how she saw the relationship: 'it was not funding for us to tell civil society what to do. It was just a kind of platform that we offered for civil society to self-organise'.[47] This intention is noted in the experiences of several, but not all, of those who led civil society networks and movements. Ignacio Packer of the International Council of Voluntary Agencies (ICVA), who was one of the founding members of the Action Committee explained: 'we would send [IOM] the list of people identified by a civil society self-organised process that we would want invited to a meeting and they would have their travel department arrange it and then cover the flight costs and the accommodation'.[48] And a regional network coordinator explained that in their region, they 'decided on the substance, on the participants, and then who to bring in as resource people'.[49] This included making use of the expertise of officials from ILO and IOM. This positive view was not shared by all. Eni Lestari of IMA, for example, told me: 'they don't really open the process. They just select people who they want to be part of [it] and that's all'.[50] This taps into a larger challenge of insider–outsidership mentioned in Chapter 3, and what happens when those fighting for access in turn find themselves forced to make decisions about access.

As the civil society movements grew in size and in strength, there has emerged a growing tension regarding who could authentically represent 'migrant civil society'. The networks of networks often included migrant-led organizations and community-led organizations as well as religious groups, charities, academics and others. Some interviewees told me that the diversity produced challenges. While it was important to maintain solidarity among those dedicated to migrant rights and to use their diverse positionalities, they explained that sometimes academics or NGO employees, who did not have direct experience of the difficulties resulting from migration governance, had the resources to dominate civil society discussions. Subsequent chapters will show how efforts at including a broader civil society took place against a backdrop of structural challenges and power imbalance, which had implications for its possibility of success.

This is complicated by what is a complex, diverse and messy arrangement of global civil society actors. Recall Maulik's observation that unlike trade unions, UN agencies and NGOs, civil society movements do not have simple mechanisms for allocating representatives and coming to consensus. It is instead painstaking, relying on recognizing a diversity of positions and perspectives. This includes a constant need to create and recreate legitimacy. When he took up the civil society liaison position, Rajah was already an insider–outsider in global governance discussions, though he told me that his background in grassroots organizing was central to how he understood his work at the global level. Some of those I interviewed, however, saw Rajah solely as a UN or an IOM insider, divorced from the realities of migrants on the ground. Such individuals did not see him as 'one of them'. This endless jostling within civil society is perhaps a core challenge for the insider–outsider, resulting in a need to perpetually reaffirm legitimacy.

Rajah's role within IOM could be seen as a co-optation by IOM as some have said. However, it could also be seen within a trajectory of claiming space and seizing greater control over discourse by some constituencies within civil society. At the same time as Bingham and ICMC were setting up a Civil

Society Coordinating Office for the GFMDs in Geneva, in 2011 members of the PGA were applying for funds and setting up a new network of networks: the Global Coalition on Migration. The intention behind the Coalition was to enable a longer-term overview approach to policy and strategizing, which enabled the creation of the '8-point 5-year action plan' mentioned earlier and which enabled civil society actors to push a shift in discourse, including within IOM. This has happened in stages.

IOM's 2013 World Migration Report focused on 'outcomes for migrants themselves and on how their lives have been affected in positive or negative ways as a result of migrating'.[51] A major recommendation in that IOM document was that 'instead of being the passive subjects of enquiry, migrants should be given the opportunity to tell their stories'.[52] However, civil society actors were also not willing to be seen only as storytellers. Rajah has observed that during one meeting in 2013, there was a lunchtime opportunity for attendees to listen to the personal experiences of migrants. They were invited to provide anecdotes, but they were not asked, as he put it, 'about policies they think are important'. He went on: 'those voices are not central when you go back to the 'serious' panels about policy discussion', and as a result, 'policies that emerge from those discussions are flawed because they're missing some important perspectives'.[53] When he decided to take the controversial liaison role with IOM, it seems that his intention was to try to contribute to addressing this. The unprecedented level of consultation with and participation of civil society in the process towards the Global Compact for Migration are evidence of this, as are the new mechanisms for bringing in a broader range of civil society actors and indeed the substantive content of the Global Compact for Migration document itself.

# A Global Compact for Migration, for better or for worse

At the end of just over two years, in December 2018, UN Member States met in Marrakech to adopt a 'Global Compact for Safe, Orderly and Regular Migration'. This was confirmed shortly afterwards by the General Assembly in New York. The Global Compact for Migration is unique. Not only is it the first globally negotiated, widely supported, framework for migration, but it is also the first time that the role of civil society was mainstreamed and acknowledged throughout migration governance discussions in an institutionalized way. The culture of the process towards the Compact noticeably differed from that of previous global discussions of migration governance, with implications for the document's content. The right to a nationality and to legal migration pathways, and the idea that irregular migration status should not affect a person's entitlement to human rights, were explicitly stated in the zero draft. And while the wording changed and the substance thinned during the negotiation process, the final document made commitments that had not been possible at the global level in this formalized way before. The final document falls short in some areas that had begun to seem possible, but it also for the first time introduces topics that had previously been off the table.

When States adopted the New York Declaration which, in its annexes, committed them to produce 'compacts' regarding migrants and refugees, there was still no clear idea of what a 'compact' among UN Member States would look like.[54] At that time, there were some regional 'pacts' between States and between regions,[55] and at the global level, there was 'The Global Compact', launched in 2000, through which thousands of private sector actors have voluntarily committed to uphold key tenets of the UN Charter.[56] But that was all. When I learnt that there would be a Compact on Migration, I asked those I knew that were central to these discussions what it would mean, but no one could tell me. Indeed, this unknown quality was perhaps part of why it was able to proceed in a new way. Interviewees told me that the modalities and mechanisms for the process were still being worked out as the process unfolded. There would sometimes even be a modalities meeting in the morning to agree on how the formal meeting in the same afternoon should proceed. Some of those civil society actors who had been part of this told me that it allowed unprecedented flexibility and access. Laurel Townhead of the Quaker United Nations Office (QUNO) told me that a saying commonly used by people at the time was of 'building the plane as we flew it'.[57] However, since agreements about the process were being made sometimes minutes before meetings were held, it was difficult to ensure that global civil society actors would know about them in time to participate, particularly those based far from locations of meetings. Efforts at dissemination were impressive, but inevitably people were left out. This is discussed further in Chapters 5 and 6.

The idea for a new sort of process was beginning to form in 2014 and 2015. During this period, powerful States in several regions were being confronted with increasing numbers of people who, denied access to the global system's peace and security and denied access to regular mobility, were crossing borders without permission. In Europe, this was being referred to as a 'migration crisis', terminology which will be problematized in Chapter 7. The actions States were taking to prevent the movement were leading to increasingly publicized human tragedies, such as that of the Kurdish child, Alan Kurdi, who was photographed, dead, on a Libyan beach and whose role in the development of the discussion will be examined in Chapter 7. In their book on the Global Compacts for Migration and on Refugees, Elizabeth Ferris and Katharine Donato observe that '[t]raditionally, migration, refugees and humanitarian issues have been marginal to the great issues of war and peace. Suddenly they were catapulted into the center ring of the global diplomatic stage'.[58] Some organizations had been connecting migration and peace for a long time. As scholar Elaine Lebon-Mcgregor observes, this was a key tenet of the ILO's 1919 founding document. However, the launch of the Migration Compact process also mainstreamed this in UN discussions. And it took place upon the foundations that had been built in previous decades.

Two relevant discourses were arising at this time in the international community. The first was about security. The second was moral. There was a number of official statements, reports and agreements, which urged that the ill-treatment of people forced to migrate irregularly must be addressed. In 2015, a series of new international agreements were adopted, most notably the Sendai Framework for Disaster Risk Reduction 2015–2030, the Sustainable Development Agenda 2015–2030 and the COP-21's 2015 Paris Agreement on Climate Change. Each featured migration. A report of the Secretary General in April 2016 opened with the observation that 'the images of the past few years have shocked the world's conscience' and '[u]nable to find safe ways to move, people suffer and die in search of safety'. He went on to demand that 'all members of the international community must do better'.[59] It seemed like change was in the air. Various explanations can be heard for the initiation of the GCM process, but Michele Klein Solomon and Suzanne Sheldon of IOM write that in 2015, Peter Sutherland suggested convening 'a major international conference' to galvanize international response.[60] In September 2016, an extraordinary summit of Heads of State gathered in New York to address large movements of refugees and migrants, 'with the aim of bringing countries together behind a more humane and coordinated approach'.[61] However, by the time that summit took place, the political winds in some powerful quarters were already changing.

The discussion changed from one of people moving per se to a split between 'migrants' and 'refugees', though initially no definition of 'migrant' was offered. At that high-level summit in September 2016, a 'New York Declaration' was unanimously adopted by UN Member States, setting out parameters for the development of a Global Compact for Migration and a Global Compact on Refugees. These processes would unfold in record time, with the deadline in 2018. Each was coordinated by different agencies, focused in different major UN cities and for the most part different people participated in each.

When the tight timeline was declared in 2016, it seemed extraordinary to think that a document which had seemed impossible for so long could be

drafted, negotiated and adopted in less than two years.[62] The process towards
the Global Compact for Migration would depend upon the spaces and
traditions that had been developed over the previous decades. As such, some
saw this as partly the culmination of Peter Sutherland's vision, arising from
the 'marriage' of migration and development and the processes associated
with it.[63] However, significant credit needs to be given to all those involved
in civil society mobilization since the 1990s. Ben Lewis of OHCHR, who had
himself also come from a civil society organization, observed of the Global
Compact for Migration process: 'I don't think any of this exists without
NGOs and migrants themselves demanding to be seen and heard.'[64] Not only
did global migrant civil society create spaces for themselves to be part of
discussion, but, as we have seen earlier, they also in some senses modelled for
States how this topic could be approached.

It became apparent that while there was disagreement between civil
society and some States, there was also observable solidarity across sectors.
Gemma Adaba who we met in Chapter 3, who coordinated the Global
Unions delegation to the Global Compact process, observed:

> the co-facilitators [from the missions to the UN of Mexico and of
> Switzerland] realised that they had natural allies in civil society. [...] they
> realised that they wanted to have a progressive enlightened document
> and that their best bet was to have civil society on their side.[65]

And civil society actors were consulted and incorporated into the process
in an unprecedented way. Several civil society actors told me that they had
been able to directly affect the wording of the zero draft of the document
and to speak with States and the UN in ways that had been impossible
before. One interviewee from a civil society organization reflected that in
their organization's area of expertise, 'I drafted the language that essentially
became the zero draft language for that document.' This relied on a culture of
shared spaces that had developed, including meeting in rooms which allowed
movement between the seating for States and that for others.

However, while there was much that was novel, this still took place against
a State-centric and citizenist backdrop. For example, in the 2016 summit in
New York, after presentations from General Assembly Presidents past and
future, the Secretary General and the heads of various international entities,
the floor was given to three 'representatives of the global refugee and migrant
community', which included Eni Lestari who we met in Chapter 3. While
they did tell their stories, they also used the space to make direct demands
of the international community. Arguably, in the moment when they spoke,
these individuals had power. However, some told me this was tokenistic

in a number of ways. First, they said there had been no open process for deciding who would speak in this forum. Second, though they opened the meeting and were able to make demands, even these invitees were not part of the negotiating and drafting of the document. Third, some worried that the extraordinary people who opened the meeting did not stand in for the many ordinary people living mundane lives made more difficult by migration policies. On this last point, it's worth noting that no one speaking from the podium in that meeting was particularly 'normal'. They all held extraordinary positions, with consequently peculiar experiences of the world. This last is a challenge to global governance discussions more generally.

The moral discourse that was in the air when the decision was made to produce the Compact made it seem like it might be possible to have a more humane approach to global migration governance. However, this air was soon changing. As the process unfolded, some civil society organizers maintained their optimism, while others became increasingly disillusioned. People who sat broadly in this second constituency told me that the Compact was not intended to stop the deaths, injury and violence experienced during migration. It was instead directed at stopping those tragedies from encroaching on the smooth running of the international system. This position is compelling. At the same time, analyses of the process and the resulting documents indicate that, while the position taken on migrants' human rights could be stronger, they are addressed in ways that they had not been before,[66] and core international principles protecting people moving are reiterated.[67] This seems like a radical shift from those meetings in 2006 in which human rights could not even be mentioned. Noncitizen power played a role in this, though it was constrained.

## Migrant civil society and noncitizen power

There is no singular understanding of the composition and role of civil society, and global migrant civil society is particularly complex. However, insofar as people are able to engage directly and substantively in global migration governance discussions, it seems that it must in some way be through a citizen relationship with the international system. Noncitizen perspectives, then, are mostly mediated through citizenship. As has been shown, this does not mean that noncitizen power is absent. This final section first sets out challenges in defining the composition of global civil society in this context, including structures affecting who is able to participate. It then argues that this affects the narratives that are able to emerge. It suggests that instead of focusing only on the role of 'civil society' per se, it might be important also to address access for people insofar as they have experience of noncitizenship and to trace the possibilities for noncitizen power.

First, 'civil society' has long been difficult to define, and so much more so for 'global civil society'. Historically, civil society has at different times *included* the institutions of government and *been in opposition* to them.[68] It has also referred to people living cooperatively without the need for a State.[69] A new usage for 'civil society' emerged in Anglophone discourses, at least, in the 1980s, to describe those pushing against Soviet power in East Central Europe.[70] In the 1990s, this meaning began to expand further, to refer more generally to those challenging State power and/or against the power of the market. This set the scene for the emergence of 'global civil society' and the NGOs mentioned in Chapter 2 that began meeting at the 1994 Cairo Conference.

In the epilogue to her 1990 book, *Justice and the Politics of Difference*, Iris Marion Young asks: 'Is there, then, in international politics something like an international civil society that repoliticizes public life outside or at the margins of these official state activities?' She suggests that studying international civil society 'can reveal a promising underside to the future of international relations'.[71] In the 1990s, a new language of 'global civil society' *would* emerge, as a way to promote peace and to democratize global politics.[72] Space was created for recognized NGO members of the UN's Economic and Social Council (ECOSOC) to contribute to intergovernmental discussions.[73]

Alongside the emergence of a global civil society has been a critique of it. One set of concerns identifies colonial tropes in its framing. This relates to both its conceptual cosmopolitan universalism[74] and the tendency to root current discussions in terms of European historical trajectories of domestic civil society.[75] It also relates to the concern that couching global civil society in terms of large NGOs based in Europe and North America may provide new mechanisms for domination.[76] Another set of concerns relate to moving power away from elected governments towards unelected employees of large NGOs with opaque accountability mechanisms.[77] These critiques have not gone away.

Those mentioned in this book who identify themselves as part of global civil society are not only members of NGOs but are also not merely extensions of domestic civil societies. The difference between domestic and global civil society is illustrated through interviews with some activists who only understood civil society on the global level. When I asked Pefi Kingi, a Pacific Island Indigenous activist engaging in the Migration Compact process, what she meant by civil society, she replied: 'civil society? I mean to be fair before we came into this process I never thought of our engagements in the community as civil society [. . .]. *We* talk about community.'[78] Another Pacific activist who was sitting nearby added further reflections on their relationship with governments domestically: 'We're related to them. We party with them. They come to our functions. We, we have a better relationship than we've heard *haoles* [non-Indigenous people] do. Because our distances are so limited. Our spaces are small and so our relatives actually work for agencies. So they are actually MPs.'[79] To these activists, the language of 'civil society' did not reflect the world as they lived it on the ground. They adopted it in order to engage in the movements of affected persons aiming to participate in global governance discussions. They didn't need a local language of civil society in order to enter into a global one.

For the most part, to those I interviewed, the composition of global civil society and global migrant civil society in particular was presumed to be progressive, to be rights-focused and to share the same broad political convictions as whoever I was interviewing at a particular time. Most told me, for example, that they didn't see a place for anti-migration, anti-multilateralism constituencies within this, though some added that it was still necessary to reach out to them. The truth is that in the research for this book, I also did not reach out to interview anyone who viewed the Compact from this perspective, and I did not observe their meetings and their protests in the way I did for global migrant civil society. However, this constituency made itself heard in different ways, with implications for how both citizen and noncitizen power are understood at the global level. This will be examined in Chapter 7.

Typically, contemporary definitions of State-level civil society push back against both the State and the market. This made it particularly interesting to hear the diversity of views about how global migrant civil society should relate to both States and the private sector.

First, participants in global migrant civil society often formed relationships with specific States. This includes Rhodora Abano of the Center for Migrant Advocacy in the Philippines who observed that 'the civil society is recognized as partner of government in working [. . .] to promote and protect the right of migrant workers'.[80] In fact, she added that by law NGOs are recognized as partners. Another interviewee observed that this went a step further so that there were 'CSOs that were fully funded by their government and accepted by the host country'.[81] Where civil society actors were paid for by governments and accompanied governments to the meetings, some felt that the line between civil society and government was blurred. Others did not see this as a problem. As mentioned earlier, the work of ICMC directly challenges the idea that there is a clear line between civil society and the governmental UN. This uncovers a tension in the diverse ways in which those engaging as part of global civil society understood their own position within it. It may also indicate that one difference between civil societies which function at the State level and global civil societies is that, while the global structure is State-centric, it is one in which States also come as participants.

Second, there were also diverse understandings of the relationship of global migrant civil society with the private sector. Previously, there had been little private sector participation in global migration governance discussions, but this increased since the creation of the GFMD.[82] Initially, business occupied an ambiguous position within civil society, with an often contentious relationship with other civil society constituencies. In 2015, States at the GFMD agreed to establish a new GFMD 'Business Mechanism', distinct from civil society. The next year the Mechanism was established, coordinated by the International Organisation of Employers (IOE) and the World Economic Forum Global Future Council on Migration, with an annual meeting specifically for the private sector at the GFMD.

When I asked interviewees to list global civil society constituencies, most lists included grassroots groups, diaspora communities and academics (though this last might have been in deference to me as an interviewer). Many also added labour unions, but interestingly some intentionally excluded them. Conversely, the list of one official from an international organization included only: 'NGOs, but I would also include academia and the trade unions'. Business and the private sector was usually excluded, but not by Ignacio Packer of ICVA and the Action Committee. When I asked him about this, he explained that for him the private sector is part of civil society and often an important ally of organizations such as his. He referred to 'the leadership of IOE' and explained:

> in 2018 we worked on common wording [. . .] for the global compact on migration, which would be pushed by civil society but at the same time by the business community. This mainly around issues around migrant rights, migrant workers rights.[83]

Other civil society activists took a very different approach. Eni Lestari of IMA said that including the private sector explicitly entrenched a framing of migration and development according to private interests and the role of the private sector in supporting States to control migration. Raúl Delgado Wise shares Lestari's view, but he argues that for this reason, the private sector *should* in fact be seen as part of civil society and that the creation of the Business Mechanism and explicit inclusion of the private sector in spaces inaccessible to other civil society actors meant that 'the business sector was given preferential status'.[84]

Those I spoke to from the business community did initially see themselves as part of civil society, though told me that they largely felt that other parts of civil society didn't agree. This was in fact a key factor in the creation of the Business Mechanism. Murtaza Khan, Fragomen's Regional Managing Partner for the Middle East, who engaged in the Business Mechanism of the GFMD, told me that there was a tendency among civil society actors to 'tar all business with one brush'.[85] He explained that he and those he represents want further regulation, to ensure that all companies keep to the same ethical and legal standards, rather than disadvantaging businesses who want to uphold both rights and national and international law. This was reiterated by Lynn Shotwell, who specializes in employee transfer and was Vice-Chair of the Business Mechanism of the GFMD when I spoke to her.

Shotwell told me that in other parts of the UN, business *is* part of civil society, but that in the global migration discussions, it is more complicated:

> what became difficult at least in the migration sphere is that so many other parts of civil society were hostile to business interests and the private sector interests. I saw very much an alignment between the labour movements and civil society, but what happened is that [. . .] the civil society actors often, when they are focused on migration, they see the worst part of the business, they see the abuses that happen in some parts of business. [. . .] So I think that we need a different mechanism.[86]

She explained that while some civil society actors did try to work with business on substantive matters, to others the private sector was only useful when it was providing funding. To Shotwell, the private sector has much to contribute beyond this. In an email, she explained that the creation of the Business Mechanism which explicitly separated the private sector from civil society 'has provided us a greater voice and more clarity on our role. It's also facilitated our efforts to recruit businesses to speak at the meetings as they don't receive the negative reception that they sometimes did when we were part of civil society'.[87]

Echoing Sutherland's WTO's affirmation of the importance of migration for business (mentioned in Chapter 3), Shotwell observes that existing systems of borders and visas inhibit global and multinational business. In this regard, she argues, often the interests of wider civil society may align with the interests of business. In her published work over several decades, Shotwell has argued in favour of visa policies that enable companies greater flexibility in hiring, training and moving staff. In 1999, she wrote that in a world in which '[t]here is global competition for the best and the brightest', it is in the interests of a State to support its employers – and so its business environment

– by having attractive visa schemes which would also be advantageous to workers.[88] This aligned with the views of some interviewees while others raised challenges with seeing migrants as units of development or labour, valued only as much as the particular labour they can provide is valued. In any case, the perceptions of who makes up global civil society differed from State-level understandings.

Global governance structures affect who is able to participate as part of civil society and how they are able to do this. Not least, the possibility of becoming part of active civil society is spread unevenly. If on the local level, '[t]he capacity for civil society is distributed disproportionately, depending on time, availability, adequacy of resources, communication networks, education and other unequally distributed resources',[89] this is even more marked at the global level. In practice, the global civil society landscape is dominated by people from certain regions and certain types of organizations. One interviewee, speaking about how this functions in the context of global migration governance and the need for a greater diversity of voices, observed: 'everything was very White'.[90] When I asked who they thought was missing from the Global Compact process, they went on to observe: 'the migrants themselves. Everything was through experts or through organizations that work with migrants. But in very few cases we heard from the migrants themselves'.[91] There is no formal mechanism for ensuring that, insofar as people encounter the international system as noncitizens, their perspectives are represented within it. Instead, they must rely on institutional insiders. And while there isn't any formal mechanism to include them, there are also structural barriers preventing their participation. These will be considered in more detail in the following chapters.

While global civil society since the 1990s has officially been composed of NGOs, several grassroots interviewees told me that they thought that 'BINGOs' (Big International NGOs) could smother migrant voices from reaching centres of power. To them, small and ill-funded grassroots organizations couldn't compete for resources and access. This is a version of a broader problem not only of economic and political power but also of epistemic injustice.[92] In her research into the impact of this on decision-making in development aid, Susanne Koch identified a perception that experts local to the site of a particular development initiative were less credible than those coming from overseas, and 'a general doubt in aid circles that local actors are able to succeed without external advice'.[93] This has implications for the kind of knowledge that can be brought to international discussion tables.

In the migration context, I was told by some that when staff from BINGO head offices in Europe and the United States, often receiving government funding, were invited to give 'the civil society perspective', this could be unhelpful. Some who work for what could be classed as large NGOs also told me that they were aware of this risk and sought efforts to mitigate it. One interviewee described one way in which this occurred. He recalled that, looking for how the large international NGO for which he worked could contribute to the Compact process, he reached out to someone from IOM in the Americas. He explained:

> So I told him, well, I am from [a particular international NGO] and we are intensely following this process from the Americas general level. So, I'd be happy to contribute in wherever I can. I think that's where the brand kind of like play a role because they were like: ok, ok. I mean, once I said I was from [that NGO] they were more interested to hear what we had to say than if I were to say I am from another organization, you know? So I think that was why later I was invited as an expert to the panel.[94]

The way things are currently structured often makes small organizations dependent upon larger NGOs and the inclination of their coordinators in order to gain a platform. As such, some of the same interviewees who criticized the gatekeeping of NGOs also said that this was made necessary by wider structures and celebrated examples in which that role had been used to include and facilitate grassroots perspectives.

Colin Rajah also recognized that leaving civil society representation to large international NGOs was problematic. He told me that to him, a crucial element of his liaison role with IOM would be to develop mechanisms to begin to address this. He said of BINGOs:

> [t]hey have offices in New York and Geneva and in other international centres. They have staff dedicated to it and [. . .] have relationships with governments and agencies working on that and have resources that are dedicated. That's good and important. But grassroots organisations which by and large make up the bulk of the work on the ground have very little to none of that at the global level. Maybe they might have some of that on the national, maybe on the regional, but very little on the global level. So I knew right from the start that that was going to be a huge gap: accessibility.[95]

With the financial and institutional support of IOM and a handful of States and of the governmental co-facilitators, he helped to support regional civil society consultations led by regional civil society networks, with the resources to grow diversity of voice. This included reaching out to organizations that had not been part of global discussions before and to the Pacific region which had previously been overlooked. However, in this work, Rajah told me that while the UN as an organization says that it is open to civil society and stakeholder participation, the institutional structures are not conducive to it. As such, it was necessary to 'move around the bureaucratic structures of the UN'.[96] This may have lessened the reliance on large NGOs to ensure civil society voice to a certain extent, but it still had to do this within a structure that was not designed for it.

This had implications for how narratives developed. Some interviewees highlighted challenges relating to the strong presence of religious organizations among global migrant civil society, though none named any specific organization. Those who mentioned this observed that religious organizations were crucial to bringing a humanitarian and broadly progressive approach to global governance discussions. However, several drew attention to particular challenges involved in discussing reproductive health and contraception and the rights of LGBT+ migrants. Some interviewees from large civil society networks told me that they believed that the strong involvement of religious organizations in their networks had forced some issues which many of their members thought were important off the table.

The landscape is complex. When I spoke to her in New York in 2019, Gemma Adaba explained: 'you have a number of faith groups who are completely in line with the secular groups.'[97] Towards the end of our discussion, she added:

> but then within these progressive groups you have religious values which dictate positions against endorsing very progressive statements upholding the human rights of LGBTQ+ migrant workers [. . .] or women's reproductive rights as human rights. These positions must be countered.

Monami Maulik also mentions this tension. For example, she told me that in 2017, the Global Coalition on Migration, under her leadership, committed to producing a 'platform for action' regarding what should be included in the Global Compact for Migration. This was developed with the input of the many diverse member organizations who submitted their initial ideas and their bottom lines. These were then debated. She explains that it 'took a while to come to consensus' and that 'at the end of the day we had to take out reference to upholding and protecting the rights of LGBTI migrants and issues of sexual orientation and gender identity'.[98] She told me:

> it's not to say our members are personally themselves discriminatory, or don't understand, or aren't fully clear that LGBTI people or migrants fully have rights [. . .] but they represent institutions that cannot take that position.

This draws attention to a broader structural problem in how civil society participation in global governance discussions is currently forced to function. That is, looking at issue areas that create tensions with religious commitments helps to make a much larger challenge become visible, one which occurs wherever there is tension between the concerns of grassroots groups and the commitments of the larger organisations that facilitate their access to global discussions.

As can be seen from the struggles to gain access and the institutional insidership, the existing system makes those in a noncitizen relationship with the international system reliant on others to put what is important to them onto agendas and convey input into a process which is not designed to include them. While there were significant efforts to make discussions more open, this was hampered by a reality in which the very structures that make people experts-by-experience on migration governance also make it difficult for them to travel to the places where key meetings were held or to be heard if they made it. This means that overwhelmingly, decisions about migration governance are made by people who have little experience of how it really functions. Those with the greatest expertise-by-experience of systems of migration governance also carry the greatest burdens of them, yet there is no formal mechanism to include them in policy discussions. This suggests a need for explicit focus on the inclusion of people insofar as they must live *despite* the international system (i.e. insofar as they experience noncitizenship) and an examination of how to facilitate noncitizen power.

# The power of place

When I spoke to migrant civil society activists who had been unable to access rooms hosting key discussions of the Global Compact for Migration, their comments often echoed elements from the song 'The Room Where It Happens' from the 2015 hit musical 'Hamilton'. One reason for this was that crucial discussions were located in countries with restrictive migration policies. An international organization representative explained in an interview: 'our approach has been to keep the space as open as possible and to meet with whoever wants to engage with us.' However, in practice, not everyone could make it into those open spaces. The organizers had to contend with a structure in which people with the most direct experience of the effects of the migration governance systems under discussion were also constrained by those systems from travelling to key locations. Some of those I spoke to believed that migrants, and irregular migrants, in particular, would always be sacrificed to enable agreement among States. A key reason for this was that they could not access the places where discussions were held and so would never be able to make those in power understand the problems of access. It was a vicious cycle.

In the discussion of migration governance, two ways of understanding the power of place collide. First, there are the places to and through which people move in the world in order to live out their lives. These places are powerful because they are where life is lived. Their power is further framed by lines that border them; affecting who can live out what parts of their lives where. These borders have power because people who wield power believe in the divisions created and protect them. Second, there are the places where power is concentrated. These are the places to which people go in order to participate in decision-making. A physical place of this second sort is powerful insofar as it supports a particular sort of 'social space',[1] made powerful because people see it as powerful and use it accordingly. The reference above to 'the room where it happened' is to a place which gains its meaning and power from the people that use it and from the legal and political structures both that those people impose upon access to it and which emanate from it.[2] Figure 5.1 shows the UN Headquarters at Turtle Bay in New York, where the Global Compact for Migration was negotiated. It is just such a place. However, Turtle Bay is also located within a State (the United States), as are all the sites where formal parts of the process towards the Migration Compact took place and

**Figure 5.1** The United Nations Headquarters at Turtle Bay in New York. Flags of member nations fly at United Nations Headquarters [1993]. Image courtesy of the United Nations Photo Library.

where most of the photographs from chapters 3 and 4 were taken. This chapter shows how in global migration governance discussions, the mechanisms affecting access to both forms of the power of place come together. The same mechanisms that affect where people can move in order to live out their lives also affect who is able to access those places where decisions are made.

## The power of movement and a crisis of agency

It is sometimes observed that the Global Compact for Migration came about because of a 'European migration crisis'.[3] Yet, confronting wealthy States in several regions in 2014 and 2015 was a crisis not of migration but of agency: the problem was not that people were moving but that too many of the 'wrong' people were trying to move.[4] When those States, confronted by unwanted people at their borders, doubled down, another crisis developed. This also wasn't a crisis of migration but a humanitarian crisis, produced as a result of deliberate policy, in which large numbers of people were trapped. This left people unable to access shelter, food, clean water and sanitation within some of the world's wealthiest States.[5] The process towards the Global Compact for Migration came about because people moved across borders that they had been told not to cross by States which had, till then, mostly been able to keep them out. This included States in Europe. Examining how things developed in Europe over this period helps to illustrate how these two types of power of place interact.

In the lead-up to the 2010s, European countries were particularly concerned about the northward movement of people from sub-Saharan Africa and parts of Asia.[6] It was framed as a concern about 'irregular migration'. However, underlying this is a concern about the arrival of people in certain unwanted categories who have been told not to move. This has echoes of colonial racialized tropes, including about who should have agency about their mobility. European countries put particular constraints on people moving from those regions. As such, European concern about irregular migration at that time was specifically about movement of people from those regions. While the period leading up to 2014 saw a focus in Europe upon Africa as a region of emigration, in fact, like Europe, African migration is also largely within the continent, and several sub-Saharan countries are countries of net immigration (i.e. they have more people arriving than leaving).[7] However, the European perception of threat from migrants travelling from sub-Sahara gives rise to policies that make that movement particularly difficult. As is shown in Chapter 2, this includes both restrictive visa policies and discrimination in visa profiling, with direct implications for who will need to travel irregularly in order to travel.

Migration decision-making is complex, especially when people face significant barriers to movement.[8] There are structural factors as well as individual 'triggers',[9] in a complex and evolving context.[10] In the period 2010–2017, nearly 75 per cent of sub-Saharans living in Europe were in the UK, France, Italy and Portugal.[11] This is not coincidental. The UK and France in particular are countries with centuries of colonial history in sub-Sahara, creating connections of language and culture, as well as indebtedness for past wrongs and dependence. The choice to move to Europe is also affected by demographic factors. For example, decreasing birth rates and increasing life expectancy in some European countries since the 1970s have produced labour shortages,[12] while continuing population growth in those parts of Africa with weak economies (made weaker by servicing international debts) has led to saturated labour markets.[13] Increasingly, the movement from Africa as well as other regions to fill those shortages has been made irregular by the new barriers imposed on migration over the same period.

In the 1960s and 1970s, while outside Europe one country after another declared independence from mostly European colonial governments, there were also growing racialized fears within European former metropoles about immigration. This contributed to increasingly restrictive immigration laws.[14] Since that time, European restrictions on the movement of people from some regions have continued to increase. In a world of more connectivity and freer movement for some, others have been confronted with increased barriers to accessing the global community and stronger constraints on movement.[15]

Particularly since the 1990s and early 2000s, European States had seen North Africa as a buffer against migration from sub-Sahara.[16] More recently, as North African countries became less stable, this buffer became less effective. At the end of 2010, popular protests arose in Tunisia and then in other countries in North Africa and the Middle East. Since the 1990s, Libya's then President Muammar Gaddafi had made agreements with sub-Saharan States, facilitating the movement of workers into Libya, but a number of factors including heightened anti-migrant racism meant many were looking to continue northwards. In the early 2000s, European leaders agreed to lift economic sanctions against Libya in exchange for Libyan cooperation in preventing migration of sub-Saharans to Europe.[17] When his regime began to teeter in 2010, Gaddafi reportedly warned that Europe would 'turn into Africa'[18] or 'turn black'[19] without his help. This reflects both the anti-Black racism of Gaddafi, and his appeal to anti-Black racism in Europe. After Gaddafi was assassinated in 2011, anti-Black racism that had long existed in Libya exploded.[20] Those identified as sub-Saharan were increasingly directly and indiscriminately targeted as 'mercenaries', forced to shelter in coastal villages or to flee.[21] Meanwhile, in nearby countries, some sub-Saharans were stranded[22] or facing unimaginable exploitation and ill-treatment as they tried to escape.[23] Reports emerged of slave markets and extortion for example.[24] Meanwhile, some citizens of North African States were themselves now also emigrating in greater numbers. And at the same time, new barriers were placed on their movement.[25]

In 2011, the violent government response to popular protests in Syria moved the country into civil war. Ordinary people, including members of the large migrant and refugee communities in the country, began to flee in larger numbers. Between 2009 and 2018, the global number of forcibly displaced people almost doubled, reaching 70.8 million. The UNHCR observed that most of this increase was from the period 2012–15, 'driven mainly by the Syrian conflict'.[26] And yet, escape routes were becoming increasingly dangerous and elusive. Those who had previously fled wars in Afghanistan and Iraq, or untenable conditions elsewhere, found their adoptive countries in the Middle East and North Africa now increasingly violent and unstable. They also began looking for ways out. In response, and through this period, the EU Border Protection agency, FRONTEX, monitored emerging routes and tried to block them.[27] In 2014, 'Mare Nostrum', the EU's search and rescue operation in the Mediterranean Sea, operated by the Italian Navy, was discontinued after a year in operation.[28] At the same time as some countries were experiencing instability, others responded by strengthening their border regimes. This continued in a tradition of European externalization of border controls.[29]

Facilitating mobility, particularly as a result of anti-colonial struggles, had been a key tenet of the Organisation for African Unity since its creation in 1963. The African Union and some regional organizations have made efforts at both securing borders and greater freedom of movement, though there also continues to be resistance to this.[30] It is in this context that European Union programmes associated with preventing movement were being established in parts of Africa. By 2015, there were outposts for European migration control in Somalia, the Sahel and West Africa, Niger, Mali and Libya; then EUNAVFOR, which was established off the East African coast in 2008, was extended to the Mediterranean Sea. This affected individuals without access to visas, who were trying to travel to Europe. The pressure exerted by the EU on countries hosting migration hubs led to people being detained or even returned to places from which they had fled without any assessment of their claim to refugee status for example.

Consequently, people continued to take their chances on unstable boats, buses, trains and by foot. As travel became more difficult, those travelling also became increasingly reliant on a growing private sector network of migration facilitators, including both smugglers and traffickers.[31] This drove an iterative growth in the role of the private sector both in supporting people to move and in supporting States to block them.[32] As demand grew, shippers allowed the human cargo on boats to become dangerously large. In April 2015, for example, in Libya, an estimated 700 people, mainly from West Africa, boarded a single boat headed for Italy. Still 180 kilometres from the Italian island of Lampedusa, it capsized.[33] It is reported that at least five boats sank in the Mediterranean in that month alone. The scale of the loss of life over this period is enormous.[34]

As migration from Libya through Italian ports became increasingly difficult, a new route began to emerge. In the spring of 2015, people began

deciding to board boats in Turkey, aiming for Greece. Greek Islands like
Lesvos hosted growing refugee camps. From there, people would try to take
land routes through Europe's Baltic periphery, heading for Western Europe.
By August, the situation along this route too was becoming increasingly
intense. The border between Hungary and Austria became a new flashpoint.
In August, the number of people boarding trains from Budapest to cities in
Austria and Germany began growing, while others sought road routes. One
group of seventy-one people, for example, climbed into a refrigerated lorry
somewhere in Hungary. On 28 August, the abandoned lorry was found on
the Austrian side of the border. All on board were dead.[35] On 1 September,
Budapest central train terminal was closed to migrants hoping to travel
onwards into Germany and other parts of Europe, leaving thousands of
people stranded in the city.

People unable to stay where they were, prevented from travelling
by plane or by sea, blocked from boarding trains and buses, started
walking into the European Union. And populist leaders in Europe started
circulating images of lines of people with barely any possessions, walking
through European fields and into European cities. This continued through
the summer of 2015. Meanwhile, European institutions scrambled to
construct new ways of talking about migration in Europe. There arose
in quick succession: the 2015 European Agenda on Migration, the 2015
Valletta Summit, the EU's Emergency Trust Fund for Africa and the
2016 Partnership Framework. However, in practice, these did not really
represent any shift of approach away from control and containment
and they didn't really acknowledge what was happening in European
borderlands.[36] A perfect storm was being created.

Once they found their way to European cities, many people were stranded
a second time. Iddrisu Wari, who had arrived as an irregular migrant in Spain
some years earlier, observes: 'how do you want that person to survive [. . .]
The law is the crime, not the person. If there's a law that says you can't earn
anything or eat anything, you have to wait three years, then of course, this
is not a law.'[37] The fact of people arriving in European countries prevented
from claiming the peace, security and prosperity available there directly
challenged those countries' self-image as progressive and promoters of rights.
Countries in the European region had long resisted coordinated UN efforts
relating to migration. By 2015 that had changed. Crucial to this change was
the fact that ordinary people with few other options were demanding entry
to European territories and European societies, while governments of those
countries largely tried to keep them out. In Chapter 7, I will suggest that this
movement is perhaps better understood using the language of 'civil disobedience'.
It is because of those people moving despite the barriers they faced that the

process towards the Global Compact for Migration was launched. And yet those very same barriers also blocked access to the process that they had initiated.

## Getting to where the power is

The mechanisms that make safe and secure migration near impossible for some also create impediments to participation in discussions about migration governance. As delegates from all over the world gathered in Marrakech to attend the Intergovernmental Conference to Adopt the Global Compact for Migration, a group of seventy civil society organizations from across sub-Saharan Africa issued a statement.[38] In that statement, they observed that not one of their key representatives had been granted a visa to attend the meetings in Marrakech. They mentioned difficulties obtaining visas throughout the two years of the process, impeding participation.

Indeed, for those affected, there were difficulties travelling to the sites of several key meetings. The process towards the Global Compact was launched in 2016. This year saw a new administration in the United States, where a large number of key meetings would be held. The new President, Donald Trump, imposed a series of constrictions on entry to the country, including specifically on people from a list of majority-Muslim countries.[39] Similar concerns also affected meetings held elsewhere. When I asked Roula Hamati, who coordinated regional civil society consultations in the Middle East and North Africa, about barriers to participation in global migration governance discussions, she told me: 'I think nightmare number one is the visa issue.'[40] She explained that she believed racist visa decisions were affecting who could attend meetings in her region. Others in other regions expressed similar views. One regional coordinator told me that racism led to delays in the processing of visa requests from what they euphemistically called 'nationalities [considered] to be problematic'.[41] Given the discrimination inherent in the global passport and visa regime identified in Chapter 2, it would be unsurprising to find that these challenges to attendance particularly affect people from countries in Africa and parts of Asia or countries experiencing conflict. And it could be a factor in why, as one interviewee quoted in Chapter 4 observed, 'everything was very White'.[42] Such barriers risked affecting the demographic of civil society participants and so also the sorts of issues discussed. This is exemplified by the fact that some civil society organizers who did not themselves encounter these problems, whether in person or in a coordinating role, told me that visas *didn't* present a significant barrier to participation.

It isn't new for passport and visa regimes to affect who can participate in governance discussions.[43] For the Global Compact for Migration process, I was told of cases where, for example, visa problems meant that an organization's sole representative, or the only representative from a particular sub-region or constituency, was unable to attend a key meeting. I was told that some grassroots activists in countries with 'weak' passports did not even bother applying. Others became dependent upon particular organizations or advocates for visa support. While some said that this affected what they felt able to say, others said that once they had a visa, how they had obtained it did not affect their participation.

One interviewee who was in the latter category had been part of engagement in a regional civil society network. On a Skype call, she explains her experience of obtaining a visa to attend the Global Compact meetings in New York:

> I was denied [a visa] during my first try [. . .] because the US embassy here [. . .] is very strict [. . .]. For example, single young [. . .] women going to the States; they are thinking people might not go back [. . .] any more. So they wanted to really secure all of the letters that I had to provide. So I had to ask IOM if they can provide me with a visa letter or an official invitation letter at least so that I can present it to the embassy. And then the second time they accepted it.[44]

This interviewee explains that she was grateful that her attendance was made possible and that she did not feel any pressure from IOM regarding her participation as a result of their help. Another interviewee mentioned that they were funded by IOM to join one meeting. They also said that this did not affect what they felt they could say at the meeting.[45] However, they did mention the *risk* of silencing. A third interviewee, who was involved in securing visas for others, mentioned the need to partner with other organizations in order to do this. They observed: 'the bigger the institution the more weight it will have to actually help get a visa'.[46] These experiences highlight a two-layered effect of the visa regime on participation: (1) discrimination in the visa process and (2) consequent need for some to rely on a decision about their eligibility to participate from a third party.

Representatives of several organizations, both governmental and non-governmental, reported that they had supported visa applications. A representative of one major funding body reflected that providing visa letters is simply part of facilitating civil society meetings and platforms. I spoke to a number of people who had received this sort of help from different entities. Some spoke only positively. Others mentioned that while they were grateful for the help, this need for support made them more cautious about what they said at meetings – fearing that if they were too critical of the entity that had supported them, they might not receive the same level of support the next time a visa was needed. Obtaining a visa also did not guarantee that a person would be able to travel to a meeting. I was told, for example, about a key speaker who was due to present at a regional preparatory event but was turned back at a transit hub because they lacked a transit visa. They had to return home, missing the event. Others, like myself, for the most part didn't need any pre-entry or transit visas at all and so would not have been affected in this way.

Several people said that it is simply too expensive and too much hassle to apply for visas for travel to meetings in Europe or North America, especially when the likelihood of approval is slim. They mentioned significant economic costs in the visa application resulting from the delays and uncertainty during the processing. Several people said that time wasted on visa applications (which often required cross-country, if not international, travel) detracted from more useful activities on the ground. These additional financial and time barriers to participation arose from the unequal effects of migration controls, but they also overwhelmingly affected people who were already time-poor and lacking financial resources. This made it harder for precisely these perspectives to be directly part of deliberations.

The coordinators of some regional networks explained that given these constraints and because of the limited time available to apply for visas (meetings and venues were often announced at the last minute), they ended up selecting people who already had visas for the relevant countries rather than those most qualified to speak on the topic at hand. Everyone who told me that they adopted this strategy said that they were not happy with it, but that this was required in order for a representative to attend at all. Some grassroots organizers said that no one in their organization was likely to be able to travel to somewhere like the United States, Switzerland or Austria, the locations of key meetings of the Global Compact for Migration meetings, so they could not consider participation as an organization at all. One local activist at a civil society event outside of these regions told me that it was better to acknowledge they had no say and would never have a say in the functioning of the international system. They should instead focus on making life better *despite* the system's malfunctioning. For them, noncitizen power in the international system was impossible.

The time constraints didn't only affect people with potential visa problems. Pefi Kingi who represented key Pacific region organizations recalled that the tight timeline between being brought into the process and travelling to Mexico for the stocktaking meeting meant that in the end, while there were three places, she was the only Pacific representative who was able to go. She recalls, 'As it transpired, I was the one of the three that was available to go.' She described this as 'a terrible tragedy, simply because the Pacific is diverse and it should be represented diversely'.[47]

For the most part, the formal parts of the Global Compact process were conducted in person and without the possibility to intervene from afar. This meant that those affected by visa problems, for example, were further removed from being able to participate. There was the possibility to send written interventions. But these went into a black box and were not part of the discussion. In addition, not all meetings and not all interventions were made available online. This meant that those not in the room would not be able to know what was said unless someone who had been there told them – and civil society organizers took it upon themselves to try to disseminate information about discussions to their networks. The formal aspect of this is also not the most important. Informal discussions, ephemeral posters and notes were also important in order to learn what was happening in the process. This was the case among States and it was also the case for civil society organizations.

In-person participation was also key to the creation of the informal networks that facilitated the transfer of information. Meeting people in person was part of forming informal caucuses and WhatsApp groups for example. In this way, despite the best efforts of those involved, in practice lack of access to physical participation could also further affect access to information about what had been discussed. The organizer of one series of civil society meetings that took place within UN compounds said of the meetings: 'People felt that it was an open and inclusive space that anyone could come to.' This was the case for those who were already there. However, for those who did not have access, this space was not open. Those involved tried to mitigate the impacts of migration policies on access to the process, but the task was enormous.

## Knowing your place

One labour activist I met at a large migrant civil society meeting laughed out loud when I asked informally whether they had considered participating in the meetings towards the Global Compact for Migration. They said that they had been a migrant worker in one of the countries where key meetings were held. Following unfair treatment at work, they had been deported. They told me that they didn't stand a chance of being re-admitted to the country, let alone to talk about migration policies while there. With this mark on their passport, it is also unlikely that they would be allowed entry to other countries hosting key meetings. They found the idea of participating ludicrous. I asked whether they had considered trying to participate from afar. They told me that they believed that their experience of how migration policies work is vital, but that no one in power would want to listen. Previous experiences of the visa infrastructure produced a range of psychological barriers, whether preventing a person from engaging at all, as in this example, or altering the way in which they felt about the process.

Eni Lestari of the International Migrants Alliance (IMA) who we met in Chapter 3 described an encounter she had on the way to a UN meeting:

> One time the UN bought me a ticket, transit in Texas. I [was] supposed to go to New York, right, and then [when I arrive in Texas,] I have to exit the immigration.
>
> > And they ask me: where I am going?
> > And I say: I'm going to New York.
> > What are you going to do there?
> > I'm going to speak at the UN.
> > What is your job?
> > I say: I'm actually a care-giver.
> > They say: why should the UN ask [a] care-giver to speak?
>
> And I don't know how to answer [their] questions, so I gave the letter [of invitation from the UN]. And then he was not convinced so he called to another officer to ask further. And they asked the same questions. And then finally they asked me to another customs [area] and then [they] check all my bag and so on and so on. Well, I assume it's a very normal procedure, because some of [the others in the arrivals hall] also get checked by the custom. But what I was very shocked was the fact that the letter that the UN gives me was not even enough for immigration and the border. [. . .] Because I told them I am just [a] care-giver and so, yeah, they saw the letter and they were just like [. . .] why the UN ask the care-giver to speak?[48]

Lestari explained that at the time, this experience rattled her confidence in her place at the meeting. Initially, she did not want to attend any UN events again. She went on to change her mind about this, but others do not. It is impossible to estimate how many people gave up on the idea of participating in international discussions about migration for these and similar reasons. And yet their experience of the disenfranchising and excluding impacts of the international migration governance infrastructure is crucial to understanding how the system works.

## Presumed absent: Irregular migrants

While there were efforts by organizers to ensure that global civil society would be present at key tables and their voices heard, there seemed to be a presumption that this would not include irregular migrants. For many in global civil society, this was not acceptable, but there wasn't much they could do. When I asked one grassroots organizer how they approached talking to members about the Global Compact for Migration, they explained:

> When we talk to migrant workers the first thing they ask is, you know, does it protect *all* migrant workers? We know the global compact only talks about regular migrants, documented migrants, right?[49]

For this organizer and their members, the legitimacy and usefulness of the Global Compact for Migration would be severely impaired to the extent to which it allowed a differentiation regarding fundamental rights according to a migrant's status. For grassroots migrant civil society, there was also concern that even if irregular migrants' rights were officially addressed in the document, this wouldn't mean much in practice.

Formerly irregular migrants did join some discussions, though, and there was a successful effort to have a member of the organization Deportados Unidos (deportees united) speak at the key stocktaking meeting in Puerto Vallarta in Mexico. One interviewee explained, 'we were saying it's gonna be in Mexico and it's very offensive that you won't take the voices of migrants that are in Mexico.'[50] So a Mexican person who had been deported from the United States spoke at the meeting. When the first draft of the Global Compact for Migration document was circulated, it was received positively by members of migrant civil society because of the extent to which it did not distinguish between migrants on the basis of status when it came to accessing basic rights. During the negotiations, some States, particularly in the Africa Group, continued to emphasize the need to maintain this lack of a distinction. The Common African Position (CAP), which set out African States' position towards the Compact, explicitly rejected the distinction. It stated, for example,: '[t]he protection of all migrants (regular and irregular, documented and undocumented) has become an imperative issue for consideration by all stakeholders', demanding that 'efforts to counteract irregular migration should not undermine the strict observance of human rights, human dignity and equal treatment before the law.'[51]

When I asked organizers about the inclusion of irregular migrants in the discussions, some were surprised. An official from an intergovernmental organization explained that it would not be in the interests of irregular immigrants themselves to be surfaced by attending meetings:

> I mean it wouldn't be smart to just have a person who is an irregular migrant in Belgium come and speak on a panel at the UN. I don't know what migrant would want to do that, right? I mean, I think we'd have a hard time recruiting that person.[52]

However, as one person in Kos put it to researchers: 'We just want our voice to be heard in the world. We want safety. And we want them to treat people like they are humans, not animals.'[53] This suggests that perhaps some irregular migrants do want to intervene in discussions about the policies that affect them. Enabling this would require mechanisms to mitigate the burdens of migration policies which currently prevent participation. This would include addressing challenges of trust produced by being irregularized.[54] Such mitigations *are* found in other realms and include, for example, anonymized live streaming.

The absence of these mitigations put a reliance on the NGOs and CSOs that choose to do so to bring irregular migrants' perspectives to the table. When I asked about irregular migrant representation in the Compact process, I was most commonly told that this was provided by the Platform for International Cooperation for Undocumented Migrants (PICUM). However, Michele Levoy, who represented PICUM in the Compact process, said that this reflected a misunderstanding.[55] She explained that PICUM didn't claim to *represent* undocumented migrants but did work to bring consideration of the rights and needs of undocumented migrants into the discussion. PICUM is a network of member organizations which work with undocumented migrants, mainly based in Europe. Some of PICUM's members are migrant-led, but the organization should not be seen as representing undocumented migrants tout court.

The initial intention of PICUM had been to try to bring the perspectives of those working with undocumented migrants into discussions at European Union institutions. PICUM has been engaging with global migration governance discussions for nearly two decades, bringing consideration of the rights and interests of undocumented migrants into that discussion. In the absence of any organization explicitly representing undocumented migrants themselves, PICUM often ends up being a key voice in advocating for their interests, but this isn't representation. Consequently, those most affected by migration policies and bearing the greatest burden of migration governance were presumed absent from the discussions and were unrepresented at discussion tables. They were reliant on others to bring their insights into meetings, and reliant on them to prioritize addressing the challenges faced as a result of being irregularized. This included actors like those mentioned in Chapters 3 and 4 as well as civil society organizations including PICUM and UN entities such as OHCHR and UNICEF and some Member States.

The need to protect irregular migrant rights became an important topic of debate among States during the final negotiations, with African States represented by Comoros on the one side and twenty-seven EU Member States led by Austria on the other.[56] The final version of the Compact indicates a tension between sovereignty and human rights of migrants, but it still affirms a commitment to ensure rights for migrants irrespective of status. In the preamble, there is a paragraph headed 'National sovereignty'.[57] It sets out that

> States may distinguish between regular and irregular migration status, including as they determine their legislative and policy measures for the implementation of the Global Compact, taking into account different national realities, policies, priorities and requirements for entry, residence and work, in accordance with international law.

This is followed on the same page by a paragraph headed 'Human rights', which states:

> By implementing the Global Compact, we ensure effective respect, protection and fulfilment of the human rights of all migrants, regardless of their migration status, across all stages of the migration cycle.

These two dimensions come together particularly in Objectives 11 and 14. Objective 11's opening includes the following:

> We further commit to implement border management policies that respect national sovereignty, the rule of law, obligations under international law, human rights of all migrants, regardless of their migration status, and are non-discriminatory, gender-responsive and child-sensitive.

This acknowledges that border management policies need to be tempered by the need to respect the human rights of people irrespective of their migration status, but does not explain how this should be done. Levoy and Adaba have both told me that this should be acknowledged as a promising development, but they and some grassroots activists also said that they would wait to see what this meant in practice before getting too excited. It is also important to see this language in the context of the complex and varied meanings given to 'sovereignty' and 'migrant' as set out in Chapter 2, including the deference to States in identifying who is a 'migrant' and which migrants are 'irregular'.

## Invisible: Those treated as migrants irrespective of movement

A catchphrase of the Compact was 'people on the move', but migration policies do not only affect people who move. Without a clear international definition of 'migrant', some people are defined as migrants irrespective of movement. This constituency is the focus of this section. Chapters 1 and 2 introduced Ekaterina E and Paulette Wilson, respectively. They have both been affected by migration policies not because they moved but in the form of exclusions from their home societies. Crucially, in both cases, migration governance was experienced in ways that are invisible to those who are unaffected. And crucially both have used noncitizen power to push for policies to be re-examined and changed. Both because of their expertise and because they bear such a burden of systems of migration governance, it is also crucial to ensure the inclusion in global migration governance discussions of those who are treated as migrants irrespective of movement.

Paulette Wilson had moved from Jamaica to the UK during a period of free movement between the two. She had been eligible for British citizenship but had not realized that she needed to confirm this with documents. Changes in migration policies in the UK meant that after living, working and raising a family in the UK as a citizen, she suddenly found herself being defined as an 'illegal immigrant' unless she could prove otherwise. She was in the process of trying to demonstrate the details of her half a century in the country when she was taken into immigration detention pending removal. Wilson knew that what had happened was terribly wrong. She spoke to a reporter and the publication of her story began a snowball of others coming forward to say that similar things had happened to them. This led to outrage in the public, debates in the UK Parliament, international intervention from other heads of government and academic investigation into what had gone wrong. Policies were changed thanks to the work of Wilson and others.

Ekaterina E travelled to the United States from the Soviet Republic of Uzbekistan as a teenager. While she was away from home, her Soviet passport ceased to be recognized. By the time she tried to obtain the citizenship of the new country, she was unable to do so. Without access to the citizenship of either Uzbekistan where she is from and where her family lives or the United States where she has now lived for most of her life, she is left 'stateless'.

That is, she does not have citizenship of any State. In the United States, there is no way to be formally recognized as stateless and she has no route to citizenship. Without a citizenship, she also doesn't have a regular way to travel elsewhere and is at risk of being treated as an irregular immigrant where she lives. E discovered that there were others in similar situations in the United States and together they tried to address their situation. They discovered that official UNHCR data indicated that there were zero stateless people in the United States. She and others successfully pushed for this to be changed. As a result a major mapping project was launched which indicated that hundreds of thousands of people may be stateless in the country.

Both Wilson and E have been affected by policies apparently directed at controlling migration, but not because they have moved. Any high-level discussion of migration governance needs to take into account experiences like theirs. This is not easy. Their realities are not only invisible; both E and Wilson have pushed for a change in situations of 'meta-blindness'. That is, it is not only the case that those who are unaffected don't know about the problems produced by underlying policies. In fact, those who are unaffected may also not know that there is something that they do not know. This means that evidence-based and sustainable policy making is dependent on the input of experts like Wilson, E and millions of others, who must live *despite* systems of governance and so have crucial insights and expertise into how they function. That is, it is crucial to look to those with expertise-by-experience of living in a noncitizen relationship to the international system. It is, then, crucial to adopt a noncitizenist lens and to recognize the value of noncitizen power. Overlooking such individuals in global migration governance discussions means that policies may be developed without full understanding of their implications. This is a problem for sustainability. It is also a problem for the UN's democratizing project. Those who must live *despite* governance structures may bear the heaviest burdens of those structures without a say in how they are designed nor how they function.

## The power of place and noncitizen power

In 2004, a Panel of Eminent Persons led by Fernando Henrique Cardoso published a report on civil society engagement in the United Nations.[58] This report raises some key matters also mentioned here. It emphasizes the importance, for example, of covering travel costs to enable wider participation and enhancing capacity among civil society actors. However, a further iteration of this report would need to engage with a more fundamental matter affecting the ability of those with expertise-by-experience of migration policies to engage meaningfully in discussions about migration governance. That is, in order to join discussions about the regime of passports and visas, it is necessary to have access to that system. The process towards the Global Compact for Migration shows the complexity of the power of place in this context. The process was launched because people moved. But the same mechanisms that politicized their movement meant that those people couldn't participate in that process.

Some said that they thought that key meetings should be held in those locations with the fewest visa restrictions. This is not a new idea.[59] Research carried out by the WHO found that when key meetings were held in the Global South, more CSO representatives from the Global South have been able to attend, thanks to both fewer travel restrictions and reduced costs.[60] I was unable to follow what happened during the move to online engagement in response to Covid, but research conducted during this time suggests that 'zoomification' enabled new voices to join UN sessions and provided for 'comparatively very open and inclusive' civil society discussions, including people who would not have participated had travel been required.[61] Stefan Rother predicts that this will lead to an increased use of online, along with in-person, meetings in the future. This could provide additional opportunities for noncitizen power.

The power of place and noncitizen power intertwine in ways that are important to recognize. This makes it necessary to address directly those elements of the migration control infrastructure which make it difficult for those key stakeholders to participate. This is also part of a much broader consideration. In order to ensure civil society access to global policy discussions, it is not only crucial to address problems of funding and capacity, though these are important, but also necessary to address the problem of citizenship.[62] That is, it is necessary to address the reality in which some people have access to the international system of mobility and others do not, and the significant impact of this on who is able to participate formally in reshaping that reality.

# When talk is cheaper for some

About a decade ago, a meeting I was observing at the UN Headquarters in New York was overrunning. An announcement was made. We were told that the interpreters would have to go home soon and that any further interventions would have to be in English. It was troubling, not because the interpreters would go home (they have working hours like anyone else), but because rather than allowing people to intervene in the UN language in which they felt most comfortable, the default language would be English. The people sitting on either side of me, observing, like myself, all spoke more than one UN language. Presumably, this was true of many of those in the room. The switch to English would privilege even further those who find it easiest to express themselves in an already dominant language. This chapter explores to what extent the default use of English makes talk cheaper for some and more costly or even impossible for others. It suggests what this means for the possibility of noncitizen power in global discussions of migration governance.

As in other global contexts, English was the presumed lingua franca of the process towards the Global Compact for Migration. It functioned almost like a national language of that process. This is an instance of a wider phenomenon which has been referred to negatively in French as 'tout-à-l'anglais'.[1] On one level, it makes sense. English is a widely spoken second language globally, a widely used language of politics,[2] and a common working language of the agencies involved in global migration governance. However, privileging English in this way can also be seen as a form of the epistemic injustice introduced in Chapter 4. As with migration policies presented in Chapter 5, language can both produce noncitizenship and prevent the expertise of those experiencing noncitizenship (including on the basis of language) from being heard directly. In addition, as with the different experiences among States of territorial sovereignty discussed in Chapters 2 and 5, the use of English as the common language also produces and reproduces structural inequalities among both States and individuals.[3]

Chapter 5 showed how the same migration governance mechanisms that control access to migration routes also control access to the spaces in which migration governance is discussed. This chapter demonstrates that something related but different occurs in the context of language. It identifies both practical problems and symbolic problems with presumed privileging of English.[4] This not only affects the discussion of migration. The UN has been called upon repeatedly not to capitulate to monolingualism.[5] And yet still, as some scholars have observed: '[English] is the language in which the fate of most of the world's citizens is decided, directly or indirectly'.[6] In this sense, then, addressing English dominance in global migration governance processes has the potential to have wider implications.

## القوة السياسية لاختيار اللغة

اختيار لغة العملية السياسية له آثار كبيرة. كانت اللغة الرئيسية للعملية نحو الميثاق العالمي للهجرة هي اللغة الإنجليزية. تمت صياغة الوثيقة باللغة الإنجليزية وكانت صياغة نص اللغة الإنجليزية التي تم التفاوض بشأنها. هذا الكتاب بين يديك مكتوب باللغة الإنجليزية. هذا يعني أنه من المعقول افتراض أن قرّاءها يجيدون اللغة الإنجليزية. أكتب هذا المقطع باللغة العربية لإعطاء إحساس بسيط بما يعنيه أن يتم منع المشاركة الكاملة والفهم الكامل بسبب اللغة المستخدمة. [7]

The title and opening of this section are written in Arabic. Some readers will be able to read the above text. It is likely that many cannot. The latter constituency will simply be excluded from the information contained within it and blocked even from knowing the title of the section they are now reading.[8] The United Nations has six official languages: Arabic, Chinese, English, French, Russian and Spanish. The principal language of the process towards the Global Compact for Migration was English. The document was drafted in English, and there were no official translations of the interim drafts. Official events were mostly held in English, with interpretation sometimes available. For formal State-led meetings, there was interpretation between the six UN languages. For more informal meetings, interpretation was either non-existent or focused on some combination of English, French, Spanish and Arabic. For the events that I attended, English was always available. For those most affected by this choice of language, there was little opportunity to push back against the dominance of English.

Like visas, which were discussed in Chapter 5, several interviewees referred to language as one of the most overwhelming barriers to accessing information and to participation. However, also like visas, for those who had not encountered this barrier (either personally or in a coordinating role), it was not seen as a problem. Some fluent speakers of English (whether as a mother tongue or as an additional language) seemed surprised that I would mention language as a potential barrier to participation. However, among those who had experienced the language barrier, the problem of language was mentioned repeatedly. As they reiterated, the Global Compact was drafted in English and the default language for discussions was English. Emails from organizers were in English, as were signs at venues. Sometimes other languages were used. Sometimes they were not. Those affected told me that this had radical implications for who could participate and how they could participate.

Some of the people from global civil society who were sending emails and information out mentioned the difficulty in deciding between sending out information only in English and not sending information out at all, given their capacity. Laurel Townhead of QUNO told me that while her organization sent out emails and information only in English, this was taken up by others and shared further. For example, she mentioned that the Bloque Latinoamericano translated into Spanish the key documents that they cascaded through their network. Indeed, one interviewee who was involved in the Bloque said that he had seen this as a key contribution.[9] When I asked Eni Lestari if the language used in emails was a problem among her networks, she added that the medium of email itself caused difficulties: 'if you are a grassroots migrant, email is your last thing, you know. You don't check email every day and you don't read long emails.'[10] Indeed, in her communications with me, Lestari preferred to use WhatsApp instead of email. Implications of diversity among the forms of communication that reach beyond named languages will be developed shortly.

Professional interpretation is expensive, but civil society organizers found ways around this. While sometimes funders provided interpretation at civil society meetings, at other times volunteers offered interpretation including on an ad hoc basis. This drew on a wealth of excellent and experienced community interpreters available among the diaspora and migrant civil society groups. Sometimes, in the absence of any alternative, interpretation in informal meetings was offered by people like myself. The quality of my interpretation was not good. When I apologized for this, I was told by people who would otherwise not have had any access to the discussion that it was better than nothing. Ignacio Packer, who organized meetings for the Action Committee, told me that 'we try to translate in Arabic, Spanish, French', but that this often wasn't possible and as a result, 'English is the main language, which is a handicap for many people'.[11] Of the civil society events I attended myself or discussed with interviewees, where interpretation was available, it was usually available in three languages, either English, French and Spanish or English, French and Arabic, depending on where the meetings were held.

The ad hoc voluntary interpretation available at civil society events arguably made some informal civil society meetings more language inclusive than some informal governmental meetings. Monami Maulik explained that this came from the culture of social movements and migrant community organizing. She explained:

> When I was running a grassroots organisation with low wage migrant workers who are sitting in a membership meeting who really don't speak English [. . .] we always had to run meetings in about four languages.[12]

She explained that this was managed using staff and community members who could step in informally and interpret where needed. For meetings of DRUM:

> days before a membership meeting, we would look at the list of [. . .] people that we know are coming, the organisers would break out who speaks Bengali only or Hindi only or who can speak English, and what should be the functional language for that meeting. We would have to figure it out and then look amongst us who can translate into that language or split up and separate the room in a way that we can be in small groups with a few volunteer simultaneous translators.[13]

This can help to explain some approaches to language in global migrant civil society discussions.

Linguistic challenges did not only arise for civil society. State delegates were also largely restricted to intervening in the six UN languages. In addition, despite the availability of interpretation, sometimes individuals from countries where the main language is one of the five other UN languages chose to intervene in English. This isn't unusual. One survey of Heads of State speeches at the UN General Assembly between 2004 and 2018 found that English was used for 52.7 per cent of the 1,540 speeches studied.[14] This all meant that those who did not speak English simply could not participate in some discussions and participated in others at a disadvantage. This impact of English-language dominance at the international level has been described as a process of 'minorization' of speakers of other languages alongside a 'naturalization' of the dominance of English.[15] While linguistic discrimination may be key to this domination, it is the domination which drives the 'minorization'.[16] There are two parts to this. First, the linguistic discrimination allows domination of those less comfortable or less able to function in English. Second, this domination risks putting those less comfortable or less able to function in English into a position that in some ways echoes that of a speaker of a minority language within a State.

One civil society activist who I interviewed in a UN language other than English said that they personally didn't feel confident to engage in the process themselves *solely because of* their lack of English.[17] Meanwhile, when those who could use English, but with some discomfort, did engage, they needed more time in order to do so. One such individual, who I in fact interviewed in English, told me they had to make heavy use of Google translate. The impact, at least in part, of language choice on who participates in discussions more generally could be seen in the different constituencies attending different civil society meetings: the People's Global Action (PGA) and the World Social Forum for Migrations (WSFM), for example, which were introduced in Chapter 3. Both of these sets of meetings make significant efforts to provide translation and interpretation, but the WSFM is traditionally dominated by the use of Spanish and the PGA by English. One of the efforts made to help include speakers of various languages is illustrated in the badges available for those staffing welcome and help desks at these events. Figure 6.1 shows some of the badges available at the 2018 WSFM in Mexico City. While there were badges to indicate that welcome staff spoke English, French, or Arabic, there was no badge to indicate Spanish, since this was presumed. At the 2018 WSFM, the absence of first-language English speakers

**Figure 6.1** At the WSFM, there were badges for people who could help speakers of French, English or Arabic. There was no badge for Spanish as this was presumed. Photograph taken by author.

was marked. Instead, there was a much larger proportion from Spanish- and French-dominated contexts. These are global civil society meetings, explicitly dependent on network formation. The official meetings at the UN are not, but may be affected similarly by English language dominance.

Some entities had tried to provide translations of the Global Compact for Migration drafts, but the combined effort of producing the translations and trying to disseminate them to everyone who might need them was overwhelming. An official from an international agency told me that the intergovernmental bloc, La Organisation Internationale de la Francophonie, made efforts to produce standard translations of key documents in French. Meanwhile, Spanish-speaking participants from both governmental and civil society perspectives came together to form the network the Bloque Latinoamericano,[18] and I was told that members of the Bloque volunteered to produce translations of key documents into Spanish on an ad hoc basis, which were then circulated among the network. However, these were not official translations and they were only available to those who came to know of their availability through their networks. Some who had tried to engage in the process and were solely Francophone or Hispanohablante told me that they were unaware of any translations.[19] One official who had been involved in organizing the process explained that it was difficult to invest in the translation of a text that would only be valid for three weeks.[20] However, the lack of funding provided for producing informal translations, or for dissemination of those translations, created problems for people without easy access to English.

In the Middle East and North Africa region, for example, this came to a head in one Arabic-language discussion of the draft Compact. As Roula Hamati, who was then the Research and Advocacy Officer of the Lebanese migrant rights organization Insan and a regional coordinator, explained:

> [T]he Compact says 'working towards eliminating detention'. But they read it as the Compact 'allows for detention' and says that 'detention is sanctioned, is allowed'. And we've had this big debate because these groups as a result were going to denounce the Compact. So it was a lot of discussing back and forth [...] and I mean, no one really being convinced because this is how they understood it and there was nothing to be done about it.[21]

From this comment, it is apparent that the barriers created by the sole use of English had implications beyond the State-led negotiation rooms. When I put this case to the official mentioned in the paragraph above, their response was simply 'wow'. They said they had not been aware of this implication.

This has implications for how the possibility of consultation is understood. Jacqueline Mowbray puts it bluntly. She observes that language is 'what allows us to communicate with each other', and consequently, language is fundamental in creating or impairing the conditions for democratic decision-making.[22] If people are unable to communicate or to understand what is being communicated, then it is difficult to see how they can meaningfully be said to be part of a policy process. Mowbray observes that there is problematically little international law and policy addressing language in global-level political institutions.[23] This, she argues, produces a 'democratic deficit' in the UN,[24] with implications for linguistic justice.[25] The dominant use of English affected how people were able to organize their engagement in the process. In the case above, the debate ended up being one of how to translate the English text rather than about the content of it. That is, while for some, the language was not even visible, for others the language was all that was visible, obscuring the content. A noncitizenist approach is needed with regard to language because (1) it uncovers structures that are invisible to those without such a perspective and (2) those who carry the heaviest burden of the international system are least able to be part of shaping it.

## Political problems with English-language dominance

English-language dominance is not limited to the Global Compact for Migration process.[26] Indeed, when I asked about the use of English, several of those who did not see language as a problem informed me that English is simply the most widely spoken international language and widely used working language in international politics. This is what made it a good choice for the lead language of this process. In 2020, with 1,268 million speakers, English is the most spoken language in the world. It is followed by Mandarin Chinese, with 1,120 million speakers. The next most commonly spoken languages have only half as many speakers or fewer.[27] However, this dominance of English is self-reinforcing. As English in its various forms[28] is increasingly dominant, it becomes increasingly important to be able to speak English in order to participate, thus making it even more true that English is dominant. As one scholar notes:[29]

> [English]'s use in particular domains, especially professional, may exacerbate different power relationships and may render these domains more inaccessible to many people; its position in the world gives it a role also as an international gatekeeper, regulating the international flow of people; it is closely linked to national and increasingly non-national

forms of culture and knowledge that are dominant in the world; and it is bound up with aspects of global relations.

That is, using English as a 'native language' of global politics risks reinforcing the sorts of hierarchies that are created when a language is privileged on a State level. It makes certain spaces inaccessible and reinforces other barriers, such as those spatial ones discussed in Chapter 5. To see this, consider what would happen to the existing landscape of participants and narratives in global migration governance if a wholesale switch were made from English to Mandarin Chinese, the second most widely spoken language.

In the case of the Global Compact for Migration, the fact of English-language dominance itself created political problems and barriers to participation. This unfolded in two ways. First, several of those who raised the problem of language also observed that the dominance of English as well as of French and Spanish – and one also mentioned Arabic – is not accidental. They observed that this dominance is a result of histories of colonial domination. This is reinforced by contemporary coloniality and neocoloniality,[30] giving rise to a feeling that capitulating to the drive to communicate in English was a capitulation to that ongoing colonial dominance. This meant that the very use of English in global political discussion was alienating for some political actors, including some who spoke English fluently. Second, some people explained that they felt insufficiently qualified to participate in discussions because though they spoke English, and sometimes fluently, their English was 'not good enough'. That is, the dominance of English in fact did dominate these participants. I will now expand on these in turn.

For some civil society actors who understood and spoke English well, the symbolic dominance of English in the process towards the Global Compact for Migration was disaffecting. Many of those trying to engage in this process were coming from countries that had experienced British colonialism in the previous century. Some said they did not want to be forced to engage in what they perceived to be a language of domination. For example, interviewees from the Middle East and North Africa region told me that many people spoke Arabic, which is also a UN language and yet found themselves forced to communicate in English. Some participants from African countries which use French as a language of politics told me informally that they were already speaking in a foreign colonial language of French and yet often felt blocked from participation because, as one person put it, French was 'not enough'. This seems to echo Frantz Fanon's description of a hierarchy of recognition channelled through language, that 'mastery of language affords remarkable power'.[31] Several interviewees observed that English, like other UN languages, dominates because of active efforts at domination.[32]

It is important though not to focus tokenistically on the use of English without seeing the broader complexity of structures of linguistic domination.[33] More than one person I spoke to from the Middle East and North Africa region observed that the insistence on speaking Arabic in some local and regional civil society consultations relating to the Global Compact for Migration in fact had detrimental effects on the most marginalized civil society constituencies in the region. Whereas Arabic may be a mother tongue for many people who have grown up in the MENA region, they told me that for migrant workers who are often from African countries where French dominates or Asian countries with dominant English, the refusal to use French or English, respectively, in some meetings prevented their participation. For them, it was Arabic-language dominance that was exclusionary. And as one told me, this also reinforced Arab colonialism.

The need for discussions to be accessible in major languages of migrants was also mentioned. Eni Lestari of IMA observed that documents relating to migration governance should be translated into the key global migrant languages as a matter of course. She went on: 'they also have to translate it into Asian languages, one or two major supplier[s] of migrants.' For her, the dominance of English was being used as an intentional method of exclusion. For her, the only way to ensure genuine participation in migration governance discussions would be to ensure that all those affected, or at least the key constituencies of those affected, by migration governance infrastructure should be able to participate in the process in their own language. However, as seen in Chapter 5, not every migrant experiences the global migration infrastructure in the same way. This is also apparent when it comes to language. There are those national languages which are not official UN languages. There are also minority languages which lack State recognition. A speaker of a minority language in a State may already have to speak an additional State language for local political engagement. International engagement, then, may require additional layers of linguistic challenges which don't affect others.

One interviewee from the Americas region observed:

> all the information that was produced in the GCM was in English so there wasn't any Spanish translation to anything. So many of my colleagues couldn't understand English as well, or didn't speak English. So that was a big challenge for us to find the people that could speak English to be able to communicate in the negotiations and in the next stages.[34]

It also became clear that it was not only the language used that was important but also the *register and form* of the language that was used. Those who had learnt English as migrant workers in manual jobs in majority-English-speaking countries, or in countries where employers spoke to employees in English, had learnt the style of English necessary for their job. This did not include the formal style and technical language used in the documents associated with the process towards the Global Compact for Migration. Some such individuals explained that although they could function fluently and confidently in English, their level of English wasn't 'good enough' to participate in global governance discussions. Several people stated that they had to read documents using Google translate as they also struggled with the formal style of English or struggled to read the quantity of documents required of them. Glorene Das of IMA explained that even when people speak English,

> there was a gap in the language, the narratives, right?, because when you consult a grassroots migrant organisations or people who are working at the roots level, the language that they use is not in line with the language of the state or the corporation.[35]

This meant that it was necessary not only to translate and interpret between named languages such as from English to Spanish, but also from English of a formal style to more accessible English. Some organizations tried to do this for some documents, but there was not time or human resources to do this for all the documents emerging during the process or even all the iterations of the Compact document. This risked excluding key people from participating in a meaningful way.

One official from the International Organisation for Migration (IOM), who had been involved in organizing the Global Compact process, observed that this was about more than register and style. It was also about the *culture* of communication at the international level which wasn't only challenging to members of global migrant civil society:

> the global processes, it always has its own language. It has its own sort of dynamics and sometimes it is difficult to bring people from the field into the global level and be able to speak the language. Because it's really two different worlds.

Indeed, the IOM had also worked with large civil society networks to provide training for civil society organizers who were new to engaging at the UN. Two people who had received this training told me that they had found it invaluable. But they also said that capitulating to the culture of the UN felt like capitulating to a colonial way of conducting discussions.

Speaking about how governance discussions take place in her region, Pefi Kingi observed: 'Pacific and Maori and indigenous Pacific in particularly, they'll only trust you if it's face to face [. . .] so you have to bring people together.'[36] This made it difficult for Pacific islanders to mobilize their responses to key documents in time. She also described cultural traditions relating to how important conversations should be conducted. This suggests that a more complex understanding of linguistic diversity is needed, including more varied forms of 'meaning making'.[37] This need for face-to-face engagement, Kingi explained, derives from a distrust of external actors as a result of past experience: '[t]hey have developed a strategy to avoid what is thrust on them. So we are [suspicious], not by nature, we are suspicious because of our experience of colonialism'. She describes how it was not only English language which dominated but also certain norms of discussion, norms which another interviewee, from a large civil society organization based in a European capital, described as 'anglo-saxon'.[38]

As was set out in Chapters 3 and 4, there are also different norms of decision-making among those in different sectors. Leading a network of networks, Monami Maulik would need to feed information to member networks and wait for them to feed information through to their members. She would then need to wait until the various organizations would respond. She explained that this affected the speed with which their advocacy message could be shared with policy-makers: 'sometimes it feels very frustrating because it ties your hands from being able to respond in the time needed to impact a negotiation or document'. She contrasted this with other organizations which 'have staff [. . .] who carry the authority and the mandate of the organisation to analyse and speak on its behalf'.[39] This suggests that efforts to 'democratize' global politics would need to take into account a broader conception of linguistic diversity and to also include cultures of communication and consultation.

Meanwhile, several of those I spoke to from large organizations mentioned that they did not think that the language question was as serious as it might appear. They explained that this was because all of those engaging at the international level in fact speak English fluently already. Fluency in English, and in the sort of English needed for such engagement, is simply one of the skills that you have to develop when becoming involved in international policy processes. However, as was mentioned by some interviewees, particularly from grassroots organizations, this effectively sets fluency in English as a pre-requisite for such participation. One told me that it was a shame that this might exclude some voices from speaking directly, but that it would be a strategic mistake to put forward someone without the required communication skills.[40] This meant that some of those grassroots organizations which were forced to select representatives with appropriate migration documents (see Chapter 5) were also forced to select those most able to use the appropriate form of English.

It is not possible to estimate how many people were excluded as a result of language from engaging in the Global Compact for Migration process at a national to a global level because many simply did not know that they could engage or did not see a point in doing so. One migrant civil society organizer observed:

> because of the language barrier [and the lack of support from any sector] to make sure that what you want to say is going to be translated, then [activists who do not speak English] will not say anything.[41]

That is, this interviewee felt that even if people who do not speak English fluently make it to the relevant meetings, there is less impetus to say something if they believe that what they say will not be translated or understood as intended.

## Lost concepts

> The fact that I
> am writing to you
> in English
> already falsifies what I
> wanted to tell you.
> My subject:
> how to explain to you that I
> don't belong to English
> though I belong nowhere else
>
> Gustavo Pérez Firmat, in *Bilingual Blues*, 1995[42]

The dominance of one language does not only give rise to lost voices but also risks lost or insufficiently defined concepts. Gustavo Pérez Firmat's poems trace some of the many ways in which language can affect a person's relationships with the societies and States in which they live. He demonstrates how the choice of language in a particular situation can affect who can participate and how they can express themselves. Expressing the topics of discussion only in one language loses the cultural framing provided by other languages, and the insight that framing things in a range of languages can offer. One interviewee observed, 'it is much more effective when we are expressing it in our own languages [. . .] so one would have to take ownership of it through our own languages and then translate it back into a main major UN speak.'[43] This may have impacted upon the process towards the Global Compact for Migration in a variety of ways. And it affects discussions of global governance more generally.

Language is imbued with culture and tradition. By discussing the Global Compact for Migration drafts only in English, it was felt by some of those I interviewed (all of them, incidentally, mother-tongue speakers of languages other than English) that the process was also culturally located in an English-speaking tradition and world view – though interestingly some of those who expressed this perspective also told me that they did not think that English-language dominance was a problem. This is part of a bigger concern with the power dynamics involved in the global use of English and how to address them.[44] Some interviewees mentioned that the failure to translate key texts loses the benefit of constructing ideas in different linguistic and cultural frameworks. The language used affects what can be expressed. Translating between languages can force clarity in key areas or else force a confrontation of a lack of clarity.

Translation requires the meanings of terminology to be established or at least the vagaries to be identified. It is common for concepts to be distinguished in some languages and not others. Indeed, even the structure of knowledge can be framed differently in different languages. Whereas English has only 'knowledge', Romance languages like French, for example, have 'savoir' (knowledge how) and 'connaître' (knowledge that).[45] Translation between English and French, then, helps to pin down which sort of knowing is in effect. This has implications for global governance discussions. UN translators Deborah Cao and Xingmin Zhao show this through English word pairs such as 'liability' and 'responsibility' (for which there is only one word in both French and Chinese) and 'boundary' and 'frontier' (for which there is only one word in French, but multiple words in Chinese).[46] They explain that the translation of these words into Chinese calls for another layer of contextualization to establish exactly which Chinese word would be an appropriate match. This forces nuance.

Consider some core terminology used in this book like 'citizenship', 'nationality' and 'statelessness'. Article 1 of the (English language version of the) 1954 Statelessness Convention defines a person as 'stateless' if they are not recognized as a national by any State under the operation of its law. The words used to describe 'statelessness' in different languages indicate slightly different underlying understandings. In English, 'statelessness' refers to being without a State, a political institution. In Spanish, 'apatridia', and in French, 'apatridie', refer to being without 'patride' or 'patrie', respectively, which mean something like homeland (lit. *fatherland*), which is not limited to the political State. In Arabic, there is still more complexity, since there is also colloquial terminology for statelessness alongside the formal legal term.[47] The colloquial phrase 'bidoon jinsiya' (lit. *without citizenship*), often shortened to simply 'bidoon' (lit. *without*), usually refers specifically to a population of people who have been without nationality in Gulf states since their independence and who are violently targeted as such.[48] The more formal term for statelessness used in the 1954 Statelessness Convention is 'anedam aljinsiya' (lit. *lacking nationality*). In addition, in English, the word 'stateless' when referring to a person is an adjective which needs to be paired with a noun. In Spanish, French and Arabic, 'stateless' can be used as a noun to refer to a person (so it is possible to refer to 'a stateless' rather than 'a stateless person'). Moreover, in English, Spanish and French, the terminology refers to a person lacking a polity, whereas in Arabic it refers explicitly to lacking membership of a polity. This could have implications, for example, for how the situation of groups of people who are without citizenship is framed. Language carries sociopolitical milieux that reach beyond the specific words used and efforts to translate between them can help to uncover this.

## Interpretation, translation and power

In December 2018, in Marrakech, at one of the side events for the Intergovernmental Conference to Adopt the Global Compact for Migration, I am sitting near the back, taking notes. It has been organized by a UN agency. There is no interpretation available. As usual, the discussion is in English. People are arriving in dribs and drabs as they make their way from far-flung rooms. I recognize most of the people in the room. I've interviewed several of them. A man in a suit comes in with two others. He waves to me and comes to sit next to me. We know each other already. He runs a major civil society network in sub-Saharan Africa. I don't recognize the people who are with him. He sits for a while, looking at the person speaking. Then he leans over to me and whispers: 'Vous comprenez l'anglais?' (*Do you understand English?*). I nod. He indicates that he'd like me to explain what's being said. For both of us, French is a second language. As the speaker continues in English, I do my best to whisper the highlights of what is being said in French. I then notice the two people sitting next to him lean over to listen in too. I realize that they also might not have understood without me interpreting for them, even though my interpretation is halting and flawed. When the man next to me wants to make a comment, he does it in French and asks me to interpret for him. I had become a reluctant gatekeeper.

This experience was not isolated. Throughout my engagement in global migration governance processes and civil society organizing around them, I have been in several situations where if I don't interpret for the person next to me, they will not understand, and where if I don't translate their intervention, they will not be heard. And I have observed this being a common experience for others. In some cases, the person is saying something with which I disagree. I'm aware that the way in which I speak their words effectively frames them as worth listening to or not. In my small way, I have found myself in control of their access to information and the access their voice has to consideration in the discussion. The structural barriers to participation that I discuss in this book do not only create barriers for an individual to participate but also set up others as gatekeepers, reinforcing their existing positions of power.

This uncomfortable feeling of being an unwilling gatekeeper was mentioned by several of those able to traverse the structural barriers to participation in a variety of ways. One interviewee mentioned that they had found themselves with access to important information about the UN process towards the Compact. They felt an obligation to disseminate this information as widely as possible because, though not identified as privileged, it was not being disseminated by any formal ways, but they did not have capacity to do it. This interviewee described the significant human and other resources needed to disseminate information as widely as is needed. Moreover, focusing on the dissemination of this information would mean that they couldn't do anything else. Similar issues arise when translating or interpreting. When I supported people to understand the English-language discussion, I found it harder to take notes. I observed meetings where civil society actors from one organization ended up translating for those from another, with implications for the participation of the person doing the translating. In this way, while more actors would be able to *understand*, as a result two actors from a specific language community were now both less able to *contribute*.

Several of those who experienced barriers to accessing information expressed suspicion that there were intentional efforts on the part of international organizations, States and even international civil society organizations to obstruct information flow and to keep access to advocacy to themselves. Their suspicion was directed at the gatekeepers who were formally tasked to enable information flow but also at those who found themselves in the positions of informal and inadvertent gatekeeping to information. And yet most of those I spoke to who had ended up in these gatekeeping roles said that where there was any lack of transparency it resulted from a lack of capacity rather than intentionally withholding information. They had struggled to disseminate information to everyone who needed it within feasible timescales and acknowledged this with frustration.

There were other, less obvious, ways in which unequal power structures were created and recreated by language. For example, interpretation at State-led events was available for formal meetings but not at side events and not at informal conversations. In these situations, English often dominated, but not always. When interpretation was available at State-led processes, it was only available with respect to the six UN languages (Arabic, Chinese, English, French, Russian and Spanish). This puts an additional burden on the person or entity who is already carrying the heavier burden of lacking access to a dominant language. It also produced silos. The Bloque Latinoamericano (which was made up of governmental and civil society members) met to have meetings in Spanish alongside key UN meetings. An interviewee who played a founding role in the Bloque, observed that 'the Bloque Latinoamericano ended up being the contact point for talking to the like-minded group'. He explained that engagement was done via WhatsApp and via email as well as via in-person discussions. Members would then meet with governments and delegations which were not Spanish-speaking to bring information and to put forward positions.

Dissemination and the use of English had profound implications for participation and it created gatekeepers, often unknowing or inadvertent gatekeepers, who could provide conduits between dominant English and the other languages spoken. This made noncitizen power dependent one way or another upon linguistic insiders. This also included, for example, myself. Despite only being there as an academic intending to observe, I also found myself in a small way making decisions about how the voice of others would be included.

# A noncitizenist approach to language in global governance discussions

Having observed the role played by language in the construction of noncitizen relationships, it becomes necessary to look to those with the most experience of how this works to find out how to address it; that is, it is necessary to look to those who carry the heaviest burden of current language practices. The problem of language dominance is not an easy one to fix. But this doesn't mean a need either to resign oneself to what novelist Chinua Achebe has described as 'fatalistic logic of the unassailable position of English'[49] or to abandon English altogether.[50] Instead, it means changing the starting point for thinking about the role of language to a noncitizenist one.

An official from an international organization explained the challenge when I asked them how it might be possible to mitigate the difficulties that resulted from the English dominance in the Global Compact for Migration process:

> I don't know what the fix is to be frank. I mean, you see the Council of Europe, you have simultaneous interpretation for how many languages? Which is a phenomenal achievement really and something that we could all strive for. The truth is that with the current budgeting we have that we are limited.[51]

That is, the ideal solution – simultaneous interpretation and translation for all the estimated 7,000 languages of the world – is not possible. Indeed, it is not feasible even to offer interpretation for all of the world's national languages, nor even for the UN six official languages for all the documents produced.

However, decisions made in scarcity depend on whose perspectives are taken into account and which costs are counted. Critical linguist Jacqueline Mowbray advocates what looks like a noncitizenist move: 'if we shift perspective and consider those whose languages are thereby excluded, the costs of such arrangements [such as limiting the number of languages and the amount of interpretation] outweigh the benefits.' She goes on later: '[o]ne person's practicality is another person's impracticality; arguments about what is "practical" inevitably presuppose a particular standpoint.'[52] Taking this seriously will mean taking seriously two matters in particular. First, given the impossibility of providing interpretation from and to all languages spoken by all people, any language policy in global migration governance will put burdens on some which are not put on others. This needs to be considered without 'naturalizing' the dominance of any language in particular[53] and so include mitigations for those bearing the greatest burden. Second, it will be necessary to step back from focusing only on counting the number of named languages available and instead explore the context of communication, deliberation and consultation more broadly. A noncitizenist approach to this would be to look at the extent to which people are forced to communicate *despite* existing systems. I will now develop each of these in turn.

First, it is not possible to provide interpretation between all languages that people speak, so a decision needs to be taken about which languages and how many languages to privilege. This will also need to include decisions about instances where wider interpretation or translation is particularly important or easy and instances where it is less important or more difficult. Whichever language or languages are chosen, this will need to be combined with measures to mitigate the effects on those who will need to carry the greatest weight of this choice. This is not only about interpretation in events or translation of formal documents. It would also include measures to ensure that as many people as possible are able to find out what is going on, even if they are not able to access the processes themselves. In 2017, one scholar found that more than 90 per cent of the UN secretariat website was available in English, over 50 per cent in French, 30 per cent in Spanish and less than 30 per cent in Chinese, Russian or Arabic.[54] This means that access to basic information about global politics is currently difficult or impossible for some people.

Technical tools could potentially contribute to this mitigation. There have been recent radical advances in the technology of translation.[55] Free online tools can already provide indicative translations of simple texts,[56] and indeed these tools were used by those engaging in the GCM process. At the time of writing, the website of the private sector agreement within the United Nations, mentioned in Chapter 4, called 'The Global Compact', for example, uses Google translation services to provide automatic non-official translation into 104 languages.[57] Translation tools used in other sectors are evolving rapidly.[58] In international education, automatic translation tools are used to facilitate access to Massive Open Online Courses (MOOCs) which use combinations of automatic speech recognition and machine translation for the creation of multilingual subtitles. Recent research in this area has found increasing levels of accuracy using these tools.[59] However, this is still error-prone and translations are only ever indicative. Critics also warn that machine translation technology is still largely 'anchored' in English. That is, there is a worry that in these systems, as English is used as a 'pivot' language (so that translations need to involve a step to and from English), its logic still dominates.[60] This is being addressed. For example, Google moves towards 'artificial neural network translation' rather than translation that relies upon English as pivot.[61]

There is already a precedent for the use of machine-produced subtitles at the UN. The Human Rights Council, for example, designates days in each session to be more accessible.[62] This includes machine-produced subtitles of the English interpretation of any intervention.[63] Perhaps the UN could develop in-house capacity in this area as part of the regular UN budget, including adopting tools which are not rooted in one language over others. Machine translation could help to ensure greater access to migration governance discussions not only for those with hearing and sight difficulties but also for those facing language barriers. A noncitizenist approach to this would include ensuring that it does not further naturalize a particular language's dominance.

Second, as has been shown above, it is not enough to focus only on the named languages like English and French but also on broader ways in which people communicate. This includes recognizing the exclusions created by privileging formal language over forms of expression seen as 'bad' or 'inappropriate',[64] excluding speakers from comprehension or credibility. Domestic level implications of this are illustrated in analysis of the US legal case of the murder of Trayvon Martin in which the testimony of a key witness was disregarded as uncredible and difficult to understand because she used African American Vernacular English. As a result the man that evidence suggests was responsible for Martin's death was acquitted.[65] There are also implications for the international level. In my research, I met some confident and fluent speakers of English who felt unable to communicate comfortably in the formal English used in the UN. Privileging a singular form of English constructs those individuals into noncitizen relationships with the organization. Native-speakerism, which privileges certain 'native speaker' framings of a language, has been critiqued in the studies of language teaching.[66] This book suggests that forms of something like native-speakerism can be found in global politics, though global native-speakerism focuses on insiders to a certain form of English rather than on linguistic heritage. A noncitizenist move starts instead from the perspectives of those who must act and act politically despite existing structures.

In addition, people don't only communicate through those named languages but also through cultural norms and customs of debate. Tying discussion to one language at a time and to a restricted selection of verbal and written forms also impairs communication more broadly. Describing ways in which people communicate meaning through norms and practices that function beyond the words spoken, critical linguist Felix Ndhlovu demands: '[w]e have to learn how communication always works (not inspite of) but because of rampant diversity of language practices.'[67] This means that efforts to 'democratize' global politics would need to include accommodating a more diverse range of norms and practices of deliberation, consultation and communication. This may include the statements of elected representatives as with democratic states and trades unions and appointed representatives as with UN agencies and NGOs. However, it may also need to support and facilitate for example the messy consultations that are needed among diverse grassroots civil society networks mentioned in Chapter 3 and the in-person formalized discussions among Indigenous Pacific actors as mentioned earlier in this chapter. The starting point for this would be to look to those who carry the greatest burden and find out their communication needs.

The structural problems described in this chapter cannot be solved by translation alone. A noncitizenist move requires a radical rethinking, starting from the perspective of those who must function *despite* the structures in question. Rather than presuming English or any other language, as dominant (Chinese also has a similarly significant number of speakers), it is necessary to make active decisions about inclusion given both existing linguistic diversity and potential mechanisms for mitigating associated exclusions (e.g. English-language speakers also have access to a wider array of tools to help them with translation). If those who are unable to communicate in English are not part of the discussion about the support for linguistic diversity, then this discussion fails to benefit from the insights of precisely those persons who know from experience what is needed. Like so many of the structural barriers to participation mentioned in this book, it compounds itself. Visas prevent the attendance of events. However, communication barriers create more pervasive engagement difficulties. This affects those who are able to attend and impairs participation at a remove as well.

# Underlying narratives

Those presumed less entitled than others to agency when it comes to mobility are also less able to participate in producing the narratives that underlie discussions of global migration governance and which affected the Global Compact for Migration process. This has implications for noncitizen power. This chapter presents three constituencies, chosen for what they can tell us about narrative and noncitizen power. First are the journalists and academics who provide initial framings and analyses of emerging migration contexts. This has included the identification of a 'migration crisis'. Second are the migrants presumed ineligible for agency over their own mobility who have crossed borders they had been told not to cross. They forced policy-makers to acknowledge existing institutions weren't working, but they weren't consulted about how to fix them. Seeing their movement through the lens of civil disobedience shows why this is problematic. Third, the anti-migration and anti-multilateralism activists also weren't seen as interlocutors by those involved in organizing the Compact process. Yet, in the final months before the Compact was to be adopted, they forced a narrative change, and governments that had previously supported the text withdrew. The different roles played by these three constituencies indicate how underlying narratives were created for this process, the implications of their power and what it took for them to be disrupted.

While images are used throughout this book, in this chapter there are none. Instead, this chapter ends by *talking about* an image that became symbolic of this period. It is a photograph from 2015 of a small child lying dead on a Turkish beach. I reflect on the power of that image, who wielded that power and how it was used. This example helps to illustrate the structural challenges impeding the impact of noncitizen power on the underlying narratives within which global migration governance is discussed.

## Journalists and academics: Producing a 'migration crisis'

The idea of a 'migration crisis' looks at the urgent movement of people in 2014 and 2015 from the perspective of those experiencing the international community primarily as citizens, concerned about people arriving into the States where they live.[1] The sense of urgency that eventually led to the Global Compact for Migration was driven by both concern at a perceived security threat arising from a 'migration crisis' and the moral imperative produced by some well-publicized instances of migrant deaths and suffering. However, from 2016, the political winds in some powerful countries began changing quickly. The moral imperative among some of those governments was diminishing and the narrative of crisis became more central. The citizenist framing can be seen in the full title of the Compact: 'The Global Compact for Safe, Orderly, and *Regular* Migration' [emphasis added]. Noncitizenist analyses might emphasize instead the multiple crises that produced the need to move[2] and crises in governance that made the migration so dangerous and disorganized.

Chapter 3 drew on Miranda Fricker's observation that when some people's descriptions of reality are disbelieved or when their realities need to be framed in ways (and according to underlying narratives) that do not reflect their lived experience, it produces a form of injustice.[3] In an essay about gender discrimination, Fricker sets out the effect of *exclusion from* versus *access to* what she calls 'those practices by which collective social meanings are generated'.[4] She picks out 'journalism, politics, academia, and law' as professions whose practitioners are in unique positions to create and to generate social meaning. When access to these professions is restricted, it restricts the collective understandings within which everyone must live and express themselves.[5] And just as those experiencing noncitizenship in relation to the international system struggled to participate in the meetings relating to the Global Compact for Migration, it is also difficult for experts-by-experience of noncitizenship to participate in journalism and academia and so to be part of the journalistic and academic contribution to framing underlying narratives about global migration. The context of migration in 2014 and 2015 was initially described by journalists.[6] It was then analysed and researched by academics. Journalists and academics play a complex and interrelated role in framing reality. Together, they make things point-at-able, and they wield authority and credibility in how this is done.

In 2014 and 2015, the proportion of people globally reported to be outside their country of birth had risen. It had gone from 2.8 per cent in 2000 to 3.3 per cent in 2015.[7] This meant that 96.7 per cent of people still lived in the countries where they were born and many of the rest were, like myself, settled long-term residents or citizens where they lived. However, changing realities and changing policies drove changes in the experiences of migration for some. In several regions, an increasing number of people were facing desperate economic conditions, civil and international war, and persecution.

At the same time, border regimes to prevent the entry of those people were being strengthened. This meant that for an increasing number of people who needed to move there were increasing restrictions on their movement. Without alternatives, they tried to cross borders they had been told not to cross and they did this in increasingly difficult and dangerous conditions. People lost their lives; were injured; and were stranded without access to shelter, food and sanitation, including in some of the richest countries on earth. Early reports from journalists about what was happening in borderzones around the world framed the crisis as one of migration: of border crossing.[8]

As shown in Chapters 3 and 5, visa waivers and free movement agreements mean that holders of the strongest passports can travel between each other's countries with no visa at all and they can travel about most of the world collecting visas at airports.[9] For the holders of the weakest passports, the situation is very different. Holders of passports that sit low in the Global Passport Index, which mostly come from sub-Saharan Africa, some parts of Asia, and countries experiencing conflict, need to apply for a visa before travelling to most other countries. They may have to provide evidence of their bank balance and health status, along with letters of support. The visa processing may take weeks, require interviews, and end in a refusal. This makes it difficult to respond quickly to emerging international news stories, including those relating to migration. Consequently, those who are most able to respond to breaking international news stories are most likely to be those who have the least direct personal experience of the gritty impact of global migration governance.[10]

As a result, a rarefied group of journalists from a small number of countries from which travel is easiest can play a disproportionate role in selecting between, and providing the narratives for, global news stories. This affects what news is reported globally and the lens through which that news is understood.[11] It meant that most of those reporting on the emerging contexts of migration in 2014 and 2015 did not have experience of having to live their life *despite* migration policies. This is a problem because even in well-intentioned reporting, structural factors or hidden dimensions in a person's decision-making may be overlooked if the person doing the reporting has not experienced the difficulties of those about whom they are reporting.[12] Speaking to researchers about migration reporting in UK media during this period, one interviewee observed: 'if you have the people that you're talking about in the room, the discussion changes,'[13] and another: 'we are just the people being talked about'.[14] This echoes the observations of global migrant civil society organizers quoted in Chapter 3 reflecting on why they need to be part of governance discussions. I'm not referring here to storytelling, but to narrative creation.

One might think that these barriers wouldn't affect people already on the ground in an emerging context. But they do. Not only can some people respond more easily to breaking international news stories, but this also makes it easier for such individuals to gain a foothold in globally high-circulation, high-impact and high-paying media outlets. This is self-reinforcing. Individuals without these benefits risk becoming dependent upon being contracted or paid for stories according to someone else's framing. This has self-reinforcing effects. First, it contributes to a milieu in which certain ways of understanding can dominate. Second, it can in turn make it increasingly difficult for dominant narratives to incorporate reporting from different vantage points, reinforcing that milieu.[15] Scholars of the coverage of migration in the EU have suggested that 'the inclusion of diverse voices [in reporting about the "migration crisis" in Europe] was highly regulated with elite versions being largely dominant, while citizen or migrant voices consistently remained marginal or fully silenced'.[16] These factors arguably drove the framing of a 'migration crisis' in Europe in the period leading up to the decision to launch a new UN process.[17]

Like journalists, academics also play key roles in constructing and framing knowledge. Scholar Cecilia Cannon has traced how academics influence international policy processes from 'raising the red flag' and defining issues, through supporting agenda-setting and policy discussions, and then involvement in both implementation and monitoring.[18] They are often invited to speak as 'experts' at key UN meetings or to provide written evidence and analyses. Theory about the world is largely produced by and for those who experience it mostly as citizens.[19] This theory is then used to analyse and to make recommendations for global migration governance. The crucial absence here is not so much *migrant* perspectives but instead *noncitizen* perspectives. Many people migrate without friction. This includes many academics. Those who have a noncitizen relationship with the international system, irrespective of whether or not they cross an international border, have a unique insight into the institutions of global migration governance.

Visa regimes and free movement agreements impact on who can participate in the global academic community.[20] They affect where people can work, who can present at conferences and who can participate in and lead research projects.[21] Discrimination in visa systems can, then, affect what knowledge is pursued and how findings are framed. This is exacerbated by other factors such as local recruitment, workload and promotion practices.[22] This may in turn intersect with unequal challenges presented by quasi-citizen statuses.[23] In recent years, academics who have been ill-affected by migration policies have begun to write publically about this, including essays and letters to the editors of leading academic journals.[24]

Academia has always functioned internationally, with scholars moving between centres of learning and scholarship.[25] Today, top-tier well-funded internationalized universities function within a global job market, recruiting talent from around the world, while major global academic gatherings and funding are concentrated in what some refer to as 'knowledge production hotspots'.[26] This affects where knowledge is produced and who is part of producing it, privileging certain perspectives and modes of thought. This creates absurdities. For example, in his paper on the Global Compact on Refugees, which was negotiated at the same time as the Global Compact for Migration, David N. Tshimba observes:

> [a]bout 90 per cent of published work on forced migration reportedly originates from researchers/practitioners based in academic and policy institutions in the global North [while] 86 per cent of the world's forcibly displaced people are hosted in countries in the global South.[27]

Noncitizenism is necessary both because (1) it confronts presumptions about arbitrary differences in entitlement to agency and to eligibility to be interlocutors in the making of policies that affect them and (2) noncitizen expertise is crucial in the development of evidence-based policy frameworks.

Language also affects who can participate in global academia, in terms of the use of both English and dominant norms of communication. Vastly more academic articles are published in English than in any single other language. While it is true that this focuses on one form of dissemination and may hide that some fields may be centred in other languages,[28] in the context of the academic work influencing the governmental process towards the Global Compact for Migration, English was dominant. In order to participate in anglophone international academia, scholars are often expected to read, publish and present work in English. Journals hosted at institutions in countries where English isn't an official language sometimes publish in English. Courses are taught in English. This puts some scholars at a disadvantage. What is at issue is not only the unequal burden produced by the need for some to learn an additional language which is already spoken by others. A form of the 'native-speakerism' mentioned in Chapter 6 also functions in international academia.

In the context of global migration governance, I suggested that 'native-speakerism' functions not in terms of mother-tongue privilege, but rather in terms of being an insider to, and feeling comfortable in, forms of formal international English. In academia, native-speakerism seems to function more similarly to how it is framed in the literature around English-language teaching.[29] Academic English is also dominated by norms of expression, such that some quite standard ways of writing or speaking can be seen as 'bad' or 'inappropriate'.[30] As a result, people who write or speak in these ways can be seen as less expert or less credible. Meanwhile, there is an incentive in some disciplines to use formal styles and terminology that are not accessible to outsiders. Given the barriers mentioned above, this further reduces the number of people with noncitizen experience who can critique and contribute to the development of the underlying narratives about migration governance.

Constraints on who is able to participate in international academia, and how, affect whose ideas can percolate into the global framing of reality. This has implications for what research is funded; what is taught to the next generation of professionals, leaders and decision-makers; and indeed what expertise is provided to policy-makers. It affects the pool of 'experts' providing the analysis for policy discussions about migration. If knowledge developed in so-called 'knowledge production hotspots' and spread around the world is less likely to include perspectives of those with first-hand experience of the real-life implications of migration governance, then there's a higher risk of these perspectives being left out of the underlying narratives of global migration governance discussions.

This also means that those who currently work as journalists and academics in dominant contexts effectively act as gatekeepers to the construction of narratives. Just as with those inadvertent gatekeepers identified in earlier chapters, journalists for high-circulation international publications and academics in knowledge hubs perform this gatekeeping role whether or not they intend to do so.[31] People who do not experience noncitizenship may not know the implications of global migration governance for those affected, but they also may not know that they have this blind spot. That is, there is a risk of what José Medina calls 'meta-blindness'.[32] This is aggravated in the context of academia. If those who write and critique conceptual frameworks for thinking about migration and governance overwhelmingly experience the world mostly as citizens, then the conceptual frameworks developed are more likely to be flawed. This is a version of what Phillip Cole refers to as an 'insider theory problem'.[33] In turn, this means that the experts who go on to use those conceptual frameworks to analyse emerging events and test policy may do so without a sufficiently rich understanding of the world.

This is not, however, inevitable. Journalists' and academics' roles in shaping narrative also mean that they can help to drive a noncitizenist move in access to journalism and to academia as well as in how migration and migration governance is framed. Analyses of political structures often suffer from a 'banal citizenism'. That is, they unthinkingly start from, presume, and privilege the relationship of citizenship.[34] Accordingly, anything else is either a quasi-citizenship or else the absence of any relationship at all. Global noncitizenist scholarship starts from and centres the perspectives of people insofar as they must live out their lives and perform their politics *despite*, rather than thanks to or irrespective of, the institutional structures that organize our world. This is not about citizen scholars having sympathy for or empathy with those experiencing the world as noncitizens. It is about deference to noncitizen expertise. This noncitizenist move requires a presumption that people are equally entitled to agency over their own mobility and equally appropriate interlocutors for policies affecting them. A starting point for this might be to reconsider the agency of those who were migrating in the period leading up to the 2016 New York Declaration.

## Civil disobedience and noncitizen power: Highlighting a crisis of governance

The process to produce the UN Global Compact for Migration was launched in 2016 in no small part because a significant number of people had crossed borders that they'd been told not to cross. For those who enjoy comfortable citizenships and carry passports stamped with visas, crossing international borders is often mundane. For others, the situation is different. Those who have the greatest need to migrate are largely also those who encounter the greatest barriers in doing so. Where there is no legal route, such individuals must find alternatives. As a result, their migration is not mundane, but it is also not abject. It becomes politicized and it is performed with intention. When such individuals break migration rules, then, they are often breaking rules that they find unliveable. What makes this act of crossing a border politically salient is not the act itself. It is the status allocated by States to the person performing the act. This is a status most likely based on where that person was born or to whom.[35] It may be affected by discrimination on the basis of race, gender and other arbitrary factors.[36] I suggest that irregular border crossing in this context can be properly understood as a form of civil disobedience. Seen in this way it directly challenges delegitimization of migration conceived of as '(un)safe, (dis)orderly and (ir)regular'.[37]

In 2014 and 2015, several rich countries found an increasing number of people without any other option refusing to be bound by arbitrary allocations of status. Over this period, growing numbers were challenging the borders of States built on ideologies of respect for human rights, freedom and democracy. Some were making it across those borders, then finding themselves without access to basic nutrition, shelter or sanitation, often treated in a degrading manner. The actions of the people who reported on and helped those migrating have been framed as 'délits de solidarités' (crimes of solidarity), 'whistleblowing' and 'civil disobedience'.[38] However, it is the migration itself and the responses of authorities in European and other countries to that movement that created the context in which the decision was made to hold an extraordinary UN meeting addressing large movements of refugees and migrants in 2016.

The irregular migration of 2014 and 2015 does not meet the conditions for classic definitions of 'civil disobedience'. Not least, the people moving aren't citizens of the States whose rules they are breaking. However, it does meet broader understanding of this terminology and particularly when considered at a global level. There have been two main ways in which irregular migration has been framed as 'civil disobedience'. I adopt a middle way between the two. First, theorist Luis Cabrera has argued that such individuals should be seen as 'global citizens', and their migration therefore a form of civil disobedience understood in a traditional way but on the global, rather than the State, level.[39] However, this deference to citizenship risks obscuring an important dimension of the politics under discussion. Second, rather than seeing civil disobedience as being 'civil' because it is performed by citizens, others argue that the civility in civil disobedience refers broadly to disobedience that is *normatively legitimate*.[40] While 'civility' is sometimes seen to mean 'in line with hegemonic class-, race- and gender-specific norms',[41] in fact theorist Robin Celikates suggests that it is necessary to move away from bias about who can be civil and instead see disobedience as civil insofar as it is according to a 'logic of political in contrast to military action'.[42] War metaphors have been used in relation to irregular migration and response to it. Philosopher Cecline Fabre has argued that the poor of the world would be justified in rising up in violent war against the world's rich that keep them poor.[43] However, even if a war metaphor would make sense in this context, it is not being waged by people migrating.[44] As Celikates puts it, in the case of irregular migration, 'those who disobey are seen as managing to maintain civility in the face of often massive state incivility'.[45] It is, then, those who moved irregularly during this time that were keeping things civil.

The individuals under discussion are being intentionally forced to live *despite* the international system. This is not because of discrimination against them *qua* members, but rather they are not recognized as members.[46] Indeed, although she doesn't use the language of civil disobedience explicitly, Scholar Anne Mcnevin presents the claims of irregular migrants as direct challenges to the idea of citizenship as an organizing principle for rights and membership.[47] As such, I take on Cabrera's global framing, but Calikate's understanding of civility. I suggest that in fact the irregular migration of 2014 and 2015 resonates in important ways on a global level with what could be described as 'paradigmatic cases' of State-level civil disobedience.[48] The fact of the noncitizen relationship is an important part of the nature of the acts. A related approach is defended by Ali Emre Benli relating to refugees.[49] I add merely that it doesn't matter whether or not a particular individual was seeking asylum.

The cases of the African American women Claudette Colvin and Rosa Parks who refused to give up their seats on segregated buses in 1950s Alabama are paradigmatic for civil disobedience. The irregular migration of 2014 and 2015 shares important characteristics.

First, the law in Alabama meant that Colvin and Parks were presumed, because of race, not to be entitled to choose where to sit on a bus. They took action, which directly and intentionally contested this. Relatedly, the constellation of laws confronting irregular border crossers in 2014 and 2015 meant that people were denied access to travel because of their place of birth and/or their parentage. Their migration directly contested this. Migration laws and policies can seem neutral and equally applied. They are not. As is shown in Chapters 3 and 5, not only are people from some countries required to apply for visas to travel to most other countries while others are not, but visa applications are in turn treated differentially. In addition, irregular migrants aren't all treated alike. For example, citizens of the United States have consistently made up a significant proportion of the unlawful noncitizens in Australia and yet I can't find evidence of US citizens in Australia's notorious immigration detention facilities.[50]

Some of those moving in 2014 and 2015 understood themselves to be intentionally demonstrating the illegitimacy of such laws. When asked whether she believed she had the right to enter EU territory, one Nigerian woman crossing the Mediterranean irregularly during this period told researchers: 'White people normally go to Nigeria, they are safe, they are ok. I know that very well. So . . . you know God created everybody.'[51] This suggests that she was aware of the racialized injustice of the laws and was breaking them knowingly and intentionally. From 2011, those travelling across land northwards mainly from Honduras, El Salvador and Guatemala have become known as a 'migrant caravan', terminology that has evolved during the period when the Compact was being negotiated.[52] As people walked northwards, they were joined by others moving and by allies. In this way, some of those involved have said that the 'caravan' became an intentionally visible statement of the right to migrate. As one commentator puts it, the caravan movement in its various forms can be understood as 'a demand to the powers of the world to let us pass without begging forgiveness for demanding it'.[53] This indicates that at least some of those migrating against States' wishes in this period recognized the injustice they were facing and were intentionally challenging it.

Some face significant barriers to international travel at a time when, for others, international mobility is becoming increasingly free. And yet, given global inequalities of access to resources, histories of colonial and neo-colonial occupation and impacts of climate change, among other things, people from precisely these regions are also less likely to find access to the security, peace and prosperity promised by the international system at home. Globally, the demographic of those who are told not to cross borders is composed largely of people from countries that have been colonized, whose populations were racialized by White colonists in previous centuries. The logics behind racialized colonial systems, whereby some people are entitled to make decisions about their own mobility and others are not, are continuous with some parts of contemporary migration infrastructures.[54] Meanwhile, some former colonies still struggle to repel interference from the powerful interests of other States and corporations in their internal decision-making, resource use and international participation. It is the citizens of these States that enjoy the least free access to international systems of mobility. If some people migrate in rejection of these unjust systems of laws, this supports the sense that this is a form of civil disobedience.

Second, Colvin and Parks, through their action, thereby became eligible for punishment according to the laws that they were challenging, making the injustice of those laws more visible. Whether or not every one of those moving irregularly in 2014 and 2015 saw their movement as political, it was politicized and it was politically powerful. Whether wilfully or not, they made their vulnerability to the grace of the States in which they travelled hypervisible and in this way laid bare the contradictions inherent in States self-identifying according to ideals of human rights and democratic principles, while violently keeping some people from those ideals on the basis of where they were born or to whom. It became difficult for the international community to ignore the fact that some people were forced to live *despite* the structures that are supposed to promote stability, security and prosperity for all.

The form of noncitizen power described in this section is extremely burdensome on those who already carry the international system's greatest burdens. It relies on the performance of artificially politicized acts for its power. It is also blunt. Those who moved in 2014 and 2015 may have forced an acknowledgement that there are problems in the international migration regime, but for the most part, they were not then consulted about what should be done about it. Indeed, global narratives about this movement were largely constructed by others, including the journalists and academics mentioned earlier and those participating in the governance processes discussed in this book. As one grassroots activist observed, it can look like the aim of the

Global Compact for Migration is not to address the suffering and death in the migration system but instead to try to ensure that the suffering and death of migrants don't disrupt the smooth running of international politics.[55]

The quotation from a Resolution of the Second Meeting of the UN General Assembly in 1947 which opened Chapter 3 supports this observation. It expressed the need for '[i]nternational co-operation for the prevention of immigration which is likely to disturb friendly relations between nations'.[56] These migrants were seen as potentially troublesome for States and those States' citizens. Their movement was framed as problematic for the functioning of the international system. Those moving were often not seen as agents with legitimate interests. The very systems that politicized their migration also made it difficult for them to participate in the political discussions about migration and to shape the narratives underlying them. As shown in this book, they relied on global migrant civil society networks, religious organizations and some intergovernmental agencies to use the process that they had launched to bring their perspectives to the table.

# Bypassing formal politics and rejecting progressive narratives

Anti-migration and anti-multilateralism civil society was largely absent throughout the process towards the Global Compact for Migration. This constituency became vocal only in the final stages of the process. However, rather than developing shared statements and fighting for access to the UN's conference rooms like global migrant civil society, they mostly used a combination of explicitly activist news sites,[57] traditional forms of protest and social media platforms.[58] And they did this successfully, forcing several governments to change their positions with respect to the Compact and changing the content of the speeches of others.[59] As one commentator observed, a 'compact that had been provisionally agreed to five months earlier by 192 of the 193 UN Member States',[60] all of those who had participated in the process, in Morocco was endorsed by only 152 States, with twelve abstentions. The New York Declaration 2016, the document that launched the process towards the Compact, condemns 'xenophobia, racial discrimination and intolerance',[61] excluding anyone holding these views from the global constituency of interlocutors, intending instead to educate them. As the process towards the Compact proceeded, this educative aim seems to have discontinued. Given the complexity presented in earlier chapters, there was little capacity also to reach out to those who were so fundamentally opposed. This section presents how anti-migration movements were able to shape narratives underlying global migration governance discussions in unique ways and what this means for the possibility of noncitizen power regarding narrative.

In those countries that would go on to drop the Compact (at least initially), few people had heard of it before late 2018 when far-right and other extremist protestors spotlighted it, arguing that it had been intentionally kept secret.[62] Researchers suggest this was driven most strongly by German language social and activist news media, which was then taken up by others.[63] As anti-migration activists were initially the only ones reporting on the Compact, they could frame public discussions of it, including in Parliaments. The German Twitter hashtag #MigrationspaktStoppen ('stop the migration compact') was driven by far-right German activist news media. It reportedly gained traction in September 2018. By mid-October, it was being used by some German MPs.[64] One 2017 study found that of those engaging in far-right content on Twitter, 19 per cent were in France, 18 per cent in Germany, 15 per cent in the United States, 10 per cent in the UK, 7 per cent in Italy, 5 per cent in Spain, 4 per cent in Switzerland and 22 per cent elsewhere in Europe and North America.[65] In 2018, the States voting against the Compact were Hungary, Poland, the United States, the Czech Republic and Israel. The abstentions were Algeria, Australia, Austria, Bulgaria, Chile, Italy, Latvia, Libya, Liechtenstein, Romania, Singapore and Switzerland. Meanwhile, some endorsed the Compact but with reservation. The UK, for example, emphasized in their statement that they endorsed the Compact on the understanding that it would 'tackle uncontrolled migration' and reaffirm 'the sovereign right of all countries to control their own borders', and it 'does not create any new 'rights' for migrants'.

Crucial to the success of far-right news media's response to the Compact is what has been referred to as its 'activism'.[66] That is, it didn't only report on the Compact (reporting which was often wildly inaccurate) but also actively encouraged political mobilization among its audiences. In the final months before the December 2018 conference to adopt the Compact this took the form of petitions and street protests, strategies that researcher Julia Rone has called traditionally 'progressive'.[67] This had swift effects. Changes in the national approaches of Austria and Italy have been traced to a surge of anti-Compact online activity. In Switzerland, protestors carried placards denouncing the Swiss Ambassador to the UN as a traitor, so that after co-facilitating the entire process (with the Government of Mexico), Switzerland did not attend the meeting to adopt the Compact. Belgium went to the conference to adopt the Compact, but while the Belgian representative was speaking in Marrakech, back in Brussels his government was coming under increasing pressure from anti-migration and anti-multilateralism protestors both in the streets and in Parliament.[68] The Belgian government would be forced to step down over its endorsement of the Compact. In countries around the world, in the autumn and winter of 2018, anti-migration and anti-multilateralism protestors blocked motorways and occupied town squares, all while continuing to engage online.[69]

Anti-migration protestors made heavy use of social media, with implications for how ideas emerged. Earlier chapters showed how global migrant civil society networks laboriously negotiated joint statements and then fought to bring them to policy-makers. The processes by which positions emerged for anti-migration movements look more like 'a market place of ideas', as described in the 2019 book *#NewPower*.[70] That is, they engaged in mass dissemination through social media, led by YouTubers and influencers.[71] According to the norms of #NewPower, individuals could get involved from anywhere in the world by liking, sharing and creating memes for example.[72] Ideas that were shared by more people gained more traction. Less popular ideas fell away. While several platforms were important, I will focus on the surge in anti-Compact YouTube content in the months before the 2018 conference for its adoption, partly because of its importance and partly because of my own experience of its effects.

Anti-Compact YouTube mobilization followed on from a wider proliferation of previously niche far-right content on the platform. One 2020 study into right-to-far-right YouTube engagement in the United States found a steep increase in viewership and in content creation from 2014 to 2017, with a drop-off after 2017.[73] The same study found a steep increase in engagement in videos (through writing comments), particularly more extreme videos, continuing after the 2017 drop in viewing figures, suggesting growing community formation.

In 2012, moving away from 'click-bait' (attention-grabbing titles or images with possibly uninteresting videos), YouTube began rewarding videos with a higher total eyeball time rather than number of views. This favoured creators who could make longer, attention-sustaining videos, including political ones. YouTube uses algorithms to recommend videos to users to keep them on the site, clicking on ads or paid-for content.[74] While the details of YouTube algorithms aren't made public, commentators trace the rise in far-right content on YouTube to algorithm changes.[75] The platform's initial efforts at making recommendations were based on 'adjacent relationships', recommending videos which were similar to those a viewer had already seen. However, this produced repetition and users got bored. So it started recommending the more popular of the adjacent videos, which, together with the importance of eyeball time, would privilege increasingly reactionary, longer-form videos which pulled people in and kept them watching. Moreover, the longer people stayed on the site, the more reactionary the videos recommended to them would become. This led to a phenomenon which researcher Ico Maly has referred to as 'algorithmic populism'.[76]

I experienced the implications of the change in the YouTube landscape directly. In 2018, I was teaching a course on global migration governance at the Management Center Innsbruck. I wanted to show a particular UN-produced video about the Global Compact for Migration for my students to critique. This had previously always appeared as the first hit in a YouTube search. However, on the day of the class, when I searched for the video, I found instead pages and pages of videos with images of burning UN flags, demonic-looking officials and boats full of people. Indeed, researchers have traced a sudden surge in anti-Compact far-right content in 2018. By 2019, one report found that 75 per cent of the most popular YouTube videos discussing the Compact were created by 'right-wing populists and anti-migration campaigners, far-right extremists or conspiracy theorists'.[77] There were very few contributions either from the left or from mainstream conservative or libertarian sources.

These anti-migration and anti-multilateralism movements are important to consider in this book. This is partly because of their substantive impact on narrative. It is also because their impact on narrative seems on the face of it to have been produced using digital forms of communication in which traditional gatekeeping and the structural effects presented in Chapters 5 and 6 are reduced. This raises the question of whether they might provide an illustration of, or a model for, noncitizen power in narratives about migration governance. However, while there are some continuities with noncitizen power here, the anti-migration and anti-multilateralism protestors largely explicitly mobilized insofar as they were outraged citizens. This has implications for how they could act and how their narrative was able to gain traction. This can be seen through two related movements that have arisen in France around this time: the Gilets jaunes and the Gilets noirs as well as how they have been used by others.

The Gilets jaunes (lit. *yellow vests*, referring to hi-viz vests worn by truckers) movement arose in autumn 2018 in response to a rise in fuel taxes. Organized through Facebook, their mobilization was largely through petitions and weekly occupation of major roads and roundabouts in French cities, which then received substantial mainstream media coverage.[78] The movement quickly gained traction across France and at both traditional extremes of the political spectrum. Over 300,000 people reportedly attended their first mass demonstrations in November 2018.[79] In four-fifths of French regions, over half of those identifying as Gilets jaunes supporters in a 2019 survey reported having voted for candidates at extreme ends of the political spectrum in the 2017 presidential election. While in three regions, more reported having voted for far-right Marine Le Pen than for far-left Jean-Luc Mélenchon, in two others this was reversed.[80] Two issue areas had broad agreement among Gilets jaunes supporters: distrust of government (79 per cent reported 'pas du tout confiance' or 'no confidence at all', in government) and belief that there are too many immigrants in France.[81]

The Gilets jaunes also directly influenced the way in which another movement arising in Paris at around this time went on to frame their activities. Members of the Gilets noirs (lit. *black vests/jackets*) movement trace its roots to the eviction of mostly irregular immigrant workers, first from a residence in September 2018 and then from a vacant building next door in which those evicted had settled. When, on 23 November, much higher numbers than expected turned out to occupy the National Museum of the History of Immigration, they reportedly realized that they had the potential to grow momentum.[82] The movement was powerful and demanded rights and agency without tying them to citizenship. And yet, as has been observed by researcher Heather Johnson who has studied other irregular migrant protest movements in Europe: '[m]oving beyond citizenship as the guiding framework for understanding political agency, in theory or in practice, is difficult.'[83]

They claimed the name, 'Gilets noirs', in March 2019. The link to the Gilets jaunes was intentional, linking to wider struggles rejecting State violence and claiming workers' rights. This can be seen in comments from members like: '[w]e want to take this struggle out of the ghetto' and 'the immigrant's cause can be anyone's cause, *sans-papiers* [lit. paperless] or not, immigrant or not.'[84] And yet this noncitizenist move was affected by the burdens of noncitizenship. Unlike the Gilets jaunes, who used Facebook and had more of a marketplace of ideas model, the Gilets noirs were largely mobilized by word of mouth, including delegates visiting the places where irregular migrants were living. Echoing reflections from those I interviewed in relation to mobilization around the Global Compact for Migration, one reason for this was their historical and current experiences of the State, including fear of the State: '[w]hen you are *sans-papiers*, the rights of man don't apply to you, even when you contribute, even when you conduct yourself well.'[85] They reportedly held in-person meetings of hundreds of people in five languages to strategize and smaller meetings of fifty to sixty people to make emerging decisions. The Gilets jaunes were initially protesting fuel costs and infrastructure changes that threatened the livelihoods of truckers and other drivers. This situation was serious. However, the Gilets noirs were protesting evictions that had already made hundreds of people homeless, deportations of people to countries they had fled, and policies which removed them from the protections of the regular workforce.

The Gilets noirs were enacting agency. Johnson has warned that '[t]he recognition of vulnerability can quickly become an assumption that agency itself is never enacted – or cannot be enacted – because it is too dangerous'.[86] Clearly, the Gilets noirs act politically and do so in a context in which their actions are unexpected and illegalized. They act politically in a situation in which 'differences between political statuses constrain what kind of politics can legitimately occur, or even be seen and heard'.[87] The greater the weight people are already carrying as a result of the existing system, the more demanding it is for them to work to change its narratives. As Karina Gareginovna Ambartsoumian-Clough, a founding member of the organization United Stateless, which was mentioned in Chapter 1, has observed, she and others must pursue activism alongside daily fighting for their own basic rights.[88] And in response to why migrant workers themselves are often absent from global governance discussions, one grassroots worker I spoke to observed, 'how can we compete with their families?'. Moreover, while the Gilets jaunes were threatened with police and even military violence, they were largely protected by their citizenship. The Gilets noirs were deportable. From this, it is apparent that, on the one hand, the anti-migration movements made use of platforms and strategies that had different gatekeeping, which could be beneficial to noncitizen power. However, on the other hand, their use of those platforms and the traction they gained with governments was mediated by their experience as citizens. As those from the Gilets noirs quoted above observed, their cause needs to be recognized and adopted by a wider constituency, including citizens, in order to effect the greatest change.

## A struggle over narrative

In 2015, a photograph of the dead body of an infant in a red T-shirt and blue shorts who had been washed onto a Turkish beach went viral. Nilüfer Demir, the photographer, explained that the image aimed to 'express the scream of his silent body'.[89] The image tied to the hashtag #KiyiyaVuranInsanlik ('humanity washed ashore').[90] It was then shared by someone with a large Twitter following.[91] The story quickly morphed into a metaphor, and the image into an icon and then into a meme.[92] It was revealed that the child was called Aylan Kurdi. This was then corrected to Alan. The image entered the political ecosystem of the internet. Sharing the meme became performative. It said more about the sharer than about the child. On the left, it has been suggested that it allowed a form of 'solidarity without substance'.[93] On the right, it went on to be used in other ways.

Once the image started circulating, political figures responded in polarized ways, particularly in Europe, where the Kurdi family had been going, and in North America to which they had applied for resettlement.[94] Politicians in the centre and left issued statements 'expressing searing personal grief and an urgent sense of heightened collective responsibility'.[95] Initially, this was about facilitating entry. Quickly, people began using the image for their own purposes. Satirical cartoonists incorporated it. Pundits discussed it. It turned out that the child's father, Abdullah Kurdi, had survived the crossing. Initially, Kurdi thought sharing his story might be useful, so he did. By the end of 2015, he had changed his mind. He told a reporter from *The Guardian* newspaper: 'I wanted to make the international community open their hearts to the plight of refugees', [. . .] 'But no one was listening. Everyone just wanted to use that picture and what happened to me for their own purposes.'[96] The picture was powerful, but the power wasn't held by Abdullah Kurdi.

To begin with, there was a rise in empathy in the press.[97] This also led to a change in public responses in Europe. European charities supporting Syrian asylum seekers and refugees reported an increase in donations.[98] States promised to welcome more refugees. Much was written and said about what needed to change. However, the furore soon subsided and few of these commitments were upheld.[99] In 2016, the death of Kurdi was used as part of the rationale for the EU-Turkey Statement, which included measures to deter movement into the EU and incentives for countries to re-admit those who had tried.[100] This was framed as protecting those who wanted to move.[101] It is unlikely that people with Kurdi's experiences had been consulted. In the UK, a year later, new images of Syrian children seeking asylum were circulated. Alive, older and arriving on UK territory, this time they were framed as devious and dangerous.[102] They were not welcomed. In 2016, the French satirical publication, *Charlie Hebdo*, published a cartoon that linked the image of a dead child in a red T-shirt on a beach to allegations of sexual assault by refugees in Germany, asking, 'What would little Aylan have become if he had grown up?'.[103]

If there had been no image of a child dead on a beach, and if the image had not been shared by someone with a large Twitter following, then the child, Alan Kurdi, would have died invisibly.[104] Ben Lewis from OHCHR said of the process towards the Global Compact for Migration that it would not have been initiated without 'migrants themselves making that journey and insisting that they had a right to be seen'. Yet, he acknowledges that, for the most part, in order to be seen, their stories and images had to be mediated by others: by journalists and then by academics, activists and policy-makers. Shahidul Alam, whose photograph of Masud Rana appears in Chapter 1, uses photography for social activism.[105] He emphasizes that 'images may have different meanings to different people, and that the meaning of a photograph can depend to a large extent on the context in which it is used'.[106] In practice, the power of the images Lewis describes was not held by those who were experiencing the world as noncitizens. This power was held by citizens, who also chose *which* images to share and how to frame them – what narrative to give them. Even in writing this section, I have made a decision about whether and how to show the image (I chose not to) and how to name what it portrayed.

Pictures of suffering children are known to elicit sympathy and generosity.[107] One could argue, as does philosopher Peter Singer (whose book, *The Life You Can Save*, has spawned a grassroots philanthropic movement in some wealthy countries), that there is a moral imperative to use such imagery, no matter its problems, if it can make things materially better for those most in need.[108] However, this focuses superficially on the interests (albeit charitable ones) of citizens, rather than on the deeper issue of cultivating a noncitizenist lens; of deferring to those affected to find out what their interests are; and of allowing *noncitizen power* to emerge. There is a risk that using images to elicit donations, for example, treats those portrayed as objects. This reinforces the idea that they are pawns in a wider project, rather than political agents in their own right. It provokes sympathy and perhaps empathy, but not deference or respect.[109] It does not present those individuals as necessary interlocutors in policy discussion. It is necessary to interrogate how the power of the image functions – and who wields that power.

Photographs are powerful.[110] This is why I chose to use them in other chapters. This book used images to introduce the reader to the political actors described as real and individual people, and did so with permission. The intention was to show the power and individuality of those pictu red in the context in which they were acting. This can be seen in the way they hold themselves, in their surroundings, and in the images selected. For Chapters 3 and 4, I particularly asked those pictured if they might suggest photographs of themselves participating in the high-level processes they were describing. This was to help the reader to get a sense of what participation in such meetings looks like. I chose not to use any images in this final chapter because I could not see how any particular image would contribute usefully to the discussion without exploitation.

Referring to photographs of tragedies, commentator Susan Sontag has written that they 'are a means of making "real" (or "more real") matters that the privileged and the merely safe might prefer to ignore'.[111] However, the photograph that is chosen and the way it is used can itself cause harm. It depends on what the image is used for. In the now-famous image of Kurdi, the subject is not portrayed as powerful. He does not have agency. He is portrayed as dead, pathetic and pitiable. He is treated as a 'thing' (to use Sontag's wording). The reason his image became an icon and then a meme may not have much to do with the realities of him as a person or of his family and the reasons they crossed the sea. It might instead have more to do with a fascination with this sort of imagery,[112] and perhaps a need to perform a socially necessary form of solidarity. The power over the image – and the power *of* the image – has not been noncitizenist. As the child's father explained, the image and the story behind it were used by others, ostensibly on behalf of noncitizens.[113] On the left, the emphasis was on him as a vulnerable refugee. It transformed the agency of a family trying actively to find a safer life for their infant son into abject, non-agent, non-threatening, victimhood.[114] On the right, it was on him as a devious migrant. This reinforced the strange moralized distinction often made between migrants and refugees mentioned in chapter 2.[115] To reiterate, the picture was powerful, as were the narratives it drove, but the power wasn't held by Abdullah Kurdi or by his son.

# Conclusion

Built into our global system is the presumption that some people, because of where they were born or who they were born to, are entitled to less agency over their own mobility than others. In some senses, this is a continuation of colonial ideologies in which some people from some countries were decision-makers and others pawns in the decisions of others. Studying who is able to participate in designing and critiquing systems of global migration governance, as this book has done, indicates that precisely those people with presumed entitlement to agency over their own mobility are also those most likely to be seen as eligible interlocutors when including non-governmental participation in developing the structures of global migration governance. This is part of a pervasive citizenism in global politics. This book showed how this functions in both more and less visible ways. That is to say, not only does explicit selection and gatekeeping affect participation in governance discussions, but there are also structural modes of exclusion which affect agency and voice in sometimes hidden and/or unexpected ways. Indeed, the very structures which currently hamper agency over mobility also hamper access to policy discussions about those structures. This is a problem both for those directly affected and for those who are trying to bring about a more evidence-based and just, and so also more sustainable, system. This concluding chapter restates that a noncitizenist move is needed in global governance, and particularly in global migration governance.

As this book has shown, there is a banal citizenism underlying global political institutions. That is, there is a presumption that all people and their politics can be understood through citizenships. This can make it difficult to frame or even to see the realities for those who must live and act politically despite existing institutional structures. The language of 'noncitizenship' and the noncitizenist move advocated in this book can address this. Noncitizenship, as presented here, is a substantive relationship with the multistate system (and elsewhere I have presented a State-level noncitizenship) in its own right. It is not the opposite or negation of citizenship. Noncitizenship and citizenship are not in a binary. This means that a person may experience *both* citizenship and noncitizenship in relation to the multistate system. It also means that noncitizenism does not deny that citizenship is important. The noncitizenist move is to examine institutions from the perspective of people insofar as they must live and act politically despite them.

Adopting a noncitizenist lens, this book has presented two main reasons why it is a problem that those presumed least entitled to agency over their own mobility are also least likely to be seen by those in power as interlocutors in developing structures of global migration governance: (1) it is a problem of sustainability and (2) it is a problem of justice.

First, excluding those with the greatest insight into and experience of the systems of migration governance from creating and critiquing those systems is a problem for sustainability. Those who are confronted daily with the policies produced to control migration, who must think about them and negotiate them in their daily lives, are thereby most expert in those structures and most likely to have insight into how they can be improved. This is relevant insofar as people experience the international system as noncitizens, irrespective of whether they have crossed or plan to cross an international border.

Insofar as people experience the world mostly as citizens, they may be affected by 'meta-blindness'.[1] That is, not only are those who carry the least burden of the international system of migration governance unaware of the weight of the burden carried by others, but they may also be unaware that there is something about which they are unaware. This also produces an 'insider theory problem',[2] such that the conceptual understanding of the system is produced and reproduced by insiders to that system, insiders who may be ignorant, because of their positionality, to the realities of that system.

This can be seen if we consider some of those we met in Chapters 1 and 2. It took Paulette Wilson making public her experience of being treated as if an illegal immigrant in the UK, her home country, for those recognized as experts to realize that this was an issue that needed to be studied. Wilson's lived reality gave her an understanding that was unavailable to those who were unaffected. After she forced her situation to be seen, academics and others began to research what she had shown them. Ekaterina E explained how she and other members of United Stateless challenged the official statistics that indicated that the number of stateless people in the United States was zero. They said that it cannot be zero because #WeAreNotZero. Thanks to their work, the official number was changed to 'unknown' and a project was launched with UNHCR and academics in collaboration with United Stateless to map the incidence of statelessness in the country. The expert insight offered by Wilson and E and the work that they undertook to break through the meta-blindess to make their insights known more widely are instances of noncitizen power and of the importance of noncitizen power in the development of better-informed policy that reflects and responds to a more accurate picture of the world, for the benefit of all.

It is important to gain insight into the unseen practical effects of policy frameworks. It is as important to gain an understanding of how people live out their agency. This book has argued that 'agency' does not track political or legal status. In practice, people are decision-makers. They make decisions based on what is important to them and their understanding of the options available. Without knowing every person's 'life-world', it is not possible to know how that person will act, which risks they will take, and which interests they will most want to satisfy. Treating all people as agentive means assuming that they are thinking, weighing, and deciding as individuals with individual life-worlds. This makes it particularly necessary to include those with a range of life-worlds into discussions about policy. Chapter 2 presents how the Partition of India could be seen as a huge and tragic example in which failure to see all people as agentive and fully recognize what this might entail gave rise to large-scale displacement and tragedy. Seeing people as agentive forces them also to be seen as potential interlocutors in the development and critique of the governance structures that affect them, if those governance structures are to be based in reality and so sustainable.

Second, noncitizen power is also important to policy making because it is the power of people insofar as they carry the heaviest burdens of the political institutions which organize all of our lives. Yet, there is no formal mechanism to consult with or represent the views of people insofar as they experience the world as noncitizens; insofar as they must live out their lives and their politics *despite* rather than *thanks to* or *beyond* the system of States. Perhaps, in practice, there are currently two international communities.[3] Human rights are developed and defended on the basis of the community of all people. These are the rights of people insofar as they are human. However, in a world affected by an underlying banal citizenism,[4] it is implicitly presumed that all people are citizens and the universal principles developed to protect all people insofar as they are human may be available to people insofar as they are citizens or quasi-citizens.[5] This produces a foundational problem (or one could say a sleight of hand) at the heart of global systems of rights and for the legitimacy of systems of governance, including those of migration governance.

Perhaps, then, there is also the community of all people and then there is the community of all people insofar as they are seen as agentive and as appropriate interlocutors (including through representation) in the international system. When people challenge this system, for example, by crossing borders they have been told not to cross, this is rarely framed as highlighting a problem with global governance structures, but rather such individuals' actions, or even the individuals themselves, are defined as 'irregular' or 'illegal' irrespective of their reasons for acting. They are made eligible for punishment and forced relocation.[6] Underlying the position taken in this book is that if there is in fact some constituency that is properly less agentive, less eligible to be interlocutors, then this would need to be defined and defended explicitly, including to the satisfaction of those thereby excluded. That is, it would for example be necessary to justify to Ekaterina E's satisfaction why she should not be given recognition in the international community and consulted about policies affecting her. In the absence of such justification (and I don't think such justification is possible) work to amend this problem needs to be undertaken with urgency.

This book has presented the work of those who, despite existing structures, have managed to bring noncitizen perspectives into discussions of global migration governance. It suggests that existing challenges can only be addressed by a noncitizenist move in thinking about global governance and global migration governance in particular. A noncitizenist move asks that noncitizens are centred and that political structures are examined through the perspectives of people insofar as they experience the world as noncitizens. As this book has shown, this may track along traditionally recognized dimensions of oppression and exclusion, such as sex, gender, race and class. But it may also arise in dimensions that are invisible to those not confronted by them. This makes noncitizenism tricky, and particularly so for those enjoying the most privileged positions within the international system. This means that a noncitizenist move will need to include facilitating rather than blocking noncitizen power and seeking out those who live out their lives and act politically despite global structures in order to seek their input into improving them. A noncitizenist move isn't so much about sympathy for, or empathy with, noncitizens. It is about deference to and solidarity with those who have expertise-by-experience of the international system.

A noncitizenist move requires a shift in presumption so that those who carry the heaviest burdens of the global system of migration governance are recognized both as experts and as key stakeholders in that system. This means that they are both agentive and essential interlocutors in the development and critique of governance systems. This up-ends the legitimacy of business as usual. Rather than starting from a situation in which access to visas, as presented in Chapter 5, and language, as presented in Chapter 6, remain the same and efforts are made around the edges to include, the starting point should be how to ensure that those who are needed in the development and critique of the systems of global migration governance can be fully part of that process. This might mean starting by looking at which locations will be easiest for those most affected to attend. It might mean engaging hybrid engagement online and in person. It might mean using technologies to assist communication and supporting alternative forms of discussion. It might mean obscuring identities where a person's participation might put them at risk. Any decisions would depend on what is most conducive to ensuring key participants are able to participate fully.

Noncitizenism also shows that there are solidarities where sometimes it might look like there is only conflict. In fact, those anti-migration and anti-multilateralism protestors discussed in Chapter 7 had some things in common with the global migrant civil society actors trying to effect change in the Global Compact. Some on both sides of this apparent binary centred their critique around a problematization of neoliberal globalization, which treats people as expendable units in others' development. Some highlighted that they were excluded from systems of power and decision-making or from economic stability. The noncitizenist move allows that these underlying concerns arise in many forms and sees them as potentially more productively in solidarity than in tension with each other.

The noncitizenist move also has implications for how engagement in global governance structures is conceived. It requires a rethinking of the aim of 'democratizing global politics', which has been underlying efforts at increasing civil society participation in global structures.[7] This book argues for centring the perspectives and voice of people insofar as they are noncitizens as a distinct and essential project. Democratization in global politics would require that those who carry the heaviest burdens of the international system and who have unique insights into it are central to the decisions made about how it should be constructed. The starting point, then, is neither NGOs nor CSOs per se, but rather those in a noncitizen relationship.

This book has identified some mechanisms that have enabled noncitizen power to emerge. It has also identified some structural challenges to this. Chapter 3 simplified the complex landscape to identify three important ways in which noncitizen power was brought to high-level governance discussions: formal representation, bridging by those engaging in both formal discussions and social movements and engagement through claiming both noncitizenship and liminal citizenship in relation to the international system. In each of these three, noncitizen power relied on some form of citizen relationship. As presented in Chapter 4, these three were also supported by institutional insiders. However, institutional structures put the people involved in this at all levels into positions of unintentional gatekeeping. A noncitizenist move, then, cannot only focus on mitigating the effects of international structures. It must also look at how to fix them.

One interviewee told me (as mentioned in Chapter 4) that they believed that the Global Compact for Migration was never really intended to make life better for the most marginalized migrants. To them, the purpose of the Compact seemed to be for ensuring that the suffering and deaths of migrants wouldn't disrupt the smooth running of the international system. They told me this on the basis of difficulties they had experienced, both when migrating and when trying to bring their expertise into discussions of migration governance. Adopting a noncitizenist approach to talking about global migration governance would need to take this perspective seriously. It would be necessary to prove that this person's belief about the Compact's intention is incorrect, rather than the other way around.

A noncitizenist approach presumes all people to be appropriately agentive and as appropriate interlocutors in discussions about the governance structures that affect them. It starts from the perspectives of people who must live and act politically despite those structures. This is for two reasons. First, it holds that governance structures need to be at least defensible to those most affected by them. Second, it advocates that governance structures should be critiqued and developed on the basis of accurate knowledge about reality. This requires input from people with direct experience of their implications, including implications which may be invisible to others. As such, a key part of the noncitizenist approach as presented in this book is the promotion of noncitizen power: promotion of the power of people insofar as they experience political and institutional structures directly and acutely as noncitizens.

Noncitizen power is a positive force. It can drive a more just and more sustainable global politics. However, as this book has shown, the positive contribution of noncitizen power in global politics requires input both from those who experience the international system as noncitizens and from those who experience it mostly as citizens. Noncitizen power relies on a noncitizenist move in thinking about global politics, including the politics of migration.

# Notes

## Introduction

1 Tendayi Bloom (2018) *Noncitizenism: Recognising Noncitizen Capabilities in a World of Citizens*, Routledge; Tendayi Bloom (2021) 'Human Rights are Not Enough: Understanding Noncitizenship and Noncitizens in Their Own Right', in Molly Land, Kathryn Libal, and Jillian Chambers (eds), *Beyond Borders: The Human Rights of Non-Citizens at Home and Abroad*, Cambridge University Press.

2 Here are some introductions to the UN system, taking different approaches: Maggie Black (2008) *The No-Nonsense Guide to the United Nations*, New Internationalist Publications; Linda Fasulo (2015) *An Insider's Guide to the UN*, Third Edition, Yale University Press.

3 The implications of this are also discussed, for example, in Ekaterina E (2021) 'United Stateless in the United States: Reflections from an Activist', in Tendayi Bloom and Lindsey Kingston (eds), *Statelessness, Governance, and the Problem of Citizenship*, Manchester University Press, 356–64.

4 The phrase, 'parliament of man' comes from the poem 'Locksley Hall' by Alfred, Lord Tennyson and published in 1842. It is found in this couplet: 'Till the war-drum throbb'd no longer, and the battle-flags were furl'd / In the Parliament of man, the Federation of the world.'

5 William Conklin (2014) *Statelessness: The Enigma in the International System*, Hart.

6 A key proponent of this structural approach to understanding justice is Iris Marion Young, not least her classic book, *Justice and the Politics of Difference*, Princeton University Press. Young's focus is on domestic justice in the United States, but she does also consider questions of global justice. She does not, to my knowledge, address the question of justice in the context of migration.

7 Drawing on the tradition stemming from Miranda Fricker (2007) *Epistemic Justice: Power and the Ethics of Knowing*, Oxford University Press.

8 Jan Aart Scholte, for example, focuses on this in the context of citizens who do not feel represented in the international system: Jan Aart Scholte (2004) 'Civil Society and Democratically Accountable Global Governance', *Government and Opposition* 39(2): 211–33.

9 Kathleen Newland (2020) 'Will International Migration Governance Survive the COVID-19 Pandemic?', Policy Brief, Migration Policy Institute.

10  S. Irudaya Rajan, P. Sivakumar, and Aditya Srinivasan (2020) 'The COVID-19 Pandemic and Internal Labour Migration in India: A "Crisis of Mobility"', *The Indian Journal of Labour Economics* 63: 1021–39.

11  Iris Marion Young (2011) *Responsibility for Justice*, Oxford University Press, 187.

# Chapter 1

1  Noncitizenism is related in some ways to Iris Marion Young's politics of difference, but I suggest looking beyond recognized systems of oppression, to focus first on the political relationship. See Iris Marion Young (1990) *Justice and the Politics of Difference*, Princeton University Press; Iris Marion Young (2001) 'Equality of Whom? Social Groups and Judgements of Injustice', *The Journal of Political Philosophy* 9(1): 1–18; and my argument for starting from a focus on capabilities in Tendayi Bloom (2018) *Noncitizenism: Recognising Noncitizen Capabilities in a World of Citizens*, Routledge.

2  I have focused on State-level noncitizenship elsewhere. See, for example: Bloom 2018; Tendayi Bloom (2021) 'Human Rights are Not Enough: Understanding Noncitizenship and Noncitizens in Their Own Right', in Molly Land, Kathryn Libal, and Jillian Chambers (eds), *Beyond Borders: The Human Rights of Non-Citizens at Home and Abroad*, Cambridge University Press.

3  This relates to 'occlusion' as presented, for example, in: Ann Laura Stoler (2016) *Duress: Imperial Durabilities in Our Times*, Duke University Press.

4  This point is presented in Phillip Cole (2017) 'Insider Theory and the Construction of Statelessness', in Tendayi Bloom, Katherine Tonkiss, and Phillip Cole (eds), *Understanding Statelessness*, Routledge, 255–67.

5  In particular: José Medina (2011) 'The Relevance of Credibility Excess in a Proportional View of Epistemic Injustice: Differential Epistemic Authority and the Social Imaginary', *Social Epistemology* 25(1): 15–35.

6  Sean Robinson (1994) 'The Aboriginal Embassy: An Account of the Protests of 1972', *Aboriginal History* 18(1): 49–63. This action is presented dramatically in the 1972 documentary film, *Ningla* Na, which translates into *Hunger for our* Land, directed by Alessandro Cavadini and including key movement leaders, including Michael Anderson.

7  Michael Anderson (2022) 'Ghillar Michael Anderson Reflects on Starting the Tent Embassy 50 Years Ago', *NITV News*, https://www.sbs.com.au/nitv/article/2022/01/26/ghillar-michael-anderson-reflects-starting-tent-embassy-50-years-ago (accessed 8 August 2022).

8  Robinson 1994.

9  Edwina Howell (2014) 'Black Power – by any means necessary', in Gary Foley, Andrew Schaap, and Edwina Howell (eds), *The Aboriginal Tent Embassy*, Routledge.

10  Edwina Howell and Andrew Schaap (2014) 'The Aboriginal Tent Embassy and Australian Citizenship', in Engin F. Isin and Peter Nyers (eds), *Routledge Handbook of Global Citizenship Studies*, Routledge, 568–80 at 576.

11  Anderson 2022.

12  Michael Anderson Ghillar (2019) 'Historical Background to the NAIDOC 2019 Theme: "Voice, Treaty, Truth"', https://nationalunitygovernment.org /content/historical-background-naidoc-2019-theme-'voice-treaty-truth' (accessed 6 December 2019).

13  Linda Burney MP in her maiden speech to the Australian Parliament, August 2016. See, for example, BBC (2016) 'Australian Aboriginal MP Linda Burney Vows to Fight for Change', 31 August 2016.

14  Robinson 1994.

15  John Ramsland (2004) 'Bringing up Harry Penrith: Injustice and Becoming Burnum Burnum: The Formative Years of a Child of the Stolen Generation', *Education Research and Perspectives* 31(2): 94–106.

16  Elvi Whittaker (1994) 'Public Discourse on Sacredness: The Transfer of Ayers Rock to Aboriginal Ownership', *American Ethnologist* 21(2): 310–34 at n. 1, 328.

17  William Beinart and Lotte Hughes (2007) *Environment and Empire*, Oxford University Press, 342; see also discussion of this in Franke Wilmer (1993) *The Indigenous Voice in World Politics*, Sage, 16.

18  Quoted in Whittaker 1994, 310.

19  For example, Barry Hindess (2003) 'Responsibility for Others in the Modern System of States', *Journal of Sociology* 39(1): 23–30.

20  It is argued that Masud Rana has also played a key role in Bangladeshi understandings of its place in the Cold War and in post-independence nation-buidling: Projit Bihari Mukharji (2015) 'Technospatial Imaginaries: Masud Rana and the vernacularization of popular Cold War geopolitics in East Pakistan, 1966–1971', *History and Technology* 31(3): 324–40.

21  Mahmud Rahman (2008) 'Pulp Fiction in Bangladesh', *World Literature Today* 82(3): 39–42; Mukharji 2015. See also Jyoti Rahman (2019) 'A Bangladeshi superhero', *Dhaka Tribune*, 21 January 2019, https://www .dhakatribune.com/opinion/op-ed/2019/01/21/a-bangladeshi-superhero (accessed 23 July 2021).

22  Rahman 2008.

23  Shaidul Alam (2016) *The Best Years of My Life*, Drik Picture Library.

24  Joya Chatterji (2010) 'Migration Myths and the Mechanics of Assimilation: Two Community Histories from Bengal', *Studies in Humanities and Social Sciences* 17(1–2): 139–74.

25  For example, see Eli Meixler (2018) 'Journalism Is Under Threat.' Inside a Bangladeshi Journalist's Dangerous Journey from Photographer to Prisoner', *Time*, 11 December 2018, https://time.com/5475494/shahidul-alam -bangladesh-journalist-person-of-the-year-2018/ (accessed 8 August 2022).

26  1.2 million: ILO (n.d.) 'Reinforcing Ties: Enhancing Contributions from Bangladeshi diaspora Members', International Labour Organisation

and Government of Bangladesh, using 2004 data from the Ministry of Expatriates' Welfare and Overseas Employment.

27  Shaidul Alam in a series of projects. This particular story comes from his book, *The Best Years of My Life*.

28  See ADB (2020) 'Bangladesh', Asian Development Bank Member Fact Sheet, May 2020.

29  Janet Henry and James Pomeroy (2018) 'The World in 2030: Our Long-Term Projections for 75 Countries', Economics Global September 2018, HSBC Global Research, 2.

30  Human Development Index 2019 Revision; UNDP (n.d.) 'Comprehensive Disaster Management Programme Phase II', Project Factsheet United Nations Development Program Bangladesh.

31  Salahuddin Ahmed (2004) *Bangladesh: Past and Present*, A. P. H. Publishing Corporation; for implications of this for contemporary Bangladesh, see Ali Riaz (2016) *Bangladesh: A Political History Since Independence*, I. B. Tauris.

32  Shabbir Ahmed and Md. Ayatullah Khan (2022) 'Spatial Overview of Climate Change Impacts in Bangladesh: A Systematic Review', *Climate and Development* ahead-of-print.

33  Ahmed and Khan 2022; M. M. Golam Rabbani, Matthew Cotton, and Richard Friend (2022) 'Climate Change and Non-Migration – Exploring the Role of Place Relations in Rural and Coastal Bangladesh', *Population and Environment* 44: 99–122.

34  Md. Arif Chowdhury, Md. Khalid Hasan, and Syed Labib Ul Islam (2022) 'Climate Change Adaptation in Bangladesh: Current Practices, Challenges and the Way Forward', *The Journal of Climate Change and Health* 6: 1–8.

35  UNDP (2020) 'The Next Frontier: Human Development and the Anthropocene: Briefing note for countries on the 2020 Human Development Report: Bangladesh', UNDP.

36  According to Global Passport Index, 2019 iteration.

37  Alam 2016.

38  International Organization for Migration (2010) Bangladesh Household Remittance Survey 2009.

39  For example, see Ashraful Azad (2019) 'Recruitment of Migrant Workers in Bangladesh: Elements of Human Trafficking for Labor Exploitation', *Journal of Human Trafficking* 5(2): 130–50; Priya Deshingkar, C. R. Abrar, Mirza Taslima Sultana, Kazi Nurmohammad Hossainul Haque, and Md Selim Reza (2018) 'Producing Ideal Bangladeshi Migrants for Precarious Construction Work in Qatar', *Journal of Ethnic and Migration Studies* 45(14): 2723–38.

40  Alam 2016.

41  Glorene Das (2018) 'Migrant Estate Workers Toil in Tough Conditions', *New Straits Times*, 28 September 2018, https://www.nst.com.my/opinion/letters /2018/09/415872/migrant-estate-workers-toil-tough-conditions (accessed 1 September 2022).

42 Andika Wahab (2020) 'The Outbreak of Covid-19 in Malaysia. Pushing Migrant Workers at the Margin', *Social Sciences and Humanities Open*, 2: 100073.

43 Lindsay Wright (2019) 'Giving a Voice to Migrant Workers in Malaysia', *Ethical Trading Initiative*, 17 July 2019, https://www.ethicaltrade.org/blog/giving-voice-to-migrant-workers-malaysia.

44 This is reportedly particularly since a 2018 change in law. AKM Ahsan Ullah (2013) 'Irregular Migrants, Human Rights and Securitization in Malaysia: An Analysis from a Policy Perspective', in C. Tazreiter and S. Y. Tham (eds), *Globalization and Social Transformation in the Asia-Pacific*, Palgrave Macmillan, 178–88.

45 Robert C. M. Weebers (2017) 'Tanah Rata and the Development of the Cameron Highlands, 1925–2030', *Journal of the Malaysian Branch of the Royal Asiatic Society* 90(312): 101–11; Amarjit Kaur (2012) 'Labour Brokers in Migration: Understanding Historical and Contemporary Transnational Migration Regimes in Malaya/Mayalsia', *IRSH* 57: 225–52.

46 Anita Isalska (2015) 'How to Plan a Trip to Malaysia's Cameron Highlands', *Lonely Planet Online*, 18 December 2015.

47 Defined in Article 1 of 1954 Convention relating to the Status of Stateless Persons.

48 Ekaterina E (2021) 'United Stateless in the United States: Reflections from an Activist', in Tendayi Bloom and Lindsey Kingston (eds), *Statelessness, Governance, and the Problem of Citizenship*, Manchester University Press.

49 For important recent analyses of the misunderstanding and implications for wider understandings of politics, including international politics: Phillip Cole (2019) 'Taking Statelessness Seriously', *Statelessness and Citizenship Review* 1(1): 161–5; Kelly Staples (2020) 'The Ethics of Statelessness', in Birgit Schippers (ed.), *The Routledge Handbook to Rethinking Ethics in International Relations*, Routledge.

50 Ekaterina E (2020) 'A Stateless Person's Take on 'Stateless'', *European Network on Statelessness Blog*, 10 September 2020, https://www.statelessness.eu/updates/blog/stateless-persons-take-stateless (accessed 1 September 2022). Lindsey Kingston traces some reasons why it has been difficult for statelessness to emerge as an issue: Lindsey Kingston (2013) '"A Forgotten Human Rights Crisis": Statelessness and Issue Emergence', *Human Rights Review* 14(2): 73–87; Lindsey Kingston (2019) 'Conceptualizing Statelessness as a Human Rights Challenge: Framing, Visual Representation, and (Partial) Issue Emergence', *Journal of Human Rights Practice* 11(1): 52–72.

51 Medina 2011.

52 Ekaterina E 2020.

53 More information is available from their website: https://www.unitedstateless.org/organization.

54 Ekaterina E 2021.

55 Ekaterina E 2021.

56 Ekaterina E 2020.

57 Emma Batha (2019) 'Stateless Woman Tells How she Couldn't Visit Dying Dad', *Reuters*, 28 June 2019, https://news.trust.org/item/20190628153501 -a8bpz/.

58 Ekaterina E 2021.

59 Donald Kerwin, Daniela Alulema, Michael Nicholson, and Robert Warren (2020) *Statelessness in the United States: A Study to Estimate and Profile the US Stateless Population*, CMS Report, January, Center for Migration Studies, New York.

60 Kerwin et al. 2020, cited in Ekaterina E 2021, 361.

61 Email, 22 November 2022.

62 Tendayi Bloom (2022) 'Can Citizenship Studies Escape Citizenism?', *Citizenship Studies* 26(4–5): 372–81.

63 Paul Gerbaudo (2017) *The Mask and the Flag: Populism, Citizenism and Global Protest*, Oxford University Press, 3, 7.

64 Gerbaudo 2017.

65 For example, Guillaume Deloison (2018) 'Critique de la Democratie', on his blog. . . https://guillaumedeloison.wordpress.com/2018/07/02/critique-de-la -democratie/.

66 Original: 'se invitará a "participar", es decir, a ser copartícipes de su propia dominación', Manuel Delgado (2016) *Ciudadanismo: La reforma ética y estética del capitalismo*, Catarata.

67 Manuel Delgado (2016) *Ciudadanismo: La reforma ética y estética del capitalismo*, Catarata.

68 Delgado 2016.

69 This is initially set out in a series of discussion pieces on the right-wing website *VDare* and then in the form of more formal articles on *The American Conservative* and in the book, Steve Sailer (2009) *America's Half-Blood Prince: Obama's "Story of Race and Inheritance"'*, VDare Foundation.

70 Steve Sailer (2006) 'Americans First', *The American Conservative*, 13 February 2006, https://www.theamericanconservative.com/articles/ americans-first/ (accessed 22 July 2021).

71 This is presented, for example, in Park MacDougald and Jason Willick (2017) 'The Man Who Invented Identity Politics for the New Right', *New York Magazine*, 30 April 2017, https://nymag.com/intelligencer/2017/04 /steve-sailer-invented-identity-politics-for-the-alt-right.html (accessed 11 January 2022).

72 Bloom 2022.

73 Bloom 2022.

74 Michael Billig (1995) *Banal Nationalism*, Sage.

75 Alasia Nuti (2019) *Injustice and the Reproduction of History: Structural Inequalities, Gender and Redress*, Cambridge University Press.

76 Philippe Muray (2000) 'Citoyen: De la citoyennophilie', *Le Débat* 2000/5, 112: 53–7 at 56.

77 Louis Theroux (1998) 'Weird Christmas', Season 1, Episode 5, *Louis Theroux's Weird Weekends*, produced by BBC Bristol and the Independent

Film Channel for the British Broadcasting Corporation BBC released 23 December 1998.

78 Recall Nuti 2019. See also for example Catherine Lu (2011) 'Colonialism as Structural Injustice: Historical Responsibility and Contemporary Redress', *The Journal of Political Philosophy* 19(3): 261–81.

79 This reflection is attributed to two young men, Jahid and Asif, upon seeing the conditions in the migrant camp in Lampedusa after their arrival in late 2016, quoted in Hsiao-Hung Pai (2018) *Bordered Lives: How Europe Fails Refugees and Migrants*, New Internationalist.

80 Kelly Staples (2012) 'Statelessness and the Politics of Misrecognition', *Res Publica* 18: 93–106.

# Chapter 2

1 The Concise Oxford English Dictionary 8th Edition p. 751.

2 Amelia Gentleman (2019) *The Windrush Betrayal,* Faber and Faber, 8, emphasis added.

3 Gentleman 2019.

4 For example,. Paul Foot (1969) *The Rise of Enoch Powell*, Penguin.

5 Tendayi Bloom and Katherine Tonkiss (2013) 'European Union and Commonwealth Free Movement: A Historical-Comparative Perspective', *Journal of Ethnic and Migration Studies* 39(7): 1067–85; In the month after his speech, Powell received over 100,000 letters, mostly of support: Amy Whipple (2009) 'Revisiting the "Rivers of Blood" Controversy: Letters to Enoch Powell', *Journal of British Studies* 48(3): 717–35.

6 Bloom and Tonkiss 2013.

7 Immigration Act 1971. See discussion, for example, in Ann Dummett and Andrew G. Nicol (1990) *Subjects, Citizens, Aliens and Others: Nationality and Immigration Law*, Weidenfeld and Nicolson.

8 Gentleman 2019.

9 Colin Yeo traces the official beginning of the 'hostile environment' in the UK to a 2012 speech by the then Home Secretary Theresa May, though with earlier roots: Colin Yeo (2018) 'Briefing: What is the Hostile Environment, Where Does It Come from, Who Does it Affect?', *Freemovement Briefing*, 1 May 2018. Frances Webber traces it to the early 1990s: Frances Webber (2019) 'The Embedding of State Hostility: A background paper on the Windrush Scandal', Institute of Race Relations Briefing Paper No. 11.

10 Amelia Gentleman (2017) '"I Can't Eat or Sleep": The Woman Threatened with Deportation after 50 Years in Britain', *The Guardian*, 28 November 2017.

11 Gentleman 2017.

12 Gentleman 2019.

13 Gentleman 2019.

14 For example, Fiona Bawdon (2014) *Chasing Status: If not British, then what am I?* Legal Action Group.

15 Gentleman 2019.

16 Oxford Migration Observatory publication.

17 Guy Hewitt and Kevin M. Isaac (2018) 'Windrush: The Perfect Storm', *Social and Economic Studies* 67(2/3): 293–302 at 298.

18 Ruth Craggs (2018) 'The 2018 Commonwealth Heads of Government Meeting, the Windrush Scandal and the Legacies Of Empire', *Round Table* 107(3): 361–2.

19 For example, see Amelia Gentleman (2020) 'Wolverhampton Marks Life of Windrush Campaigner Paulette Wilson', *The Guardian*, 4 September 2020, https://www.theguardian.com/uk-news/2020/sep/04/wolverhampton-marks-life-of-windrush-campaigner-paulette-wilson (accessed 11 January 2021).

20 https://www.gov.uk/government/publications/windrush-task-force-data-q2-2021.

21 Nicholas De Genova (2013) '"We are of the Connections": Migration, Methodological Nationalism, and "militant Research"', *Postcolonial Studies* 16(3): 250–8.

22 Nicholas De Genova (2015) 'Extremities and Regularities: Regularity Regimes and the Spectacle of Immigration Enforcement', in Yolande Jansen, Robin Celikates, and Joost de Bloois (eds), *The irregularities of Migration in Contemporary Europe: Detention, Deportation, Drowning*, Rowman and Littlefield.

23 Tendayi Bloom (2019) 'When Migration Policy Isn't about Migration: Considerations for Implementation of the Global Compact for Migration', *Ethics and international Affairs* 33(4): 481–97.

24 See, respectively, essays by Bridget Wooding (292-305), Natalie Brinham (342-355), Maarja Vollmer (181-194), Ahmad Benswait (87-98), and Edwin O. Abuya (251-264) in Tendayi Bloom and Lindsey N. Kingston (2021) *Statelessness, Governance, and the Problem of Citizenship*, Manchester University Press. Luke de Noronha suggests that citizenship inevitably produces such hierarchies and exclusions: Luke de Noronha (2022) 'Hierarchies of Membership and the Management of Global Population: Reflections on Citizenship and Racial Ordering', *Citizenship Studies* 26(4–5): 426–35.

25 ENS (2017) 'Protecting Stateless Persons from Arbitrary Detention', European Network on Statelessness. There are also reports from around the world of citizens detained under immigration measures; E.g. Paige St. John and Joel Rubin (2018) 'ICE held an American Man in Custody for 1,273 Days. He's Not the Only One Who Had to Prove his Citizenship', *Los Angeles Times*, 27 April 2018.

26 Describing people denied citizenship of their home States, Kristy Belton introduces the terminology of 'displaced in situ' and 'rooted displacement': Kristy Belton (2015) 'Rooted Displacement: The Paradox of Belonging Among Stateless People', *Citizenship Studies* 19(8): 907–21.

27 Luke de Noronha (2019) 'Deportation, Racism and Multi-Status Britain: Immigration Control and the Production of Race in the Present', *Ethnic and Racial Studies* 42(14): 2413–30.

28 For example, Shashi Tharoor (2016) *Inglorious Empire: What the British Did to India*, Penguin; Yasmin Khan (2007) *The Great Partition: The Making of India and Pakistan*, Yale University Press; see also Tayyab Mahmud (1997) 'Migration, Identity and the Colonial Encounter', *Oregon Law Review* 73: 633–90.

29 For example, Khan 2007; Ayesha Jalal (1985) *The Sole Spokesman: Jinnah, The Muslim League and the Demand for Pakistan*, Cambridge University Press.

30 Urvashi Butalia (2000) *The Other Side of Silence: Voices from the Partition of India*, Duke University Press, 59.

31 George Kyris (2022) 'State Recognition and Dynamic Sovereignty', *European Journal of International Relations* 28(2): 287–311.

32 Kyris 2022, 74.

33 Khan 2007.

34 Butalia 2000, 55.

35 Saadat Hasan Manto (2008) 'Shyam: Krishna's Flute', in Khalid Hasan (editor and translator), *Bitter Fruit: the Very Best of Saadat Hasan Manto'*, Penguin, 485–502.

36 OHK Spate (1947) 'The Partition of the Punjab and of Bengal', *The Geographical Journal* 110(4/6): 201–18; Navdip Kaur (2011) 'Violence and Migration: A Study of Killing in the Trains during the Partition of Punjab in 1947', *Proceedings of the Indian History of Congress* 72(I): 947–54; Swarna Aiyar (1995) '"August Anarchy": The Partition Massacres in Punjab, 1947', *South Asia* XVIII: 13–36.

37 Amartya Sen (2006) *Identity and Violence: The Illusion of Destiny*, Penguin, 2.

38 See, for example, these recent analyses of the displacement: K. Hill, W. Seltzer, J. Leaning, S. J. Malik, and S. S. Russell (2008) 'The demographic impact of Partition in the Punjab in 1947', *Population Studies* 62(2): 155–70; Prashant Bharadwaj, Asim Khwaja, and Atif Mian (2008) 'The Big March: Migratory Flows after the Partition of India', *Economic and Political Weekly* 43(35): 39–49. See also the detailed analysis in Prashant Bharadwaj, Asim Ijaz Khwaja, and Atif R. Mian (2009) 'The Partition of India: Demographic Consequences', Available from SSRN.

39 Prashant Bharadwaj, Asim Khwaja, and Atif Mian (2008) 'The Big March: Migratory Flows after the Partition of India', *Economic and Political Weekly* 43(35): 39–49. I have rounded to integers.

40 Bharadwaj, Khwaja and Mian 2008.

41 Catherine Dauvergne (2004) 'Sovereignty, Migration and the Rule of Law in Global Times', *Modern Law Review* 67(4): 588–615.

42 See Introduction to Vazira Fazila-Yacoobali Zamindar (2007) *The Long Partition and the Making of Modern South Asia*, Columbia University Press.

43 Fazila-Yacoobali Zamindar 2007.

44 See, for example, the recent book: Gillian Brock (2020) *Justice for People on the Move: Migration in Challenging Times*, Cambridge University Press.

45 For example, Luis Cabrera (2019) 'Free Movement, Sovereignty and Cosmopolitan State Responsibility', in Richard Beardsworth et al. (eds), *The State and Cosmopolitan Responsibilities*, Oxford University Press.

46 Alesia Nuti (2019) *Injustice and the Reproduction of History: Structural Inequalities, Gender and Redress*, Cambridge University Press, 38.

47 Sara Amighetti and Alasia Nuti (2015) 'A Nation's Right to Exclude and the Colonies', *Political Theory* 44(4): 541–66.

48 For example, see, though using different language, Mostafa Rejai and Cynthia H. Enloe (1969) 'Nation-States and State-Nations', *International Studies Quarterly* 13(2): 140–58. For distinction between internal and external sovereignty, see, for example, Nicholas Barber (2018) *The Principles of Constitutionalism*, Oxford University Press, 25 for example. Note also, for example, Catherine Lu's analysis of how Japan saw being a colonizer as key to being seen as civilized Catherine Lu (2011) 'Colonialism as Structural Injustice: Historical Responsibility and Contemporary Redress', *The Journal of Political Philosophy* 19(3): 261–81.

49 Aníbal Quijano (2007) 'Coloniality and Modernity/Rationality', *Cultural Studies* 21(2–3): 168–78 (translated by Sonia Therborn); Barry Hindess (2003) 'Responsibility for Others in the Modern System of States', *Journal of Sociology* 39(1): 23–30.

50 Quijano 2007, 168; R. P. Anand (1966) 'Sovereign Equality of States in International Law – I', *International Studies* 8(3): 213–41 at 240; Maja Spanu (2020) 'The Hierarchical Society: The Politics of Self Determination and the Constitution of New States after 1919', *European Journal of International Relations* 26(2) 372-392.

51 Aníbal Quijano (2000) 'Coloniality of Power and Eurocentrism in Latin America', *International Sociology* 15(2): 215–32.

52 Ngũgĩ wa Thiong'o (2005) *Decolonising the Mind: The Politics of Language in African Literature*, East African Educational Publishers Ltd, Nairobi (first published 1986).

53 This sentiment is echoed in the literature. Consider, for example, Robert Goodin (1992) 'If People Were Money. . ', in Brian Barry and Robert E. Goodin (eds), *Free Movement*, Harvester Weatsheaf, 6–22.

54 Hindess 2003.

55 Yolande Jansen, Robin Celikates, and Joost de Bloois (2015) 'Introduction', in Jansen, Celikates, and de Bloois (eds), *The Irregularlization of Migration in Contemporary Europe: Detention, Deportation, Drowning*, Rowman and Littlefield.

56  Raúl Delgado Wise (2018) 'Is There a Space for Counterhegemonic Participation? Civil Society in the Global Governance of Migration', *Globalizations* 15(6): 746–61.

57  Hein de Haas, Mathias Czaika, Marie-Laurence Flahaux, edo Mahendra, Katharina Natter, Simona Vezzoli, and María Villares-Varela (2018) 'International Migration: Trends, Determinants and Policy Effects', DEMIG Paper 33 IMI Working Paper Series no. 142, 28.

58  Steffen Mau, Fabian Gülzau, Lena Laube, and Natascha Zaun (2015) 'The Global Mobility Divide: How Visa Policies Have Evolved over Time', *Journal of Ethnic and Migration Studies* 41(8): 1192–213.

59  Mogens Hobolth (2014) 'Researching Mobility Barriers: The European visa Database', *Journal of Ethnic and Migration Studies* 40(3): 424–35.

60  Mau et al. 2015.

61  Paul Asquith, Henrietta Bailey, David Hope-Jones, Ambreena Manji, and Nick Westcott (2019) 'Visa Problems for African Visitors to the UK', Joint All-Party Parliamentary Group Report by the APPG for Africa, the APPG for Diaspora, Development and Migration and the APPG for Malawi.

62  Asquith et al. 2019.

63  Esther Yei-Mokuwa, Carolin Dieterle, and Elizabeth Storer (2019) 'The UK's Self-Harming Scandal of Visa Rejections for Visiting Academics', London School of Economics Africa at LSE blog, 21 May 2019.

64  Ankebe Oqubay (2020) 'UK Visa System for African Visitors Requires Urgent Reform', *New African*, 12 February 2020.

65  For example, see Rey Koslowski (2000) *Migrants and Citizens*, Cornell University Press, 2; Mikhail Alexseev (2006) *Immigration Phobia and the Security Dilemma: Russia, Europe, and the United States*, Cambridge University Press.

66  B. S. Chemni (1998) 'The Geopolitics of Refugee Studies: A View from the South', *Refugee Studies* 11(4): 350–74.

67  For example, see Steffen Mau, Heike Brabandt, Lena Laube, and Christof Roos (2012) *Liberal States and the Freedom of Movement: Selective Borders, Unequal Mobility*, Palgrave.

68  MIO (2019) 'Africa's Youth: Jobs or Migration?', Mo Ibrahim Foundation Report; Tara Brian and Frank Laczko (eds) *Fatal Journeys: Tracking Lives Lost during Migration*, International Organization for Migration. It is worth noting that while it is clear that the mortality in the Mediterranean region is high, it is possible that reporting problems may be masking death rates in other regions.

69  Lanre Olusegun Ikuteyijo (2020) 'Irregular Migration as Survival Strategy: Narratives from Youth in Urban Nigeria', in Mora L. McLean (ed.), *West African Youth Challenges and Opportunity Pathways*, Palgrave Macmillan, 53–77.

70  Human Development Reports and information about them can be found at the website: hdr.undp.org/en/content/human-development-index-hdi (accessed 6 July 2020).

71  For a background on the Human Development Index, read autobiography of its creator: Mahbub Ul Haq (1976) *The Poverty Curtain*; based on the Capabilities Approach presented by Amartya Sen.

72  S. Castles et al. (2012) 'Irregular Migration: Causes, Patterns, and Strategies', in Irena Omelaniuk (ed.), *Global Perspectives on Migration and Development*, Springer, 117–51.

73  Natasha Basu and Bernardo Caycedo (2017) 'A Radical Reframing of Civil Disobedience: "Illegal" Migration and Whistleblowing', in Esther Peeren, Robin Celikates, Jeroen de Kloet, and Thomas Poell (eds), *Global Cultures of Contestation: Mobility, Sustainability, Aesthetics and Connectivity*, Springer; Catherine Dauvergne (2008) *Making People Illegal: What Globalization Means for Migration and the Law*, Cambridge University Press; Jonathan Simon (2007) *Governing Through Crime: How the War on Crime Transformed American Democracy and Created a Culture of Fear*, Oxford University Press.

74  Daniel Vega Macías (2021) 'La pandemia del COVID-19 en el discurso antimigratorio y xenófobo en Europa y Estados Unidos', *Estudios fronterizos* 22: 1–22.

75  Amanuel Elias, Jehonathan Ben, Fethi Mansouri, and Yin Paradies (2020) 'Racism and Nationalism during and Beyond the COVID-19 Pandemic', *Ethnic and Racial Studies* 44(5): 783–93; see also personal experience presented in Kong Pheng Pha (2020) 'Two Hate Notes: Deportations, COVID-19, and Xenophobia against Hmong Americans in the Midwest', *Journal of Asian American* Studies 23(3): 335–9.

76  For example, Saifuddin Ahmed, Vivia Hsueh Hua Chen, and Arul Indrasen Chib (2021) 'Xenophobia in the Time of a Pandemic: Social Media Use, Stereotypes, and Prejudice against Immigrants during the COVID-19 Crisis', *International Journal of Public Opinion Research* online publication, 30 April 2021; Tyler T. Reny and Matt A. Barreto (2022) 'Xenophobia in the Time of Pandemic: Othering, anti-Asian Attitudes, and COVID-19', *Politics, Groups, and Identities* 10(2): 209–32. This also included a well-documented drop in consumption of Chinese food worldwide, see for example brief note: Yulia E. Chuvileva, Andrea Rissing, and Hilary B. King (2020) 'From Wet Markets to Wal-Marts: Tracing Alimentary Xenophobia in the Time of COVID-19', *Social Anthropology* 28(2): 241–3; Carol Chan and Maria Montt Strabucchi (2020) 'Many-Faced Orientalism: Racism and Xenophobia in a Time of the Novel Coronavirus in Chile', *Asian Ethnicity* 22(2): 374–94.

77  For example, see David R. Glerum (2021) 'Tainted Heroes: The Emergence of Dirty Work during Pandemics', *Industrial and Organizational Psychology* 14: 41–4.

78  Vega Macías 2021; Vincent Geisser (2020) 'L'hygiéno-nationalisme, remède miracle à la pandémie? Populismes, racismes et complotismes autor du Covid-19', *Migrations Soicété* 2020/2 No.180: 3–18; see also Ruth Simpson and Rachel Morgan (2020) '"Gendering" Contamination: Physical, Social and Moral Taint in the Context of COVID-19', *Gender in Management* 35(7/8): 685–91.

79  Zhaohui Su, Dean McDonnell, Junaid Ahmad, Ali Cheshmehzangi, Xiaoshan Li, Kylie Meyer, Yuyang Cai, Ling Yang, and Yu-Tao Xiang (2020) 'Time to Stop the Use of "Wuhan Virus", "China Virus", or "Chinese Virus" Across the Scientific Community', *British Medical Journal Global Health* 5(9): 1–3; Reny and Barreto 2020.

80  Waihiga Mwaura (2020) 'Letter from Africa: The spread of coronavirus prejudice in Kenya', *BBC News*, 9 March 2020.

81  Keneth Iceland Kasozi et al. (2020) 'Misconceptions on COVID-19 Risk Among Ugandan Men: Results from a Rapid Exploratory Survey, April 2020', *Frontiers in Public Health* 8(416): 1–10. Uchechukwu L. Osuagwu et al. (2020) 'Misinformation About COVID-19 in Sub-Saharan Africa: Evidence from a Cross-Sectional Survey', *Health Security* 19: 1.

82  Adewale Maja-Pearce (2020) 'Rich Man's Disease', *London Review of Books Blog*, 31 March 2020, https://www.lrb.co.uk/blog/2020/march/rich-man-s-disease (accessed 23 June 2020); ETB Sivapriyan (2020) 'COVID-19 is a Rich Man's Disease: Tamil Nadu CM', *Deccan Herald*, 16 April 2020, https://www.deccanherald.com/national/covid-19-is-a-rich-man-s-disease-tamil-nadu-cm-826123.html (accessed 23 June 2020); Shashank Bengali, Kate Linthicum, and Victoria Kim (2020) 'How Coronavirus – A "Rich Man's Disease" – Infected The Poor', *Los Angeles Times*, 8 May 2020, https://www.latimes.com/world-nation/story/2020-05-08/how-the-coronavirus-began-as-a-disease-of-the-rich; Robin Oryem (2020) 'Xenophobia and Behavioural Responses to COVID-19 in Uganda', London School of Economics blog, 1 May 2020, https://blogs.lse.ac.uk/africaatlse/2020/05/01/xenophobia-racism-ebola-behavioural-change-covid19-uganda/.

83  For example, Lorenzo Tondo (2020) 'Salvini Attacks Italy PM over Coronavirus and Links to Rescue Ship', *The Guardian,* 24 February 2020, https://www.theguardian.com/world/2020/feb/24/salvini-attacks-italy-pm-over-coronavirus-and-links-to-rescue-ship (accessed 10 September 2021).

84  Human Rights Watch (2020) 'China: Covid-19 Discrimination Against Africans: Forced Quarantines, Evictions, Refused Services in Guangzhou', *Human Rights Watch News*, 5 May 2020, https://www.hrw.org/news/2020/05/05/china-covid-19-discrimination-against-africans (accessed 10 September 2021).

85  Ani Movsisyan et al. (2021) 'Travel-Related Control Measures to Contain the COVID-19 Pandemic: An Evidence Map', *British Medical Journal Open* 11: e041619.

86  UN News, 'COVID-19: Agencies Temporarily Suspend Refugee Resettlement Travel', 17 March 2020.

87  UNHCR (2020) 'Beware Long-Term Damage to Human Rights and Refugee Rights from the Corona Virus Pandemic', Press release, 22 April 2020.

88  For example, Jean N. Lee, Mahreen Mahmud, Jonathan Morduch, Saravana Ravindran, and Abu S. Shonchoy (2021) 'Migration, Externalities, and the

Diffusion of COVID-19 in South Asia', *Journal of Public Economics* 193: 104312; S. Irudaya Rajan, P. Sivakumar, and Aditya Srinivasan (2020) 'The COVID-19 Pandemic and Internal Labour Migration in India: A "Crisis of Mobility"', *The Indian Journal of Labour Economics* 63: 1021–39.

89  For example, see Matthew Charles (2020) '"Disease of the Rich, Killer of the Poor" How Covid-19 brought Latin America to its Knees', *The Telegraph*, https://www.telegraph.co.uk/global-health/science-and-disease/ coronavirus-in-latin-america/.

90  Bengali et al. 2020; Yves Genier (2020) 'Une maladie de l'élite', *Pour La Tête*, 7 April 2020, https://bonpourlatete.com/analyses/une-maladie-de-l-elite (accessed 18 February 2021); Jason Beaubien (2020) 'COVID-19's Global Spread among the Relatively Rich Has Been Remarkable', *NPR*, 14 March 2020, https://www.npr.org/2020/03/15/815828858/coronavirus-and-the -rich-beaubien (accessed 18 February 2021).

91  For example, see Kathryn Libal, Scott Harding, Marciana Popescu, S. Megan Berthold, and Grace Felten (2021) 'Human Rights of Forced Migrants During the COVID-19 Pandemic: An Opportunity for Moblization and Solidarity', *Journal of Human Rights and Social Work* 6: 148–60.

92  World Health Organisation (2020) *ApartTogether Survey: Preliminary Overview of Refugees and Migrants Self-Reported Impact of Covid-19*, World Health Organisation; Lorenzo Guadagno (2020) *Migrants and the COVID-19 Pandemic: An Initial Analysis*, International Organisation for Migration.

93  Eric Reidy (2020) 'The COVID-19 Excuse? How Migration Policies are Hardening Around the Globe', *The New Humanitarian*, 17 April 2020.

94  With exceptions. For example, the region of Kerala in India made preparations for returning citizens. See, for example, discussion in S. Irudaya Rajan (2020) 'Migrants at a Crossroads: COVID-19 and Challenges to Migration', *Migration and Development* 9(3): 323–30.

95  Solon Ardittis and Frank Laczko (2020) 'Introduction – Migration Policy in the Age of Immobility', *Migration Policy Practice* 8(10): 2–7.

96  Quote published on the site of France24 on 13 March 2020.

97  Tim Hume (2020) 'Corona Virus Is Giving Europe's Far Right the Perfect Excuse to Scapegoat Refugees', *Vice News*, 19 March 2020.

98  Gupta, Surojit (2020) '30% of Migrants will Not Return to Cities: Irudaya Rajan', *Times of India*, https://timesofindia.indiatimes.com/india/30-of -migrants-will-not-return-to-cities-irudaya-rajan/articleshow/76126701 .cms.

99  S. K. Singh, Vibhuti Patel, Aditi Chaudhary, and Nandlal Mishra (2020) 'Reverse Migration of Labourers Amidst COVID-19', *Economic and Political Weekly*, 8 August 2020, LV.32 25-30, 26.

100  Rajan et al. 2020; Singh et al. 2020, 27.

101  World Health Organisation 2020; F. Landis Mackellar (2020) 'COVID-19: Demography, Economics, Migration and the Way Forward', in *Migration Policy Practice* 10(2): 8–14 at 11; Guadagno 2020.

102 For example, Jens Brockmeier (2009) 'Reaching for Meaning: Human Agency and the Narrative Imagination', *Theory and Psychology* 19(2): 213–33.

103 Marilyn Frye (1983) 'Oppression', in Marilyn Frye (ed.), *The Politics of Reality: Essays in Feminist Theory*, Crossing Press, 1–16 at 4.

104 I take the phrase 'reach for meaning' from Brockmeier 2009.

105 Following the work of critical economist Amartya Sen on the one hand and anti-colonial theorist Aníbal Quijano on the other. Amartya Sen (1977) 'Rational Fools: A Critique of the Behavioral Foundations of Economic Theory', *Philosophy and Public Affairs* 6(4): 317–44; Aníbal Quijano (1992) 'Colonialidad y Modernidad/Racionalidad', *Perú Indígena* 13(29): 11–20.

106 This is argued through an example in: Saba Mahmood (2005) *Politics of Piety: The Islamic Revival and the Feminist Subject*, Princeton University Press.

107 Guido Calabresi and Philip Bobbitt (1971) *Tragic Choices*, W.W. Norton and Company.

108 For example, see the ways in which this affects narratives of victimhood, villainousness, and so forth, in Cetta Mainwaring (2016) 'Migrant Agency: Negotiating Borders and Migration Controls', *Migration Studies* 4(3): 289–308.

109 I took this poetic framing from Guillermo E. Acuña González (2016) 'Estructura y agencia en la migración infantil centroamericana', *Cuadernos Inter.c.a.mbio sobre Centroamérica y el Caribe* 13(1): 43–62 at 46.

110 Stefan Rother (2018) 'Angry Birds of Passage – Migrant Rights Networks and Counter-Hegemonic Resistance to Global Migration Discourses', *Globalizations* 15(6): 854–69.

111 OHCHR refers to the UN Office of the High Commissioner for Human Rights.

112 Original: 'Les migrants ne manquent pas d'agentivité: ils prennent des décisions vitals tous les jours, avec courage et determination: ils essaient cependant de le faire dans la discretion.'; François Crépeau (2016) 'La mobilité et la diversité, défis des sociétés contemporaines', presentation to Organisation internationale de la Francophonie, Conseil constitutionnel de France, Paris, les 31 mai et 1 juin 2016.

113 See in particular Vicki Squire (2017) 'Unauthorised Migration beyond Structure/Agency? Acts, Interventions, Effects', *Politics* 37(3): 254–72.

114 Nando Sigona (2014) 'The Politics of Refugee Voices: Representations, Narratives, and Memories', in Elena Fiddian-Qasmiyeh, Gil Loescher, Katy Long, and Nando Sigona (eds), *The Oxford Handbook of Refugee and Forced Migration Studies*, Oxford, 369–82.

115 Edward W. Said (2003) *Orientalism*, Penguin Random House (first published 1978).

116 Quijano 1992; also Hugh Tinker (1977) *Race, Conflict and International Order: From Empire to United Nations*, MacMillan.

117 Turn of phrase from Chielozona Eze (2014) 'Rethinking African Culture and Identity: The Afropolitan Model', *Journal of African Cultural Studies* 26(2): 234–47 at 244.

118 Marie-Pier Lemay (2020) 'Erreur de diagnostic: préférences adaptives et impérialisme', *Philosophiques* 47(1): 139–64.

119 Mahmud 1997, 637.

120 Jacqueline Bhabha (2018) *Can We Solve the Migration Crisis?*, Polity, 18.

121 Joseph E. Inikori (2003) 'The Struggle against the Transatlantic Slave Trade: The Role of the State', in Sylviane A. Diouf (ed.), *Fighting the Slave Trade: West African Strategies*, Ohio University Press.

122 https://www.slavevoyages.org/about/about#.

123 For some studies of the complex and changing landscape of the slave trade over this period, see, for example, Sylviane A. Diouf (ed.) (2003) *Fighting the Slave Trade: West African Strategies*, Ohio University Press.

124 David Eltis and David Richardson (2008) 'A New Assessment of the Transatlantic Slave Trade', in David Eltis and David Richardson (eds), *Essays on the New Transatlantic Slave Trade Database*, Yale University Press.

125 Alvin O. Thompson (1976) 'Race and Colour Prejudices and the Origin of the Trans-Atlantic Slave Trade', *Caribbean Studies* 16(3/4): 29–59.

126 Patricia M. Muhammad (2004) 'The Trans-Atlantic Slave Trade: A Forgotten Crime Against Humanity as Defined by International Law', *American University International Law Review* 19: 883–948.

127 Patricia Ihuoma Ogu (2016) 'Africa's Irregular Migration to Europe: A Re-enactment of the Transatlantic Slave Trade', *Journal of Global Research in Education and Social Science* 10(2): 49–69.

128 Julia O'Connell Davidson (2012) 'Absolving the State: The Trafficking-Slavery Metaphor', *Global Dialogue* 14(2): 31–41.

129 Matthew J. Gibney (2013) 'Is Deportation a Form of Forced Migration?', *Refugee Survey Quarterly* 32(2): 116–29; Vincent Chetail (2016) 'Is There Blood on my Hands? Deportation as a Crime of International Law', *Leiden Journal of International Law* 29(3): 917–43.

130 Joseph Carens (1987) 'Aliens and Citizens: The Case for Open Borders', *The Review of Politics* 49(2): 251–73.

131 Zetter (2015) *Protection in Crisis: Forced Migration in a Global Era*, Migration Policy; Heaven Crawley and Dimitris Skleparis (2018) 'Refugees, Migrants, Neither, Both: Categorical Fetishism and the Politics of Bounding in Europe's "Migration Crisis"', *Journal of Ethnic and Migration Studies* 44(1): 48–64.

132 Crawley and Skleparis 2018.

133 Shahram Khosravi (2010) *'Illegal' Traveller: An Auto-Ethnography of Borders*, Palgrave, 23.

134 Jill I Goldenziel (2017) 'Displaced: A Proposal for an International Agreement to Protect Refugees, Migrants, and States', *Berkeley Journal of International Law* 35(1): 47–89.

135  Crawley and Skleparis 2018.
136  This isn't a new discussion. For example, Norman Myers (1997) 'Environmental Refugees', *Population and Environment* 19(2): 167–82; David Keane (2004) 'The Environmental Causes and Consequences of Migration: A Search for the Meaning of "Environmental Refugees"', *Georgetown International Environmental Law Review* 16(2): 209–24.
137  For example, see Sonja Fransen and Hein de Haas (2021) 'Trends and Patterns of Global Refugee Migration', *Population and Development Review* 48(1): 97–128.
138  Katy Long (2013) 'When Refugees Stopped Being Migrants: Movement, Labour and Humanitarian Protection', *Migration Studies* 1(1): 4–26.
139  Long 2013, emphasis in the original.
140  Esther Rosenfeld (1995) 'Fatal Lessons: United States Immigration Law during the Holocaust', *University of California Davis Journal of International Law and Policy* 1(2): 249–66.
141  James Hathaway (1984) 'The Evolution of Refugee Status in International Law: 1920–1950', *International Comparative Law Quarterly* 33(2): 348–80.
142  Long 2013.
143  Erika Feller (2005) 'Refugees are not Migrants', *Refugee Survey Quarterly* 24(4): 27–35.
144  Thomas Gammeltoft-Hansen (2011) *Access to Asylum: International Refugee Law and the Globalisation of Migration Control*, Cambridge University Press.
145  Tazreena Sajjad (2018) 'What's in a Name? "Refugees", "Migrants" and the Politics of Labelling', *Race and Class* 60(2): 40–62.
146  I took this phrase from Paul Kockelman (2007) 'Agency: The Relation between Meaning, Power, and Knowledge', *Current Anthropology* 48(3): 375–401. Kockelman is playing with Jean-Paul Sartre's mantra that 'man is condemned to be free', from Jean-Paul Sartre (1970) *L'existentialisme est un humanisme*, Les Éditions Nagel (first published 1946).
147  Hsiao-Hung Pai (2018) *Bordered Lives: How Europe Fails Refugees and Migrants*, New Internationalist.
148  See, for example, the discussion in Phillip Cole (2017) 'Insider Theory and the Construction of Statelessness', in Tendayi Bloom, Katherine Tonkiss and Phillip Cole (eds), *Understanding Statelessness*, Routledge.

# Chapter 3

1  'International Co-Operation for the Prevention of Immigration Which Is Likely to Disturb Friendly Relations Between Nations', 17 November 1947, A/467, A/RES/136(II).

2 Alexander Betts (2011) *Global Migration Governance*, Oxford University Press, 2; Stefan Rother and Elias Steinhilper (2019) 'Tokens or Stakeholders in Global Migration Governance? The Role of Affected Communities and Civil Society in the Global Compacts on Migration and Refugees', *International Migration* 57(6): 243–57.

3 The language of 'epistemic injustice' was introduced in Miranda Fricker (2007) *Epistemic Injustice: Power and the Ethics of Knowing*, Oxford University Press. With thanks to Andrew Reid for first introducing me to this language. Some of his reflections on the political philosophy of epistemology: Andrew Reid (2019) 'What Facts Should be Treated as "Fixed" in Public Justification?', *Social Epistemology* 33(6): 491–502; Andrew Reid (2019) 'Buses and Breaking Point: Freedom of Expression and the "Brexit" Campaign', *Ethical Theory and Moral Practice* 22: 623–37.

4 Related to Stefan Rother's inside–outside strategies: Stefan Rother (2022) *Global Migration Governance from Below: Actors, Spaces, Discourses*, Palgrave; Stefan Rother (2009) '"Inside-Outside" or "Outsiders by Choice"? Civil Society Strategies Towards the 2nd Global Forum on Migration and Development (GFMD) in Manila', *ASIEN* 111: 95–107.

5 Some important long-form analyses of global migrant civil society activities have been published recently. Notable examples include: Rother 2022; Sandra Lavenex and Nicola Piper (2022) 'Regions in Global Migration Governance: Perspectives "from above", "from below" and "from beyond"', *Journal of Ethnic and Migration Studies* 48(12): 2837–54; Carl-Ulrik Schierup, Branka Likic-Brboric, Raúl Delgado Wise, and Gülay Toksöz (eds) (2019) *Migration, Civil Society and Global Governance*, Routledge.

6 Interview, New York, 26 February 2019.

7 Gemma Adaba (1997) 'How International Financial Institutions Undermine Worker Rights', *Guild Practitioner* 54: 219–23.

8 ILO Constitution 1919, preamble.

9 Co97 – Migration for Employment Convention (Revised), 1949 (No. 97).

10 Adaba explained that Global Unions is the partnership between the ITUC, the Global Union Federations (GUFs) and the Trade Union Advisory Committee (TUAC) to the OECD.

11 Gemma Adaba (2016) *Financing Social Protection Floors*, Financing for Development Working Paper Series II.A/1, 30 November 2016, 4.

12 Clarified via email 25 October 2022.

13 See a discussion of the tripartite system, its uncertain origins and its potential benefits, in: Bernard Béguin (1959) 'ILO and the Tripartite System', *International Conciliation* 32: 448; David Waugh (1982) 'The ILO and Human Rights', *Comparative Labor Law* 5(2): 186–96.

14 ILO (1956) 'Report of the Committee on the Extent of the Freedom of Employers' and Workers' Organisations', *International Labour Office Official Bulletin* xxxix: 9 (cited in Béguin 1959, 408).

15 'The General Conference recommends that each Member of the International Labour Organisation shall, on condition of reciprocity and upon terms to be agreed between the countries concerned, admit the foreign workers (together with their families) employed within its territory, to the benefits of its laws and regulations for the protection of its own workers, as well as to the right of lawful organization as enjoyed by its own workers', ILO (1919) R002 – Reciprocity of Treatment Recommendation, 1919 (No.2), available at Information System on International Labour Standards: https://www.ilo.org/dyn/normlex/en/f?p=1000:12100 :1889755223957::NO::P12100_SHOW_TEXT:Y: (accessed 1 August 2021).

16 Jean Grugel and Nicola Piper (2011) 'Global Governance, Economic Migration and the Difficulties of Social Activism', *International Sociology* 26(4): 435–54 at 441.

17 Katy Long (2013) 'When Refugees Stopped Being Migrants: Movement, Labour and Humanitarian Protection', *Migration Studies* 1(1): 4–26 at 9.

18 Elaine Lebron-McGregor and Nicholas R. Micinski (2021) 'The Changing Landscape of Multilateral Financing and Global Migration Governance', in Tesseltje de Lange, Willem Maas, and Annette Schrauwen (eds), *Money Matters in Migration: Policy, Participation, and Citizenship*, Cambridge University Press, 19–37 at 27.

19 Vincent Chetail (2022) 'The International Organization for Migration and the Duty to Protect Migrants: Revisiting the Law of International Organizations', in Jan Klabbers (ed.), *The Cambridge Companion to International Organizations Law*, Cambridge University Press, 244–64.

20 With reference to the Domestic Workers Convention, see, for example, Nicola Piper (2015) 'Democratising Migration from the Bottom Up: The Rise of the Global Migrant Rights Movement', *Globalizations* 12(5): 788–802.

21 Roger Böhning (1991) 'The ILO and the New UN Convention on Migrant Workers: The Past and Future', *The International Migration Review* 25(4): 698–709; Antoine Pécoud and Paul de Guchteneire (2006) 'Migration, Human Rights and the United Nations: An Investigation into the Obstacles to the UN Convention on Migrant Workers' Rights', *Windsor Yearbook of Access to Justice* 24: 241–66 at 247.

22 For example, see this contemporary discussion of the process leading to and following from the Convention: Roger Böhning (1976) 'The ILO and Contemporary International Economic Migration', *The International Migration Review* 10(2): 147–56.

23 For example, discussed in Böhning 1991.

24 6 November 1974 (A/RES/3224(XXIX)); 9 December 1975 (A/RES/3449(XXX)); 16 December 1976 (A/RES/31/127); 16 December 1977 (A/RES/32/120); 20 December 1978 (A/RES/33/163); 17 December 1979 (A/RES/34/172); 15 December 1980 (A/RES/35/198); 16 December 1981 (A/RES/36/160); 17 December 1982 (A/RES/37/170); 16 December 1983

(A/RES/38/86); 14 December 1984 (A/RES/39/102); 13 December 1985 (A/RES/40/130); 4 December 1986 (A/RES/41/151); 7 December 1987 (A/RES/42/140); 8 December 1988 (A/RES/43/146); 15 November 1989 (A/RES/44/155).

25  For example, see James Nafziger and Barry Bartel (1991) 'The Migrant Workers Convention: Its Place in Human Rights Law', *International Migration Review* 25(4): 771–99.

26  This is particularly helpfully set out in Nafziger and Bartel 1991, 778 and in the appendix which starts at 789. See also Pécoud and de Guchteneire 2006, 246.

27  Tendayi Bloom (2014) *Extended Report: Global Migration Governance: A Decade of Change?*, Policy Report No. 02/07, United Nations University Institute on Globalization, Culture and Mobility.

28  Skype interview 29 November 2018.

29  Pécoud and de Guchteneire 2006, 250.

30  For example, François Crépeau and Bethany Hastie (2015) 'The Case for "Firewall" Protections for Irregular Migrants', *European Journal of Migration and Law* 17(2–3): 157–83.

31  For example, François Crépeau and Idil Atak (2016) 'Global Migration Governance: Avoiding Commitments on Human Rights, Yet Tracing a Course for Cooperation' *Netherlands Quarterly of Human Rights* 34(2): 113–46.

32  UNGA (2002) 'Strengthening of the United Nations: An Agenda for Further Change, Report of the Secretary-General', United Nations General Assembly Fifty-seventh session Item 53 on the provisional agenda A/57/387, 10.

33  Elaine McGregor-Lebron (2020) *International Organizations and Global Migration Governance*, Doctoral Thesis, Maastricht University, 86.

34  McGregor-Lebon 2020.

35  UN Press Release (2006) 'Secretary-General Appoints Peter Sutherland as Special Representative for Migration', 23 January 2006, SG/A/976/BIO/3735, https://www.un.org/press/en/2006/sga976.doc.htm (accessed 1 August 2021).

36  Jagdish Bhagwati (1994) 'The World Trading System', *Journal of International Affairs* 48(1): 279–85; Peter Gallagher (2005) *The First Ten Years of the WTO 1995–2005*, Cambridge University Press; Deborah Cass (2005) 'The Sutherland Report: The WTO and its Critics', *International Organizations Law Review* 2: 153–66; Fernando Henrique Cardoso, Sara Regine Hassett, and Christine Weydig (2005) 'An Interview with Fernando Henrique Cardoso', *Journal of International Affairs* 58(2): 211–19.

37  McGregor-Lebon 2020, 85.

38  McGregor-Lebon 2020, 115–16.

39  For example, Peter Sutherland (2010) 'The Age of Mobility: Can We Make Migration Work for All?', *Global Policy*, February 2010.

40  Interview. New York. 26 February 2019. This was also mentioned by others, for example, as quoted in Bloom 2014.

41  For example, see Crépeau and Atak 2016; David Weissbrodt (2009) *The Human Rights of Non-Citizens*, Oxford University Press.

42  For example, Susan Martin and Rola Abimourched (2009) 'Migrant Rights: International Law and National Action', *International Migration* 47(5): 115–38. Not explicitly about migration, but for an analysis of how people are in fact removed from human rights in practice see William Conklin (2014) *Statelessness: The Enigma of the International System*, Hart.

43  For example, 'migrant rights has become a serious human rights issue that deserves dire attention' Peter D Sutherland (2013) 'The International Migrants Bill of Rights: Why it Matters', *Georgetown Immigration Law Journal* 28: 269–71.

44  Sutherland 2013.

45  Katherine Tonkiss (2018) 'The Narrative Assemblage of Civil Society Interventions into Refugee and Asylum Policy Debates in the UK', *Voluntary Sector Review* 9(2): 119–35; Maria Lorena Cook (2010) 'The Advocate's Dilemma: Framing Migrant Rights in National Settings', *Studies in Social Justice* 4(2): 145–64.

46  Lu 2011, 266.

47  Interview, New York, 26 February 2018.

48  Monami Maulik (2011) 'Our Moment Is for the Long Haul: Ten Years of DRUM's Community Organizing by Working-Class South Asian Migrants', *Race/Ethnicity: Multidisciplinary Global Contexts* 4(3): 455–67; Susan Matloff-Nieves, Dana Fusco, Joy Connolly, and Monami Maulik (2015) 'Democratizing Urban Spaces A Social Justice Approach to Youth Work', in Michael Heathfield and Dana Fusco (eds), *Youth and Inequality in Education: Global Actions in Youth Work*, Routledge.

49  Skype interview, 7 March 2019.

50  Skype interview, 7 March 2019.

51  Skype interview, 7 March 2019. Clarified by email, 28 October 2022.

52  Skype interview, 8 November 2018.

53  Maulik 2011, 459, with inserted clarification from email from Maulik.

54  Maulik 2011.

55  Mary Kaldor (2003) 'The Idea of Global Civil Society', *International Affairs* 79(3): 583–93.

56  Debora Spini problematizes this, in Debora Spini (2010) 'Civil Society and the Democratization of Global Public Space', in David Armstrong, Valeria Bello, Julie Gilson, and Debora Spini (eds), *Civil Society and International Governance: The Role of Non-State Actors in Global and Regional Regulatory Frameworks*, Routledge.

57  Neera Chandhoke (2005) 'How Global is Global Civil Society?', *Journal of World Systems Research* XI(2): 355–71; Helmut Anheier, Marlies Glasius, and Mary Kaldor (2001) 'Introducing Global Civil Society', in Anheier, Glasius, and Kaldor (eds), *Global Civil Society*, Oxford University Press, 3–22.

58  This paper provides an interesting analysis of some of these debates, albeit not specific to the discussion of migration: Louise Amoore and Paul

Langley (2004) 'Ambiguities of Global Civil Society', *Review of International Studies* 30: 89–110.

59  Crépeau and Atak 2016.

60  Kathleen Newland (2005) *The Governance of International Migration: Mechanisms, Processes and Institutions*, Paper prepared for the Policy Analysis and Research programme of the Global Commission on International Migration, September 2005.

61  For example, see UNFPA (2004) *Meeting the Challenges of Migration: Progress since the ICPD*, 88.

62  Skype interview, 15 March 2019.

63  The two approaches are referred to as 'inside–outside' and 'outsiders by choice' by Stefan Rother 2009, 97. See also Stefan Rother (2013) 'Civil Society and Competing Visions of Global Migration Governance from Below', in Geiger et al. (eds), *Disciplining the Transnational Mobility of People* Palgrave Macmillan.

64  Interview, New York, 26 February 2019.

65  Skype interview, 25 October 2018. Clarified by email, 28 September 2022.

66  Skype interview, 7 March 2019. Clarified by email, 28 October 2022.

67  Anheier, Glasius, and Kaldor 2001, 10.

68  Skype interview, October 2018.

69  Skype interview, 25 October 2018.

70  Skype interview, 1 November 2018.

71  Skype interview, 7 March 2019.

72  Maulik 2011, 462.

73  Skype interview, 7 March 2019.

74  Eni Lestari, interview by Annalee Lepp (2016) 'Eni Lestari in Conversation with Annalee Lepp', *Migration, Mobility, and Displacement* 2(1): 55–66 at 57–8.

75  Information clarified and elaborated by Lestari, email 19 October 2022. Asia Pacific Forum on Women, Law and Development (2016) 'In conversation with Eni Lestari: From Domestic Worker to Global Advocate', web post, 16 September 2016, https://apwld.org/in-conversation-with-eni-lestari -from-domestic-worker-to-global-advocate/ (accessed 30 July 2021). See also: Stefan Rother (2017) 'Indonesian Migrant Domestic Workers in Transnational Political Spaces: Agency, Gender Roles and Social Class Formation', *Journal of Ethnic and Migration Studies* 43(6)" 956–73 at 966.

76  Lestari and Lepp 2016, 58.

77  Skype interview, 16 November 2018.

78  Lestari and Lepp 2016, 61, emphasis added.

79  Lestari and Lepp 2016.

80  This role of emotion is explained for example in research into the views about immigration detention among those with different experiences of it in the UK: Katie Tonkiss and Luis Cabrera (2022) '"I Felt Like a Bird Without Wings": Incorporating the Study of Emotions into Grounded Normative Theory', *Contemporary Political Theory*, Early View, 1–22.

81 UNGA (2000) 'United Nations Millennium Declaration', General Assembly Resolution 55/2, 8 September 2000.

82 Skype interview, 6 March 2019.

83 Skype interview, 16 November 2018.

84 For example, see Aníbal Quijano (2007) 'Coloniality and Modernity/ Rationality', *Cultural Studies* 21(2–3): 168–78 (translated by Sonia Therborn); Aníbal Quijano (2000) 'Coloniality of Power and Eurocentrism in Latin America', *International Sociology* 15(2): 215–32.

85 Note that Fricker has been criticized for a distinction she draws between epistemic injustice and epistemic bad luck. There is not scope to engage with this in detail here, except to suggest that some of this may derive from a disagreement about the scope of Fricker's categories. These are set up with helpful examples in Miranda Fricker (2006) 'Powerlessness and Social Interpretation', *Episteme* 3(1–2): 96–108.

86 Fricker 2007.

87 Fricker 2007.

88 José Medina (2011) 'The Relevance of Credibility Excess in a Proportional View of Epistemic Injustice: Differential Epistemic Authority and the Social Imaginary', *Social Epistemology* 25(1): 15–35; Emmalon Davis (2016) 'Typecasts, Tokens, and Spokespersons: A Case for Credibility as Testimonial Injustice', *Hypatia* 31(3): 485–501.

89 Medina 2011.

90 Davis 2016.

91 Medina 2011; Cole 2017.

92 Harper Lee (2010) *To Kill a Mockingbird*, Arrow Books.

93 I'm adopting Catherine Lu's notion of background conditions here: Catherine Lu (2017) *Justice and Reconciliation in World Politics*, Cambridge University Press.

# Chapter 4

1 Amnesty International was a notable exception.

2 For example, Donald Kerwin (2020) 'International Migration and Work: Charting an Ethical Approach to the Future', *Journal on Migration and Human Security* 8(2): 111–33.

3 This is tabulated in Tendayi Bloom (2014) *Extended Report: Global migration Governance: A Decade of Change?*, UNU-GCM Policy Report 02/07 at 15.

4 For example, see Chukwu-Emeka Chikezie (2012) 'Civil Society, the Common Space, and the GFMD', in Irena Omelaniuk (ed.), *Global Perspectives on Migration and Development: GFMD Puerto Vallarta and Beyond*, Springer.

5 Bloom 2014, 15.

6  Richard Blue, Danielle de García, and Kristine Johnstone (2012) *Study of the Outcomes and Impacts of the Global Forum on Migration and Development Civil Society Days*, Social Impact Inc.

7  Stefan Rother (2019) 'The Global Forum on Migration and Development as a Venue of State Socialisation: Stepping Stone for Multi-Level Migration Governance?', *Journal of Ethnic and Migration Studies* 45(8): 1258–74; Kellynn Wee, Kudakwashe P. Vanyoro, and Zaheera Jinnah (2018) 'Repoliticizing International Migration Narratives? Critical Reflections on the Civil Society Days of the Global Forum on Migration and Development', *Globalizations* 15(6): 785–808.

8  See also the strategic follow up on the plan, for example, Elaine McGregor (2017) 'Movement: A Global Civil Society Report on Progress and Impact on Migrants' Rights and Development: Through Year 3 of Civil Society's 5-year 8-point Plan of Action', International Catholic Migration Commission Europe.

9  Raúl Delgado Wise (2018) 'The Global Compact in Relation to the Migration-Development Nexus Debate', *Global Social Policy* 18(3): 328–31.

10  Rother 2019.

11  Bloom 2014, 35.

12  Bloom 2014.

13  Bloom 2014, 18 (chart 6); Rother 2019.

14  Kevin Ostoyich (2009) 'Emigration, Nationalism and Church Identity in Europe: The Legacy of the German St Raphael Society in International Catholic Migration Assistance', *International Journal for the Study of the Christian Church* 9(3): 240–54.

15  James J. Norris (1958) 'The International Catholic Migration Commission', *Catholic Lawyer* 4(Spring): 118–22 at 118.

16  Norris 1958, 120.

17  https://holyseemission.org/.

18  John Bruton (2018) 'Peter Sutherland: A Gifted Administrator and Humanitarian', *The Irish Times*, 8 January 2018, https://www.irishtimes.com/news/politics/peter-sutherland-a-gifted-administrator-and-humanitarian-1.3347580 (accessed 31 July 2021); ICMC (2018) 'Peter Sutherland, In Memoriam', ICMC website, 8 January 2018, https://www.icmc.net/2018/01/08/peter-sutherland-in-memoriam/# (accessed 31 July 2021).

19  Skype interview, 1 November 2018.

20  Skype interview, 1 November 2018.

21  Skype interview, 1 November 2018.

22  For helpful reviews of literature on IOM in light of its new position, see, for example: Antoine Pécoud (2018) 'What Do We Know About the International Organization for Migration?', *Journal of Ethnic and Migration Studies* 44(10): 1621–38; Jan Klabbers (2019) 'Notes on the Ideology of International Organizations Law: The International Organization for Migration, State-Making, and the Market for Migration', *Leiden Journal of International Law* 32: 383–400.

23  This is found across Rother's impressive corpus. See, for example, Rother 2022.

24  Nicola Piper and Stefan Rother observe that this was initially explicitly formulated by the Migrant Forum in Asia (MFA) in 2009, see Nicola Piper and Stefan Rother (2012) 'Let's Argue about Migration: Advancing a Right(s) Discourse via Communicative Opportunities', *Third World Quarterly* 33(9): 1735–50. See: Migrant Forum in Asia (2009) 'Mobilizing Migrant Community and Civil Society Voices for the Second Global Forum on Migration and Development (GFMD): The Migrant Forum in Asia Experience'.

25  Bloom 2014, 22.

26  Skype interview, 25 October 2018, clarified by email 28 September 2022.

27  Skype interview, 25 October 2018.

28  Though international law scholar Vincent Chetail argues that this does not mean it is not committed to protect migrant rights, given the broader body of laws that govern international organizations. Vincent Chetail (2022) 'The International Organization for Migration and the Duty to Protect Migrants: Revisiting the Law of International Organizations', in Jan Klabbers (ed.), *The Cambridge Companion to International Organizations Law*, Cambridge University Press, 244–64.

29  For example, see Ishan Ashutosh and Alison Mountz (2011) 'Migration Management for the Benefit of Whom? Interrogating the Work of the International Organization for Migration', *Citizenship Studies* 15(1): 21–38; Pécoud 2018.

30  Skype interview, 21 December 2018.

31  See, for example, Younes Ahouga (2021) 'Transforming the International Organisation for Migration: An Analysis of the IOM Strategic Vision', Working Paper No. 2'21/5, Ryerson Centre for Immigration and Settlement.

32  Pauline Gardiner Barber and Catherine Bryan (2018) 'International Organization for Migration in the field: "Walking the Talk" of Global Migration Management in Manila', *Journal of Ethnic and Migration Studies* 44(1): 1725–42; Anissa Maâ (2020) 'Manufacturing Collaboration in the Deportation Field: Intermediation and the Institutionalization of the International Organisation for Migration's "Voluntary Return" Programmes in Morocco', *The Journal of North African Studies* 26(5): 932–53; Frances Webber (2011) 'How Voluntary are Voluntary Returns?', *Race and Class* 53(4): 98–107.

33  Klabbers 2019, 387.

34  Klabbers 2019, 384.

35  Elaine Lebron-McGregor and Nicholas R. Micinski (2021) 'The Changing Landscape of Multilateral Financing and Global Migration Governance', in Tesseltje de Lange, Willem Maas, and Annette Schrauwen (eds), *Money Matters in Migration: Policy, Participation, and Citizenship*, Cambridge University Press, 19–37 at 25.

36  Ashutosh and Mountz 2011, also quoted in Klabbers 2019.

37  Cecilia Cannon and Thomas Biersteker (2020) 'The Governance of International Organisations: Structural Components, Internal Mechanisms, and Contemporary Challenges', in Helmut K. Anheier and Theodor Baums (eds), *Advances in Corporate Governance: Comparative Perspectives*, Oxford University Press, 203–29.

38  Chetail 2022.

39  Michele Klein Solomon and Suzanne Sheldon (2018) 'The Global Compact for Migration: From the Sustainable Development Goals to a Comprehensive Agreement on Safe, Orderly and Regular Migration', *International Journal of Refugee Law* 30(4): 584–90 at 587.

40  https://www.iom.int/member-states.

41  Kathleen Newland (2010) 'The Governance of International Migration: Mechanisms, Processes, and Institutions', *Global Governance* 16(3): 331–43 at 338.

42  Lebon-Mcgregor and Micinski 2021, 24–5.

43  E.g. see Philip Martin and Manolo Abella (2009) 'Migration and Development: The Elusive Link at the GFMD', *The International Migration Review* 43(2): 431–9.

44  See for example Elspeth Guild, Stefanie Grant, and Kees Groenendijk (2020) 'Unfinished Business: The IOM and Migrants' Human Rights', in Martin Geiger and Antoine Pécoud (eds), *The International Organization for Migration: The New 'UN Migration Agency' in Critical Perspective*, Palgrave Macmillan.

45  For example, Ahouga 2021.

46  Skype interview, 21 December 2018.

47  Skype interview, 21 December 2018.

48  Skype interview, 8 November 2018.

49  Skype interview, 19 October 2018.

50  Skype interview, 16 November 2018.

51  IOM (2013) *World Migration Report 2013: Migrant Well-Being and Development*, IOM, 24.

52  IOM 2013, 2.

53  Rachel OConnell (2013) 'Migrant Life: An Interview with Colin Rajah', *The Politic,* 12 July 2013.

54  For example, see essays in Thomas Gammeltoft-Hansen, Elspeth Guild, Violeta Morena-Lax, Marion Panizzon, and Isobel Roele (2017) *What Is a Compact? Migrants' Rights and State Responsibilities Regarding the Design of the UN Global Compact for Safe, Orderly and Regular Migration*, Raoul Wallenberg Institute of Human Rights and Humanitarian Law.

55  For example, see some examples in the essays in Rahel Kunz, Sandra Lavenex, and Marion Panizzon (eds) *Multilayered Migration Governance: The Promise of Partnership*, Routledge.

56  Andreas Rasche (2009) '"A Necessary Supplement": What the United Nations Global Compact Is and Is Not', *Business and Society* 48(4). For a helpful book of essays on the Global Compact, see Andreas Rasche and

Georg Kell (eds) *The United Nations Global Compact: Achievements, Trends and Challenges*, Cambridge University Press.

57  Skype interview, 21 January 2019.

58  Elizabeth G. Ferris and Katharine M. Donato (2020) *Refugees, Migration and Global Governance*, Routledge, 2.

59  Ban Ki Moon (2016) 'In Safety and Dignity: Addressing Large Movements of Refugees and Migrants: Report of the Secretary-General', A/70/59, 2.

60  Klein Solomon and Sheldon 2018.

61  See statement on website of the Summit: https://refugeesmigrants.un.org/ summit (accessed 19 September 2022).

62  See also reflections of Kathleen Newland (2018) 'The Global Compact for Safe, Orderly and Regular Migration: An Unlikely Achievement', *International Journal of Refugee Law* 30(4): 657–60.

63  E.g. Peter Hilpold (2021) 'Opening up a New Chapter of Law-Making in International Law: The Global Compacts on Migration and for Refugees of 2018', *European Law Journal* 26(3–4): 226–44.

64  Skype interview, 26 October 2018.

65  Interview, New York, 26 February 2019.

66  For example, see Ferris and Donato 2020, 12.

67  Vincent Chetail (2020) 'The Global Compact for Safe, Orderly and Regular Migration: A Kaleidoscope of International Law', *International Law in Context* 16(3): 253–68.

68  Adam B Seligman traces the re-emergence of the terminology of civil society particularly in the US: Adam B. Seligman (1995) *The Idea of Civil Society*, Princeton University Press, 16.

69  Jürgen Kocka (2004) 'Civil Society from a Historical Perspective', *European Review* 12(1): 65–79.

70  For example, Kocka 2004.

71  Iris Marion Young (1990) *Justice and the Politics of Difference*, Princeton University Press, 259.

72  For example, see Mary Kaldor (2002) 'The Ideas of 1989: The Origins of the Concept of Global Civil Society', in Richard Falk, R. B. J. Walker, and Lester Ruiz (eds), *Reframing the International: Law, Culture, Politics*, Routledge, 70–82; Mary Kaldor (2003) 'Civil Society and Accountability', *Journal of Human Development* 4(1): 5–27.

73  For example, Mary Kaldor (2003) 'The Idea of Global Civil Society', *International Affairs* 79(3): 583–93.

74  Craig Calhoun (2002) 'The Class Consciousness of Frequent Travelers: Toward a Critique of Actually Existing Cosmopolitanism', *South Atlantic Quarterly* 101: 869–97.

75  Helmut K. Anheier (2007) 'Reflections on the Concept and Measurement of Global Civil Society', *VOLUNTAS: International Journal of Voluntary and Nonprofit Organizations* 18: 1–15.

76  For example, Neera Chandhoke (2007) 'Global Civil Society and Global Justice', *Economic and Political Weekly* July 21: 3016–22.

77 Kaldor 2003.
78 Joint interview, Marrakech, 12 December 2018.
79 Joint interview, Marrakech, 12 December 2018.
80 Skype interview, 29 November 2018.
81 Skype interview, 6 March 2019.
82 Jenna Hennebry and Nicola Piper (2021) 'Global Migration Governance And Migrant Rights Advocacy: The Flexibilization of Multi-Stakeholder Negotiations', in Catherine Dauvergne (ed.), *Research Handbook on the Law and Politics of Migration*, Edward Elger.
83 Skype interview, 8 November 2018.
84 Delgado Wise 2018.
85 Telephone interview, 14 January 2019.
86 Skype interview, 23 April 2019.
87 Clarification by email, 28 September 2022.
88 For example, see Lynn Frendt Shotwell (1999) 'Temporary Worker Visa Policy: Meeting the Needs of the 21st Century', *In Defense of the Alien* 22: 55–8.
89 Kocka 2004, 73.
90 Skype interview, 6 March 2019.
91 Skype interview, 6 March 2019.
92 For example, Susanne Koch (2020) '"The Local Consultant Will Not Be Credible": How Epistemic Injustice is Experienced and Practised in Development Aid', *Social Epistemology* 34(5): 478–89.
93 Ibid.
94 Skype interview, 6 March 2019.
95 Skype interview, 25 October 2018.
96 Skype interview, 25 October 2018.
97 Interview, New York, 26 February 2019.
98 Skype interview, 7 March 2019.

# Chapter 5

1 I take this framing of 'space' from Henri Lefebvre, but I am referring narrowly to the physical elements of 'place'. Henri Lefebvre (1991) *The Production of Space*, Blackwell (translated by Donald Nicholson-Smith). Perhaps this could be seen as a form of 'public space'. For a helpful survey of different ways in which public space is understood, see Charles T. Goodsell (2003) 'The Concept of Public Space and Its Democratic Manifestations', *American Review of Public Administration* 33(4): 361–83. For an interesting application for the discussion of how some places are made politically salient see, for example: Linda Hershkovitz (1993) 'Tiananmen Square and the Politics of Place', *Political Geography* 12(5): 397.
2 Stuart Elden (2007) 'There is a Politics of Space because Space is Political: Henri Lefebvre and the Production of Space', *Radical Philosophy Review* 10(2): 101–16.

3   For a framing of this as a 'migration crisis' and one pertaining to Europe in particular, see, for example: Laurie Buonanno (2017) 'The European Migration Crisis', in Desmond Dinan et al. (eds), *The European Union in Crisis*, Palgrave; Joao Estevens (2018) 'Migration Crisis in the EU: Developing a Framework for Analysis of National Security and Defence Strategies', *Comparative Migration Studies* 6: 1–24.

4   And in the construction of who should and who should not be allowed to move, it is hard to ignore the racialized reality in which it is overwhelmingly non-White migrants are illegalized. This point is made particularly clearly in Nicholas De Genova (2018) 'The "Migrant Crisis" as Racial Crisis: Do *Black Lives Matter* in Europe?', *Ethnic and Racial Studies* 41(10): 1765–82.

5   For example, see Médecins Sans Frontièrs (2021) 'Constructing Crisis at Europe's Borders', MSF.

6   'Migration from Africa, as well as other parts of the world, is being increasingly considered as one of the key threats to European political and social security', Belachew Gebrewold (2007) 'Migration as a Transcontinental Challenge', in Belachew Gebrewold (ed.), *Africa and Fortress Europe: Threats and Opportunities*, Routledge.

7   According to World Bank estimates for 2017, sub-Saharan countries of net immigration are Angola, Botswana, Burundi, Chad, DRC, Equatorial Guinea, Ethiopia, Gabon, Mauritania, Niger, South Africa and Uganda.

8   Surveyed in Belachew Gebrewold and Tendayi Bloom (2015) *Understanding Migration Decisions*, Routledge.

9   Caroline Wanjiku Kihato (2018) 'The "Containment Compact": The EU Migration 'Crisis' and African Complicity in Migration Management', South African Institute of International Affairs Occassional Paper 288, September 2018.

10  Lorenzo Gabrielli (2011) 'European Immigration Policies Outside the Union: An Impact Analysis on Migration Dynamics in Northern African Transit Areas', in Jocelyne Streiff-Fénart and Aurélia Segatti (eds), *The Challenge of the Threshold: Border Closures and Migration Movements in Africa*, Lexington Books.

11  Pew Research Center (2018) 'At Least a Million Sub-Saharan Africans Moved to Europe Since 2010', https://www.pewresearch.org/global/2018 /03/22/at-least-a-million-sub-saharan-africans-moved-to-europe-since -2010/.

12  For example, see J. R. Hough (1988) 'Social Policy and the Birthrate', *International Journal of Sociology and Social Policy* 8(5): 35–50; Colin Crouch (2008) 'Change in European Societies since the 1970s', *West European Politics* 31(1–2): 14–39.

13  Aderanti Adepoju (2004) 'Trends in International Migration in and from Africa', in Douglas S. Massey and J. Edward Taylor (eds), *International Migration: Prospects and Policies in a Global Market*, Oxford University Press.

14  Ann Dummett and Andrew Nicol (1994) *Subjects, Citizens, Aliens and Others: Nationality and Immigraiton Law*, Weidenfeld and Nicolson; Evan

Smith and Marinella Marmo (2014) 'The Myth of Sovereignty: British Immigration Control in Policy and Practice in the Nineteen-Seventies', *Historical Research* 87: 344–69; Catherine Wihtol de Wenden (2002) 'Ouverture et fermeture de la France aux étrangers: Un siècle d'évolution', *Vingtième Siécle Revue d'Histoire* 2002/1(73): 27–38: Sylvain Laurens (2008) '<<1974>> et la fermeture des frontièrs: Analyse critique d'une décision érigée en turning-point', *Politix* 2008/2(82): 69–94.

15  Hein de Haas, Katharina Natter, and Simona Vezzoli (2016) 'Growing Restrictiveness or Changing Selection? The Nature and Evolution of Migration Policies', *International Migration Review* Early View, 1–44; Hein de Haas, Mathias Czaika, Marie-Laurence Flahaux, Edo Mahendra, Katharine Natter, Simona Vezzoli, and María Villares-Varela (2019) 'International Migration: Trends, Determinants, and Policy Effects', *Population and Development Review* 45(4): 885–922.

16  For example, see Hein de Haas (2007) 'North African Migration Systems: Evolution, Transformations and Development Linkages', International Migration Institute, James Martin 21st Century School, University of Oxford Working Paper 6.

17  Gerasimos Tsourapas (2017) 'Migration Diplomacy in the Global South: Cooperation, Coercion and Issue Linkage in Gaddafi's Libya', *Third World Quarterly* 10: 2367–85.

18  BBC (2010) 'Gaddafi Wants EU Cash to Stop African Migrants', *BBC News* website 31 August 2010, https://www.bbc.co.uk/news/world-europe-11139345

19  Sholto Byrnes (2010) 'Colonel Gaddafi warns Europe over "Turning Black"', *The New Statesman*, 1 December 2010; Ian Traynor (2010) 'EU Keen to Strike Deal with Muammar Gaddafi on Immigration', *The Guardian*, 1 September 2010.

20  Hamid Bahri (2014) 'Race and Color in North Africa and the Arab Spring', in Moha Ennaji (ed.), *Mulitculturalism and Democracy in North Africa: Aftermath of the Arab Spring*, Routledge, 135.

21  See also analysis in Lucas Mafu (2019) 'The Libyan/Trans-Mediterranean Slave Trade, the African Union, and the Failure of Human Morality', *Sage Open* January–March: 1–10.

22  For example, see William Gois and Karen Campbell (2013) 'Stranded Migrants: A Call to Rethink the Current Labour Migration Paradaigm', *Migration and Development* 2(2): 157–72.

23  See, for example, Davide Gnes (2013) 'Maghnia: Crossing the Uncrossable Border', Mission Report on Vulnerability of sub-Saharan Migrants and Refugees at the Algerian-Moroccan Border, Euro-Mediterranean Human Rights Network, Copenhagen.

24  Numerous reports of slave markets in 2017 led OHCHR to issue a letter. See Office of the High Commissioner for Human Rights AL LBY 6&2017 letter to the Government of Libya dated 28 November 2017. See also analysis by Human Rights Watch (2019) 'Trading in Suffering: Detention, Exploitation

and Abuse in Libya', Human Rights Watch, 23 December 2019. See also, for example, Glenda Garelli and Martina Tazzioli (2017) 'Choucha beyond the Camp: Challenging the Border of Migration Studies', in Nicholas De Genova (ed) *The Borders of "Europe": Autonomy of Migration, Tactics of Belonging*, Duke University Press.

25  For example, Tamirace Fakhoury (2016) 'Securitising Migration: The European Union in the Context of the Post-2011 Arab Upheavals', *The International Spectator: Italian Journal of International Affairs* 51(4): 67–79.

26  UNHCR (2019) *Global Trends: Forced Displacement in 2018*, UNHCR, 4.

27  This is explained, for example, by former FRONTEX expert for Spain, Julián Javier Pérez Quiles: Julián Javier Pérez Quiles (2018) 'La Agencia Europea de Fronteras y Guardacostas, Frontex', *Revista Jurídica Región de Murcia* No. 52: 143–56.

28  Paolo Cuttitta (2014) 'From the *Cap Anamur* to *Mare Nostrum*: Humanitarianism and Migraiton Controls at the EU's Maritime Borders', in Matera and Taylor (eds), *The Common European Asylum System and Human Rights: Enhancing Protection in Times of Emergencies*, Asser Institute.

29  For example, see Thomas Gammeltoft-Hansen (2011) *Access to Asylum*, Cambridge University Press; Bill Frelick et al. (2016) 'The Impact of Externalization of Migration Controls on the Rights of Asylum Seekers and Other Migrants', *Journal on Migration and Human Security* 4(4): 190–220.

30  Samuel Kehinde Okunade and Olusola Ogunnubi (2019) 'The African Union Protocol on Free Movement: A Panacea to End Border Porosity?', *Journal of African Union Studies* 8(1): 73–91; Okunade and Ogunnubi identify factors hindering free movement in ECOWAS, others observe that progress has been made on free movement in the region, for example: Samuel Kehinde Okunade and Olusola Ogunnubi (2021) 'A "Schengen" Agreement in Africa? African Agency and the ECOWAS Protocol on Free Movement', *Journal of Borderlands Studies* 36(1): 119–37; Aderanti Adepoju, Alistair Boulton, and Mariah Levin (2010) 'Promoting Integration Through Mobility: Free Movement Under Ecowas', *Refugee Survey Quarterly* 29(3): 120–44; Victor H. Mlambo (2020) 'Consolidating Regional Integration Through a Free Movement Protocol: The Quest for Collective Development in the SADC', *African Journal of Governance and Development* 9(2): 455–71.

31  For example, see essays in Thomas Gammeltoft-Hansen and Ninna Nybert Sorensen (2013) *The Migration Industry and the Commercialisation of International Migration*, Routledge.

32  Tendayi Bloom (2016) 'Privatised Migration Management in the Mediterranean Region and Sub-Saharan Migration Decision-Making', in Belachew Gebrewold and Tendayi Bloom (eds), *Understanding Migrant Decisions: From Sub-Saharan Africa to the Mediterranean Region*, Routledge, 99–119.

33  Amnesty International (2015) 'Italy: Lampedusa Survivors' Tales of Despair Should Shock EU into Action', *Amnesty International News*, 16 February 2015.

34  This can be seen also in *Fatal Journeys: Tracking Lives Lost during Migration*.

35  See, for example, Marton Dunai (2019) 'Four Jailed for Life Over Death of 71 Migrants in Hungarian Truck', *Reuters*, 20 June 2019, https://www.reuters .com/article/us-europe-migrants-hungary-trial-idUSKCN1TL0LX.

36  For example, see Melissa Mouthaan (2021) 'Old wine in New Bottles? The European Union's Organizational Response to Reforming the EU-African Migration Cooperation', *Journal of Common Market Studies* 59(5): 1177–84.

37  Iddrisu Wari (2016) "You Make a Decision and you Start Your Journey': Reflections of a Ghanaian Economic Migrant and Founder of the NGO, CEHDA', in Belachew Gebrewold and Tendayi Bloom (eds), *Understanding Migrant Decisions: From Sub-Saharan Africa to the Mediterranean Region*, Routledge, 194–218 at 211–12.

38  I was sent a copy of this statement at the time. It is also mentioned, for example, by: Vicki Squire (2019) 'A Milestone Missed: The Global Compact on Migration and the Limits of Solidarity', *Global Affairs* 5(2): 155–62; Samir Abi (2019) 'Global Compact: The Engagements of Marrakech', *West African Observatory on Migration*, http://www.obsmigration.org/en/2019 /02/global-compact-the-engagements-of-marrakech/ (accessed 1 October 2020).

39  For a helpful analysis of how this sits within the American politicolegal tradition, see Robert S. Chang (2018) 'Whitewashing Precedent: From the Chinese Exclusion Case to Korematsu to the Muslim Travel Ban Cases', *Case Western Reserve Law Review* 68(4): 1183–222.

40  Skype interview, 1 November 2018.

41  Skype interview, 1 November 2018.

42  Skype interview, 5 March 2019.

43  For example, Lisa L. Pike (1990) 'The Arafat visa Denial: Successful Diplomatic Persuasion, but a Violation of the Headquarters Agreement Treaty', *Suffolk Transnational Law Journal* 13: 634–55; Al Jazeera (2020) 'Iran's Zarif Says US Denied him a Visa to Attend UN Meeting', *Al Jazeera Online*, 7 January 2020; Ros Young (1986) 'Report from Nairobi: The UN Decade for Women Forum', in *Race and Class*, 67–71; Carol Ann Traut (1997) 'China and the 1995 United Nations Conference on Women', *Journal of Contemporary China* 6(16): 581–9 at 587–8; Elisabeth Reichert (1996) '"Keep on Moving Forward": NGO Forum on Women, Beijing, China', *Social Development Issues* 18(1): 89–97 at 91; Tom Lantos (2002) 'The Durban Debacle: An Insider's View of the UN World Conference Against Racism', *The Fletcher Forum on World Affairs* 26(1): 31–52 at 35; Lyndal Rowlands (2017) 'Travel Restrictions Cast Shadow on UN Women's Meeting', *Inter Press Service News Agency*, 16 March 2017; El Espectador (2013) 'Evo Morales pidió cambiar sede de Asamblea General de la ONU', *El Espectador*, 24 September 2013; Colum Lynch (2011) 'TurtleLeaks: No Visa, No Entry! How the U.S. Bars diplos from the U.N.', *Foreign Policy*, 4 May 2011; Mark Landler and Rick Gladstone (2014) 'U.S. Says Iran's Pick for U.N. Envoy Won't Get a Visa', *New York Times*, 11 April 2014.

44  Skype interview, 19 October 2018.

45 Skype interview, 21 January 2019.

46 Skype interview, 8 January 2019.

47 Interview, Marrakech, 12 December 2018.

48 Skype interview, 18 November 2018.

49 Skype interview, 6 March 2019.

50 Skype interview, 5 March 2019.

51 African Union (2017) Common African Position (CAP) on the global compact for safe, orderly and regulatory migration' AU/STC/MRIDP/4(II) at 12.

52 Skype interview, 21 December 2018.

53 Vicki Squire, Angeliki Dimitriadi, Nina Perkowski, Maria Pisani, Dallal Stevens, and Nick Vaughan-Williams (2017) *Crossing the Mediterranean Sea by Boat: Mapping and Documenting Migratory Journeys and Experiences, Final Project Report*, University of Warwick, www.warwick.ac.uk/crossingthemed.

54 Nando Sigona (2012) ' "I Have Too Much Baggage": The Impacts of Legal Status on the Social Worlds of Irregular Migrants', *Social Anthropology* 20(1): 50–65.

55 Skype interview, 15 March 2019.

56 Olawale Maiyegun (2019) 'Role of Regional Consultative Processes in the Lead up to the Negotiations of Global Compact on Migration: The Case of Africa', *International Migration* 57(6): 258–72. Note that Austria spoke as President of the EU at the time. Hungary abstained from any joint EU position, so that it was presented as the position of twenty-seven European countries rather than of the EU.

57 United Nations (2018) 'Global Compact for Safe, Orderly and Regular Migration', Intergovernmentally Negotiated and Agreed Outcome, 13 July 2018, 4.

58 United Nations General Assembly (2004) 'We the Peoples: Civil Society, the United Nations and Global Governance, Report of the Panel of Eminent Persons on United Nations-Civil Society Relations' A/58/817.

59 For example, Eric Neumayer (2006) 'Unequal Access to Foreign Spaces: How States Use Visa Restrictions to Regulate Mobility in a Globalized World', *The Transactions of the Institute of British Geographers* 31(1): 72–84.

60 Bart Cammaerts and Nico Carpentier (2006) 'The Unbearable Lightness of Full Participation in a Global Context: WSIS and Civil Society Participation', in Jan Servaes and Nico Carpentier (eds), *Towards a Sustainable Information Society: Deconstructing WSIS*, Intellect Books, 25.

61 Stefan Rother (2022) 'Global Migration Governance from below in Times of COVID-19 and "Zoomification": Civil Society in "Invited" and "Invented" Spaces', *Comparative Migration Studies* 10(1): 1–21.

62 For an explanation of this framing, see Tendayi Bloom and Lindsey Kingston (2021) 'Opening a Conversation about Statelessness, Governance, and the Problem of Citizenship', in Bloom and Kingston (eds), *Statelessness, Governance, and the Problem of Citizenship*, Manchester University Press.

# Chapter 6

1 Translates as 'all-in-English'. E.g. see, Michaël Oustinoff (2008) 'Le tout-à-l'anglais est-il inévitable?', *HERMÈS, La Revue* 51: 79–84.

2 Analysed, with its implications, for example, in Jean-Marie Le Breton (2004) 'Réflexions Anglophiles Sur La Géopolitique De L'Anglais', *La Découverte: Hérodote* 115: 11–23.

3 For example, Robert Phillipson (1999) 'International Languages and International Human Rights', in Miklós Kontra, Robert Phillipson, Tove Skuntnabb-Kangas, and Tibor Várdy (eds), *Language: A Right and a Resource*, Central European University Press, 28.

4 Presented, for example, in Jacqueline Mowbray (2010) 'Language in the UN and EU: Linguistic Diversity as a Challenge for Multilateralism', *New Zealand Journal of Public and International Law* 8(1): 91–116 at 100.

5 Robert Phillipson and Tove Skutnabb-Kangas (1996) 'English Only Worldwide or Language Ecology?', *TESOL Quarterly* 30(3): 429–53.

6 Phillipson and Skutnabb-Kangas 1996, 441.

7 Thank you to May Darwich for checking my Arabic (though any errors remaining are my own) and for her insights into the powerful role of language in framing politics. May Darwich and Tamirace Fakhoury (2016) 'Casting the Other as an Existential Threat: The Securitization of Sectarianism in the International Relations of the Syria Crisis', *Global Discourse* 6(4): 712–32; May Darwich (2019) *Threats and Alliances in the Middle East: Saudi and Syrian Policies in a Turbulent Region*, Cambridge University Press.

8 I chose Arabic because, unlike with French or Spanish, it is not possible to extrapolate any meaning from written Arabic from knowledge of English alone and it is not easy for someone unfamiliar with Arabic script to type it into an online translation tool. While Russian and Mandarin would also have provided this, I wanted to choose a language in which I would be able to draft and understand the text myself.

9 Skype interview, 5 March 2019.

10 Skype interview, 16 November 2018.

11 Skype interview, 8 November 2018.

12 Skype interview, 7 March 2019.

13 Skype interview, 7 March 2019.

14 Tomoyuki Kawashima (2021) 'English Use by the Heads of State at the United Nations General Assembly', *English Today* 145 37(2): 92–114.

15 Donna Patrick (2010) 'Language Dominance and Minorization', in Jürgen Jaspers, Jan-Ola Östman, and Jef Verschueren (eds), *Society and Language Use*, John Benjamins Publishing Company.

16 This point is well made in Philippe Hambye (2019) 'La minorisation linguistique, entre discrimination et domination symbolique. Différences et enjeux de deux lectures des inégalités', *Minorités linguistiques et société* 12: 15–30.

17 Skype interview, 11 January 2019.

18  The role of the Bloque is discussed, for example, in Natalia Debandi and Joanna Sander (2020) 'Proceso de adopción del Pacto Mundial sobre Migración. Actores, tramas y repercusiones en Sudamerica', *Revista Diarios del Terruño* 10 (julio-diciembre): 58–87. To get a sense of the position of the Bloque as a group representing both States and migrant civil society of Latin America, see its official statement: Bloque Latinoamericano (2017) 'Puntos de partida para un pacto global de migración que beneficie a la población en las migraciones y sus gobiernos', *Migración y desarrollo* 15(21): 137–40.

19  e.g. Skype interview 11 January 2019.

20  Skype interview, 21 December 2018.

21  Skype interview, 1 November 2018.

22  Jacqueline Mowbray (2012) *Linguistic Justice: International Law and Policy*, Oxford University Press, 165.

23  Mowbray 2012, 181.

24  Mowbray 2010.

25  With thanks to Alice Corr for alerting me to the linguistic justice literature, particularly through drawing my attention to this powerful article: John Rickford and Sharese King (2016) 'Language and Linguistics on Trial: Hearing Rachel Jeantel (and Other Vernacular Speakers) in the Court Room and Beyond', *Language* 92(4): 948–88.

26  For a powerful analysis of English dominance in the Sustainable Development Agenda, for example, see Lisa J. McEntee-Atalianis (2017) '"Leave no One Behind": Linguistic and Digital Barriers to the Dissemination and Implementation of the United Nations Sustainable Development Agenda', *Language Problems and Language Planning* 41(3): 217–44.

27  The third most spoken language is Hindi with 637 million speakers and then Spanish (538 million), French (277 million), Standard Arabic (274 million), Bengali (265 million) and Russian (258 million). All the data in this paragraph is according to Ethnologue 200 2020 revision: https://www.ethnologue.com/guides/ethnologue200.

28  For more on the forms of English, see, for example, Rakesh M. Bhatt (2001) 'World Englishes', *Annual Review of Anthropology* 30: 527–50.

29  Alastair Pennycook (1994) *Cultural Politics of English as an International Language*, Longman, 13.

30  For example, see Phillipson 1999.

31  Frantz Fanon (1986) *Black Skin White Masks*, Pluto Press (trans. Charles Lam Markmann), 187.

32  These sentiments echo those already expressed more broadly and analysed, for example, in the classic work Robert Phillipson (1992) *Linguistic Imperialism*, Oxford University Press.

33  For example, see Mazrui's argument that it is too simplistic to 'associate European languages with oppression and non-European languages with liberation': Alamin Mazrui (1993) 'Language and the Quest for Liberation in Africa: The Legacy of Frantz Fanon', *Third World Quarterly* 14(2): 351–63.

34  Skype interview, 5 March 2019.

35   Skype interview, 6 March 2019.

36   Interview, Marrakech, 12 December 2018.

37   For example, see Chapter 1 of Finex Ndhlovu and Leketi Makalela (2021) *Decolonising Multilingualism in Africa: Recentering Silenced Voices from the Global South*, Multilingual Matters.

38   Skype interview, 8 November 2018.

39   Skype interview, 7 March 2019. Clarified by email 28 October 2022.

40   For example, Skype interview, 8 January 2019.

41   Skype interview, 16 November 2018.

42   Gustavo Pérez Firmat (1995) *Bilingual Blues*, Bilingual Press. This poem is reprinted in Junot Díaz (2008) *Drown*, Faber, which is where I first came across it.

43   Interview, Marrakech, 12 December 2018.

44   Yukio Tsuda (1998) 'Critical Studies on the Dominance of English and the Implications for International Communication', *Japan Review* 10: 219–36.

45   Amandine Catala (2022) 'Academic Migration, Linguistic Justice, and Epistemic Injustice', *The Journal of Political Philosophy* 30(2): 324–46.

46   Deborah Cao and Xingmin Zhao (2008) 'Translation at the United Nations as Specialized Translation', *The Journal of Specialised Translation* 9: 47.

47   With thanks to Ahmad Benswait for his help with this. Benswait has writte n on both the subject of statelessness and that of barriers to narrative creation. Ahmad Benswait (2021) 'Language and statelessness: The impact of political discourses on the Bidoon community in Kuwait', in Tendayi Bloom and Lindsey Kingston (eds) *Statelessness, Governance, and the Problem of Citizenship*, Manchester University Press 87-98; Ahmad Benswait (Jaber) and Miguel Pérez-Milans (2022) 'Pressing times, losing voice: critique and transformative spaces in higher education', *London Review of Education* 20(1): 1–15.

48   See, for example, Ahmad Benswait (2021) 'Language and Statelessness: The Impact of Political Discourses on the Bidoon Community in Kuwait', in Tendayi Bloom and Lindsey Kingston (eds), *Statelessness, Governance, and the Problem of Citizenship*, Manchester University Press.

49   This phrase is attributed to Chinua Achebe in describing the use of English in African literature in a 1964 speech, see Ngugi wa Thiong'o (1986) *Decolonising the Mind: The Politics of Language in African Literature*, Heinemann, 7.

50   For example, see Catala 2021, who also provides suggestions for how to mitigate English-language dominance in international academia for example.

51   Skype interview, 21 December 2018.

52   Mowbray 2010, 108.

53   Patrick 2010.

54   McEntee-Atalianis 2017.

55   Michael Cronin (2013) *Translation in the Digital Age*, Routledge.

56   See this discussion of the history of free online machine translation: Federico Gaspari and John Hutchins (2007) 'Online and Free? Ten Years

of Online Machine Translation: Origins, Developments, Current Use and Future Prospects', *Proceedings of Machine Translation Summit* XI: Papers.

57  See top line here: https://www.unglobalcompact.org (as of 18 January 2019).

58  Harold Somers (2003) 'Introduction', in Harold Somers (ed.), *Computers and Translation: A Translator's Guide*, John Benjamins Publishing Company.

59  Juan Daniel Valor Miró, Pau Baquero-Arnal, Jorge Civera, Carlos Turró, and Alfons Juan (2016) 'Multilingual Videos for MOOCs and OER', *Educational Technology & Society* 21(2): 1–12 at 7.

60  Rita Raley (2003) 'Machine Translation and Global English', *The Yale Journal of Criticism* 16(2): 291–313 at 299.

61  Ido Ramati and Amit Pinchevski (2018) 'Uniform Multilingualism: A Media Genealogy of Google Translate', *New Media & Society* 20(7): 2550–65 at 2552.

62  See document: 'Task Force of the Human Rights Council on Accessibility for Persons with Disabilities: Accessibility Plan', dated 15 December 2017, 7–8; 9–10. For list of accessible sessions of the HRC, see: https://www.ohchr .org/EN/HRBodies/HRC/Pages/AccessibilitytoPanelswithweblinks.aspx.

63  The total cost of this combination is quoted at approximately USD 13,200 for making a three-hour meeting accessible 'through international sign interpretation, captioning, webcast, and printing of oral statements in Braille'. See document: 'Task Force of the Human Rights Council on Accessibility for Persons with Disabilities: Accessibility Plan', dated 15 December 2017, 10.

64  Nelson Flores and Jonathan Rosa (2015) 'Undoing Appropriateness: Raciolinguistic Ideologies and Language Diversity in Education', *Harvard Educational Review* 85(2): 149–71.

65  Rickford and King 2016.

66  For example, Adrian Holliday (2015) 'Native-Speakerism: Taking the Concept Forward and Achieving Cultural Belief', in Anne Swann, Pamela Aboshiha, and Adrian Holliday (eds), *(En)Countering Nativespeakerism*, Palgrave Macmillan. See also discussion beyond English in essays in Stephanie Ann Houghton, Damian J. Rivers, and Kayoko Hashimoto (eds) (2018) *Beyond Native-Speakerism: Current Explorations and Future Visions*, Routledge.

67  Finex Ndovulu (2015) 'Ignored Lingualism: Another Resource for Overcoming the Monlingual Mindest in Language Education', *Australian Journal of Linguistics* 35(4) 398–414, with thanks to Alice Corr for drawing my attention to this paper.

# Chapter 7

1  For example, see Jacqueline Bhabha (2018) *Can we Solve the Migration Crisis?*, Polity, 30; Kelly Staples (2019) '"The Problem with Refugees": international protection and the limits to solidarity', *International Politics* 56 158–174.

2  For example,. see analysis by Heaven Crawley, Franck Düvell, Katharine Jones, Simon McMahon, and Nando Sigona (2018) *Unravelling Europe's 'Migration Crisis': Journeys over land and sea*, Policy Press, 130.

3  Miranda Fricker (2007) *Epistemic Injustice: Power and the Ethics of Knowing*, Oxford University Press. The terminology she uses for the two dimensions mentioned here is 'testimonial epistemic injustice' and 'hermeneutical epistemic injustice', respectively.

4  Miranda Fricker (2006) 'Powerlessness and Social Interpretation', *Episteme* 3(1–2): 96–108 at 98.

5  For example, tracing the linkage of 'immigration' and 'delinquancy' in the French press: Éric Fassin (2011) '"Immigration et Délinqunce"': La construction d'un problème entre politique, journalism et sociologie', *Cités* 2011/2 46: 69–85.

6  For example, Mike Berry, Inaki Garcia-Blanco, and Kerry Moore (2015) 'Press Coverage of the Refugee and Migrant Crisis in the EU: A Content Analysis of Five European Countries', Report prepared for the United Nations High Commission for Refugees.

7  UNDESA (2015) *Trends in International Migrant Stock: The 2015 Revision*, UNDESA.

8  Berry et al. 2015.

9  Global Passport Index.

10  For example, see footnote 12 in Zeynep Devrim Gürsel (2010) '*U.S. Newsworld*: The Rule of Text and Everyday Practices of Editing the World', in S. Elizabeth Bird (ed.), *The Anthropology of News and Journalism: Global Perspectives*, Indiana University Press.

11  Christina Lee (2018) 'Why Visa Privilege is a Press Freedom Issue', *Hostwriter*, 30 October 2018; see also Amanda Darach (2018) 'It's Getting More Difficult for Foreign Journalists to Work in the US', *Columbia Journalism Review*, 12 September 2018; Edwin Guerrero Nova (2018) 'Censura en Colombia: ¿Se están negando visas a periodistas extranjeros?' *Latin American Post*, 7 September 2018.

12  Rodney Benson (2013) 'Why Narrative Is Not Enough: Immigration and the Genres of Journalism', in Giovanna dell'Orto and Vicki Birchfield (eds), *Reporting at the Southern Borders: Journalism and Public Debates on Immigration in the EU and US*, Routledge, 73–87. See also helpful illustration in Jelani Cobb (2018) 'When Newsrooms are Dominated by White People, they Miss Crucial Facts', *The Guardian Opinion*, https://www.theguardian.com/world/commentisfree/2018/nov/05/newsroom-diversity-media-race-journalism (accessed 19 November 2020).

13  Heaven Crawley, Simon McMahon, and Katharine Jones (2016) 'Victims and Villains: Migrant Voices in the British Media', Coventry: Centre for Trust, Peace and Social Relations, Coventry University, 12.

14  Crawley et al 2016, 8.

15  For example, see discussion in Pamela Newkirk (2002) *Within the Veil: Black Journalists, White Media*, New York University Press.

16 Lilie Chouliaraki, Myria Georgiou, Rafal Zaborowski, and Wouter Oomen (2016) 'The European "Migration Crisis" and the Media: A Cross-European Press Content Analysis', Project Report, London School of Economics and Political Science, 27.

17 For example, see Chouliaraki et al. 2016; Berry et al. 2015; Crawley et al. 2016. This isn't new. See, for example: Robert Solé (1988) 'Le journalisme et l'immigration (Entretien avec Jacqeline Costa-Lascoux)', *Revue Européenne des Migrations internationals* 1988: 157–66.

18 Cecilia Cannon (2017) 'Modes of Knowledge Mobilization by/for International Bureaucracies Throughout International Policy Processes', in Annabelle Littoz-Monnet (ed.), *The Politics of Expertise in International Organizations*, Routledge, 128–47.

19 This is a version of what Phil Cole calls an 'insider theory problem' in Cole 2017.

20 Gaële Goastellec (2016) 'La mobilité international: une qualité des carriers et des marchés académiques en Europe?', *Journal of International Mobility* 2016/1(4): 171–88; Hady Elsahar (2018) 'Highlighting Visa Issues in Scientific Conferences', *Medium*, 9 June 2018; Matthew Weaver (2018) 'WHO Voices Alarm as Academics Denied Visas to Visit UK Conference', *The Guardian*, 9 October 2018; Jeffrey Herliky-Mera (2015) 'Visa Restrictions Limit Academic Freedom', *University World News*, 17 July 2015.

21 See, for example, Virginia Gewin (2019) 'What Scientists Should Know about Visa Hurdles', *Nature* 569: 297–9.

22 Terri Kim (2017) 'Academic Mobility, Transnational Identity Capital, and Stratification under Conditions of Academic Capitalism', *Higher Education* 73: 981–97; Louise Morley, Nafsika Alexiadou, Stela Garaz, José González-Monteagudo, and Marius Taba (2018) 'Internationalisation and Migrant Academics: The Hidden Narratives of Mobility', *Higher Education* 76: 537–54.

23 Chapter 1 observed that it is incorrect to see contingent statuses like a work visa, humanitarian leave and refugee status as noncitizen statuses. They are relevant insofar as they approximate citizenship and are bestowed by States. As such, they are more properly understood as quasi citizen statuses.

24 Some examples, from across disciplines: Arwa Badran (2007) 'Equal Access to International Debate: Visas and Their Implications', *Archaeologies* 3(2): 207–9; Ahmad Benswait (Jaber) and Miguel Pérez-Milans (2022) 'Pressing times, losing voice: critique and transformative spaces in higher education', *London Review of Education* 20(1): 1-15; Elsahar 2018; Sukaina Ehdeed (2019) 'The Impact of Visa Denial in Academia', *LSE Blogs*, https://blogs.lse.ac.uk/mec/2019/08/27/the-impact-of-visa-denial-in-academia/ (accessed 27 November 2020); Gewin 2019; Izhar Khan (2007) 'Academic Apartheid by the Back Door', *The Lancet* 369(9560): 463; Katarina Zimmer (2019) 'As Visa Difficulties Persist, Scientists Push for Change', *The Scientists*, https://www.the-scientist.com/news-opinion/as-visa-difficulties-persist--scientists

-push-for-change-66114; James Lancaster (2019) 'Access Denied: Focus on Delegate Visa Issues', *AMI Magazine*, https://amimagazine.global/features/delegate-visa-issues-access-denied/ (accessed 27 November 2020); Elizabeth Redden (2019) 'Conference Visa Woes . . . in Canada', *Inside Higher Ed*, https://www.insidehighered.com/news/2019/03/28/scholars-complain-visa-problems-ahead-international-conference-canada (accessed 27 November 2020); Valéry Ridde (2008) 'Defying Boundaries: Globalization, Bureaucracy and Academic Exchange', *Promotion and Education* 15(1): 3–4; James Schultz (2003) 'Sluggish Visa Approval Process Hamstrings Scientific Conferences', *Journal of the National Cancer Institute* 95(8): 579–80.

25 Terri Kim (2011) 'Globalization and Higher Education in South Korea – Towards Ethnocentric Internationalization or Global Commercialization of Higher Education?', In R. King, S. Marginson, and R. Naidoo (eds), *Handbook of Globalization and Higher Education*, Edward Elgar Publishing Ltd., 286–305. This isn't a new thing. See also this somewhat archaic discussion: Steven Dedijer (1964) 'Migration of Scientists: A World-Wide Phenomenon and Problem', *Nature* 201: 964–7.

26 For example, Goastellec 2016; Morley et al. 2018; Ulrich Teichler (2015) 'Academic Mobility and Migration: What We Know and What We Do Not Know', *European Review* 23: S6–S37.

27 David N. Tshimba (2021) 'The Ghost of Racism in the Contemporary Global Compact on Refugees', *Journal of Refugee Studies* feab103.

28 For example, see Rainer Enrique Hamel (2013) 'L'anglais, langue unique pour les Sciences? Le rôle des modèles plurilingües dans la recherche, la communication scientifique et l'enseignement supérieur', *Synergies Europe* 8: 53–66.

29 For example, Adrian Holliday (2015) 'Native-Speakerism: Taking the Concept Forward and Achieving Cultural Belief', in Anne Swann, Pamela Aboshiha, and Adrian Holliday (eds) *(En)Countering Nativespeakerism*, Palgrave Macmillan. See also discussion beyond English in essays in Stephanie Ann Houghton, Damian J. Rivers, and Kayoko Hashimoto (eds) (2018) *Beyond Native-Speakerism: Current Explorations and Future Visions*, Routledge.

30 Terminology taken from Nelson Flores and Jonathan Rosa (2015) 'Undoing Appropriateness: Raciolinguistic Ideologies and Language Diversity in Education', *Harvard Educational Review* 85(2): 149–71.

31 Expressed and defended explicitly in Miranda Fricker (2017) 'Evolving Concepts of Epistemic Injustice', in Kidd, Medina and Pohlhaus (eds) *Routledge Handbook of Epistemic Injustice*, Routledge, 53–60.

32 I make this argument in more detail in Chapter 3. José Medina (2011) 'The Relevance of Credibility Excess in a Proportional View of Epistemic Injustice: Differential Epistemic Authority and the Social Imaginary', *Social Epistemology* 25(1): 15–35.

33 Cole 2017.

34 This is set up and defended in Chapter 1.

35 For example, Ayelet Shachar (2009) *Birthright Lottery: Citizenship and Global Inequality*, Harvard University Press.

36 Chapter 5 traced how these factors function in terms of access to visas. A now classic text sets this out in terms of access to citizenship: Laura Van Waas (2009) *Nationality Matters*, Intersentia Publishers. The essays in a recent publication explore current dimensions of this: Tendayi Bloom and Lindsey Kingston (eds) (2021) *Statelessness, Governance, and the Problem of Citizenship*, Manchester University Press.

37 For example, see Leonie Ansems de Vries and Katharine T. Weatherhead (2021) 'Politics of Knowledge Production in the Global Compact for Migration', *Interventions: International Journal of Postcolonial Studies* 23(2): 294–312.

38 Nicolas Klausser (2016) 'Les associations de défense du droit des étrangers, des lanceurs d'alerte?', *La Revue des droits de l'homme* 10: 1–10; Nandini Archer, Claudia Torrisi, Claire Provost, Alexander Nabert, and Belen Lobos (2019) 'Hundreds of Europeans "Criminalised" for Helping Migrants – As Far Right Aims to Win Big in European Elections', *Open Democracy*, 18 May 2019; Carla Festman (2019) 'Using Criminal Law to Restrict the Work of NGOs Supporting Refugees and Other Migrants in Council of Europe Member States', Expert Council on NGO Law, December 2019 CONF/EXP(2019)I; Lina Vosyliūtė and Carmine Conte (2019) 'Crackdown on NGOs and Volunteers Helping Refugees and Other Migrants', Final Synthetic Report June 2019, Research Social Platform on Migration and Asylum.

39 Luis Cabrera (2010) *The Practice of Global Citizenship*, Cambridge University Press.

40 William E. Scheuerman (2018) *Civil Disobedience*, Polity.

41 Çigdem Çidam, William E. Schuerman, Candice Delmas, Erin R. Pineda, Robin Celikates, and Alexander Livingston (2020) 'Theorizing the Politics of Protest: Contemporary Debates on Civil Disobedience', *Contemporary Political Theory* 19: 513–46.

42 Robin Celikates (2018) 'Constituent Power Beyond Exceptionalism: Irregular Migration, Disobedience, and (re-) Constitution', *Journal of International Political Theory* 15(1) with thanks to Sarah Bufkin for recommending that I read this.

43 For example, see Cecile Fabre (2012) *Cosmopolitan War*, Oxford University Press.

44 Vittorio Longhi describes migrant labour movements using mostly traditional methods of labour movements to challenge ill-treatment in the face of an often violent war from the side of authorities: Vittorio Longhi (2014) *The Immigrant War*, Policy Press.

45 Celikates 2018.

46 Recall discussions in earlier chapters of William Conklin (2014) *Statelessness: The Enigma in the international System*, Hart.

47 Anne McNevin (2011) *Contesting Citizenship: Irregular Migrants and the New Frontiers of the Political*, Columbia University Press.

48  I take this idea of aligning with paradigmatic cases from: Kimberley Brownlee (2004) 'Features of a Paradigm Case of Civil Disobedience', *Res Publica* 10: 337–51.

49  Ali Emre Benli (2018) 'March of Refugees: An Act of Civil Disobedience', *Journal of Global Ethics* 14(3): 315–31.

50  For example, discussed in Tendayi Bloom (2018) *Noncitizenism: Recognising Noncitizen Capabilities in a World of Citizens*, Routledge.

51  Vicki Squire (2019) 'A Milestone Missed: The Global Compact on Migration and the Limits of Solidarity', *Global Affairs* 5(2): 155–62.

52  Amelia Frank-Vitale and Margarita Núñez Chaim (2020) '"Lady Frijoles": las caravanas centroamericanas y el poder de la hipervisibilidad de la migración indocumentada', *EntreDiversidades Revista de ciencias sociales y humanidades* 7(1): 37–61.

53  Original: 'una exigencia hacia los poderes del mundo de dejarnos pasar sin pedir disculpas por exigirlo', in Frank-Vitale and Núñez Chaim 2020.

54  This was defended in Chapter 2.

55  Based on interview, quoted in Chapter 4.

56  'International Co-operation for the Prevention of Immigration Which Is Likely to Disturb Friendly Relations Between Nations', 17 November 1947, A/467, text available at A/RES/136(II).

57  For example, see Julia Rone (2020) 'Far Right Alternative News Media as "Indignation Mobilization Mechanisms": How the Far Right Opposed the Global Compact for Migration', *Information, Communication and Society* 25(9): 1333–50.

58  Maximilian Conrad (2021) 'Post-Truth Politics, Digital Media, and the Politicization of the Global Compact for Migration', *Politics and Governance* 9(3): 301–11.

59  Jakob Guhl (2019) 'Too little, Too Late', interview with Jakob Guhl, Friedrich Ebert Stiftung website, 7 February 2019.

60  Kathleen Newland (2018) 'An Overheated Narrative Unanswered: How the Global Compact for Migration Became Controversial', *Migration Policy Institute blog*, December 2018, https://www.migrationpolicy.org/news/overheated-narrative-unanswered-how-global-compact-became-controversial (accessed 19 September 2022).

61  New York Declaration preamble paragraph 14.

62  Conrad 2021.

63  Rone 2020.

64  Conrad 2021, 306.

65  Jacob Davey and Julia Ebner (2017) 'The Fringe Insurgency: Connectivity, Convergence and Mainstreaming of the Extreme Right', *ISD*, 11.

66  Rone 2020.

67  Rone 2020.

68  For example, see Ellen Desmet, Ine Lietaert, Jeffrey Goegiers, and Rosella Marino (2020) 'Belgium and the Global Compact for Migration: Taking

Stock After Two Years', Centre for the Social Study of Migration and Refugees, Ghent University, Belgium.

69  Rone 2020.

70  Jeremy Heimans and Henry Timms (2019) *#Newpower: Why Outsiders Are Winning, Institutions Are Failing, and How the Rest of Us Can Keep up in the Age of Mass Participation*, Pan Macmillan.

71  For example, see Laurens Cerulus and Eline Schaart (2019) 'How the UN Migration Pact Got Trolled', *Politico*, 3 January 2019.

72  Heimans and Timms 2019.

73  Kevin Munger and Joseph Phillips (2022) 'Right-Wing YouTube: A Supply and Demand Perspective', *The International Journal of Press/Politics* 27(1): 186–219.

74  Lauren Valentino Bryant (2020) 'The YouTube Algorithm and the Alt-Right Filter Bubble', *Open Information Science* 4(1): 85–90 at 87.

75  For example, see Julia Alexander (2019) 'The Golden Age of Youtube is Over', *The Verve*, 5 April 2019; Kevin Roose (2019) 'The Making of a YouTube Radical', *New York Times*, 8 June 2019. Note that there is disagreement regarding whether these algorithm changes had the effect presented here. Becca Lewis (2020) 'All of YouTube, Not Just the Algorithm, is a Far-Right Propaganda Machine', *Medium*, 8 January 2020.

76  Ico Maly (2019) 'Algorithmic Populism and Algorithmic Activism', *Diggit Magazine*, 26 November 2019.

77  Guhl 2019.

78  For example, see Pierre C. Boyer, Thomas Delemotte, Germain Gauthier, Vincent Rollet, and Benoît Schmutz (2020) 'Les determinants de la mobilization des Gilets jaunes', *Revue économique* 17(1): 109–38.

79  Winnie Lem (2020) 'Notes on Militant Populism in Contemporary France: Contextualizing the Gilets Jaunes', *Dialectical Anthropology* 44: 397–413.

80  Yann Algan, Elizabeth Beasley, Daniel Cohen, Martial Foucault, and Madeleine Péron (2019) 'Qui sont les Gilets jaunes et leurs soutiens?', Observatoire du Bien-être du CEPREMAP et CEVIPOF, no. 2019-03, 14 February 2019, 3, table 1.

81  Algan et al. 2019, 6, 7.

82  Anon (2019) 'Gilets Noirs, pour rester en colère et puissants!', *Vacarme* 2019/3(No.88): 68–79.

83  For example, see analysis of earlier movements in Heather L. Johnson (2015) 'These Fine Lines: Locating Noncitizenship in Polititical Protest in Europe', *Citizenship Studies* 19(8): 951–65.

84  Anon 2019.

85  Original: 'Quand tu es sans-papiers, les droits de l'homme ça ne te concerne pas, alors même que tu cotises, que tu te conduis bien.' Anon 2019.

86  Johnson 2015.

87  Johnson 2015.

88 Discussed further in Tendayi Bloom (2021) 'The Problem of Citizenship in Global Governance', in Tendayi Bloom and Lindsey Kingston (eds), *Statelessness, Governance, and the Problem of Citizenship*, Manchester University Press.

89 This quotation first appeared in a Turkish language CNN report. I take it here from the related English-language piece: Brandon Griggs (2015) 'Photographer Describes "Scream" of Migrant Boy's "Silent Body"', *CNN Online*, 3 September 2015.

90 Itamar Mann (2016) *Humanity at Sea: Maritime Migration and the Foundations of International Law*, Cambridge University Press, 1.

91 Rebecca Adler-Nissen, Katrine Emilie Andersen, and Lene Hansen (2020) 'Images, Emotions, and International Politics: The Death of Alan Kurdi', *Review of International Studies* 46(1): 75–95.

92 For a discussion of how this image functioned as a meme and the implications of this, see discussion in Yasmin Ibrahim (2018) 'The Unsacred and the Spectacularized: Alan Kurdi and the Migrant Body', *Social Media + Society*, October-December 2018.

93 For example, Vincent Miller (2015) 'Phatic Culture and the Status Quo: Reconsidering the Purpose of Social Media Activism', *Convergence: The International Journal of Research into New Media Technologies* 23(3): 251–69.

94 Gerhild Perl and Sabine Strasser (2018) 'Transnational Moralities: The Politics of Ir/responsibility of and Against the EU Border Regime', *Identities* 25(5): 507–23; Bhabha 2018, from 36.

95 Bhabha 2018, 38.

96 Adnan R. Khan (2015) 'Alan Kurdi's Father on his Family Tragedy: "I Should Have Died with Them"', *The Guardian*, 22 December 2015.

97 Chouliaraki et al. 2016, 7.

98 Paul Slovic, Daniel Västfjäll, Arvid Erlandsson, and Robin Gregory (2017) 'Iconic Photographs and the Ebb and Flow of Empathetic Response to Humanitarian Disasters', *Proceedings of the National Academy of Sciences of the United States of America* 114(4): 640–4.

99 Jacob Sohlberg, Peter Esaiasson, and Johan Martinsson (2019) 'The Changing Political Impact of Compassion – Evoking Pictures: The Case of the Drowned Toddler Alan Kurdi', *Journal of Ethnic and Migration Studies* 45(13): 2275–88.

100 Sevda Tunaboylu and Jill Alpes (2017) 'The EU-Turkey Deal: What Happens to People Who Return to Turkey?', *Forced Migration Review* 54: 84–7; for a helpfully thorough analysis of how readmission agreements work, albeit written before the one under discussion, see Sarah Wolff (2014) 'The Politics of Negotiating EU Readmission Agreements: Insights from Morocco and Turkey', *European Journal of Migration and Law* 16(1): 69–95.

101 Adler-Nissen et al. 2020; Perl and Strasser 2018; Bhabha 2018, from 36.

102 Carly McLaughlin (2017) '"They Don't Look Like Children": Child Asylum-Seekers, the Dubs Amendment and the Politics of Childhood', *Journal of Ethnic and Migration Studies* 44(11): 1757–73.

103 The cartoon includes an image of two men with animal-like facial features chasing two women, with a cut-in drawing of the famous image of a child lying dead on a beach. The caption reads, 'Que serait devenu le petit Aylan s'il avait grandi? Tripoteur de fesses en Allemagne', *Charlie Hebdo* Issue 1224, 6 January 2016. In English, this means 'What would little Aylan have become if he had grown up? An arse groper in Germany'. It references the stories circulating at the time of a migrant man touching women inappropriately at a winter market in Germany.

104 For example, see discussion in Heide Fehrenbach and Davide Rodogno (2015) '"A Horrific Photo of a Drowned Syrian Child": Humanitarian Photography and NGO Media Strategies in Historical Perspective', *International Review of the Red Cross* 97(900): 1121–55; and Kristine Sinclaire (2016) 'The Dead Boy and the Aftermath', Centre for Mellemøst Studies, Syddansk Universitet.

105 Eli Meixler (2018) 'Journalism Is Under Threat.' Inside a Bangladeshi Journalist's Dangerous Journey from Photographer to Prisoner', 11 December 2018 in *Time* at https://time.com/5475494/shahidul-alam -bangladesh-journalist-person-of-the-year-2018/ (accessed 8 August 2022).

106 Shahidul Alam (2007) 'The Visual Representation of Developing Countries by Developmental Agencies and the Western Media', in *Policy and Practice – A Development Education Review*, Centre for Global Education, Lisburn, 62.

107 For a collection of essays on this, see Heide Fehrenbach and Davide Rodogno (eds) (2015) *Humanitarian Photography: A History*, Cambridge University Press.

108 Peter Singer (2009) *The Life You Can Save*, Penguin. For information about the movement that this book has driven, see the website: https://www .thelifeyoucansave.org/ (accessed 27 June 2020).

109 See Kelly Staple's presentation of 'respect' in this context: Kelly Staples (2012) 'Statelessness and the Politics of Misrecognition', *Res Publica* 18: 93–106.

110 For example: Hannah Ryan and Katie Tonkiss (2022) 'Loners, Criminals, Mothers: The Gendered Misrecognition of Refugees in the British Tabloid News Media', *Sociological Research Online* Early View.

111 Susan Sontag (2003) *Regarding the Pain of Others*, Penguin, 6.

112 Sontag describes the fascination with seeing bodies in pain as almost pornographic, Sontag 2003, 36.

113 In their survey of historical image use of this sort, Fehrenbach and Rodogno observe that the image alone does not have the power. The power comes also through how it is shared, and the gatekeepers that decide this. They draw parallels with historic use of images in this way, such as that of the missionary societies: Fehrenbach and Rodogno 2015.

114 Miriam Tiktin (2017) 'A World Without Innocence', *American Ethnologist* 44(4): 577–90.

115 Erika Feller (2005) 'Refugees are not Migrants', *Refugee Survey Quarterly* 24(4): 27–35.

# Conclusion

1  José Medina (2011) 'The Relevance of Credibility Excess in a Proportional View of Epistemic Injustice: Differential Epistemic Authority and the Social Imaginary', *Social Epistemology* 25(1): 15–35.
2  Phillip Cole (2017) 'Insider Theory and the Construction of Statelessness', in Tendayi Bloom, Katherine Tonkiss, and Phillip Cole (eds), *Understanding Statelessness*, Routledge.
3  William Conklin (2014) *Statelessness: The Enigma in the International System*, Hart.
4  Tendayi Bloom (2022) 'Can Citizenship Studies Escape Citizenism?', *Citizenship Studies* 26(4–5): 362–81.
5  Lindsey Kingston (2019) *Fully Human: Personhood, Citizenship, and Rights*, Oxford University Press.
6  Matthew Gibney (2013) 'Is Deportation a Form of Forced Migration?', *Refugee Survey Quarterly* 32(2): 116–29.
7  Mary Kaldor (2003) 'Civil Society and Accountability', *Journal of Human Development* 4(1): 5–27; Fernando Henrique Cardoso, Sara Regine Hassett, and Christine Weydig (2005) 'An Interview with Fernando Henrique Cardoso', *Journal of International Affairs* 58(2): 211–19.

# Bibliography

Abi, Samir (2019) 'Global Compact: The Engagements of Marrakech', *West African Observatory on Migration*, available at: http://www.obsmigration.org/en/2019/02/global-compact-the-engagements-of-marrakech/ (accessed 1 October 2020).

Abuya, Edwin O. (2021) 'Registering Persons at Risk of Statelessness in Kenya: Solutions or Further Problems?', in Tendayi Bloom and Lindsey Kingston (eds), *Statelessness, Governance, and the Problem of Citizenship*, Manchester University Press, 251–63.

Acuña González, Guillermo E. (2016) 'Estructura y agencia en la migración infantil centroamericana', *Cuadernos Inter.c.a.mbio sobre Centroamérica y el Caribe* 13(1): 43–62.

Adaba, Gemma (1997) 'How International Financial Institutions Undermine Worker Rights', *Guild Practitioner* 54: 219–23.

Adaba, Gemma (2016) *Financing Social Protection Floors*, Financing for Development Working Paper Series II.A/1, 30 November 2016.

ADB (2020) 'Bangladesh', Asian Development Bank Member Fact Sheet, May 2020.

Adepoju, Aderanti (2004) 'Trends in International Migration in and from Africa', in Douglas S. Massey and J. Edward Taylor (eds), *International Migration: Prospects and Policies in a Global Market*, Oxford: Oxford University Press.

Adepoju, Aderanti, Alistair Boulton and Mariah Levin (2010) 'Promoting Integration Through Mobility: Free Movement Under Ecowas', *Refugee Survey Quarterly* 29(3): 120–44.

Adler-Nissen, Rebecca, Katrine Emilie Andersen and Lene Hansen (2020) 'Images, Emotions, and International Politics: The Death of Alan Kurdi', *Review of International Studies* 46(1): 75–95.

African Union (2017) 'Common African Position (CAP) on the Global Compact for Safe, Orderly and Regulatory Migration', AU/STC/MRIDP/4(II).

Ahmed, Saifuddin, Vivia Hsueh Hua Chen and Arul Indrasen Chib (2021) 'Xenophobia in the Time of a Pandemic: Social Media Use, Stereotypes, and Prejudice against Immigrants during the COVID-19 Crisis', *International Journal of Public Opinion Research*, online publication 30 April 2021.

Ahmed, Salahuddin (2004) *Bangladesh: Past and Present*, New Delhi: A. P. H. Publishing Corporation.

Ahmed, Shabbir and Md. Ayatullah Khan (2022) 'Spatial Overview of Climate Change Impacts in Bangladesh: A Systematic Review', *Climate and Development*, ahead-of-print.

Ahouga, Younes (2021) 'Transforming the International Organisation for Migration: An Analysis of the IOM Strategic Vision', Working Paper No. 2'21/5, Ryerson Centre for Immigration and Settlement.

Alam, Shahidul (2007) 'The Visual Representation of Developing Countries by Developmental Agencies and the Western Media', in *Policy and Practice – A Development Education Review*, Lisburn: Centre for Global Education.

Alam, Shahidul (2016) *The Best Years of My Life*, Drik Picture Library.

Alexander, Julia (2019) 'The Golden Age of Youtube Is Over', *The Verve*, 5 April 2019.

Alexseev, Mikhail (2006) *Immigration Phobia and the Security Dilemma: Russia, Europe, and the United States*, Cambridge University Press.

Algan, Yann, Elizabeth Beasley, Daniel Cohen, Martial Foucault and Madeleine Péron (2019) 'Qui sont les Gilets jaunes et leurs soutiens?', Observatoire du Bien-être du CEPREMAP et CEVIPOF, no. 2019-03, 14 February 2019.

Amighetti, Sara and Alasia Nuti (2015) 'A Nation's Right to Exclude and the Colonies', *Political Theory* 44(4): 541–66.

Amnesty International (2015) 'Italy: Lampedusa Survivors' Tales of Despair should Shock EU into Action', *Amnesty International News*, 16 February 2015.

Amoore, Louise and Paul Langley (2004) 'Ambiguities of Global Civil Society', *Review of International Studies* 30: 89–110.

Anand, R. P. (1966) 'Sovereign Equality of States in International Law - I', *International Studies* 8(3) 213–41.

Anderson, Michael (2022) 'Ghillar Michael Anderson Reflects on Starting the Tent Embassy 50 years ago', *NITV News*, available at: https://www.sbs.com.au/nitv/article/2022/01/26/ghillar-michael-anderson-reflects-starting-tent-embassy-50-years-ago (accessed 8 August 2022).

Anderson Ghillar, Michael (2019) 'Historical Background to the NAIDOC 2019 Theme: 'Voice, Treaty, Truth', available at: https://nationalunitygovernment.org/content/historical-background-naidoc-2019-theme-'voice-treaty-truth' (accessed 6 December 2019).

Anghie, Antony (2005) *Imperialism, Sovereignty and the Making of International Law*, Cambridge: Cambridge University Press.

Anheier, Helmut, Marlies Glasius and Mary Kaldor (2001) 'Introducing Global Civil Society', in Helmut Anheier, Marlies Glasius and Mary Kaldor (eds), *Global Civil Society*, Oxford University Press, 3–22.

Anheier, Helmut K. (2007) 'Reflections on the Concept and Measurement of Global Civil Society', *VOLUNTAS: International Journal of Voluntary and Nonprofit Organizations* 18: 1–15.

Anon (2019) 'Gilets Noirs, pour rester en colère et puissants!', *Vacarme* 2019/3(No.88): 68–79.

Ansems de Vries, Leonie and Katharine T. Weatherhead (2021) 'Politics of Knowledge Production in the Global Compact for Migration', *Interventions: International Journal of Postcolonial Studies* 23(2): 294–312.

Archer, Nandini, Claudia Torrisi, Claire Provost, Alexander Nabert and Belen Lobos (2019) 'Hundreds of Europeans "criminalised" for Helping Migrants – As far Right Aims to Win Big in European Elections', *Open Democracy*, 18 May 2019.

Ardittis, Solon and Frank Laczko (2020) 'Introduction - Migration Policy in the Age of Immobility', *Migration Policy Practice* 8(10): 2–5.

Asal, Houda (2014) 'Islamophobie: la fabrique d'un nouveau concept. État des lieux de la recherche', *Sociologie* 5(1): 13–29.

Ashutosh, Ishan and Alison Mountz (2011) 'Migration Management for the Benefit of whom? Interrogating the Work of the International Organization for Migration', *Citizenship Studies* 15(1): 21–38.

Asia Pacific Forum on Women, Law and Development (2016) 'In Conversation with Eni Lestari: From Domestic Worker to Global Advocate', 16 September 2016 web post, available at: https://apwld.org/in-conversation-with-eni-lestari-from-domestic-worker-to-global-advocate/ (accessed 30 July 2021).

Asquith, Paul, Henrietta Bailey, David Hope-Jones, Ambreena Manji and Nick Westcott (2019) 'Visa Problems for African Visitors to the UK', Joint All-Party Parliamentary Group Report by the APPG for Africa, the APPG for Diaspora, Development and Migration and the APPG for Malawi.

Azad, Ashraful (2019) 'Recruitment of Migrant Workers in Bangladesh: Elements of Human Trafficking for Labor Exploitation', *Journal of Human Trafficking* 5(2): 130–50.

Badran, Arwa (2007) 'Equal Access to International Debate: Visas and Their Implications', *Archaeologies* 3(2): 207–9.

Bahri, Hamid (2014) 'Race and Color in North Africa and the Arab Spring', in Moha Ennaji (ed.), *Mulitculturalism and Democracy in North Africa: Aftermath of the Arab Spring*, Routledge.

Ban Ki Moon (2016) 'In Safety and Dignity: Addressing Large Movements of Refugees and Migrants: Report of the Secretary-General', A/70/59.

Barber, Nicholas (2018) *The Principles of Constitutionalism*, Oxford University Press.

Basu, Natasha and Bernardo Caycedo (2017) 'A Radical Reframing of Civil Disobedience: "Illegal" Migration and Whistleblowing', in Esther Peeren, Robin Celikates, Jeroen de Kloet and Thomas Poell (eds), *Global Cultures of Contestation: Mobility, Sustainability, Aesthetics and Connectivity*, Springer.

Batha, Emma (2019) 'Stateless Woman Tells How She Couldn't Visit Dying Dad', *Reuters*, 28 June 2019, available at: https://news.trust.org/item/20190628153501-a8bpz/

Bauman, Zygmunt (1998) *Globalization: The Human Consequences*, Polity.

Bawdon, Fiona (2014) *Chasing Status: If not British, then What Am I?*, Legal Action Group.

BBC (2010) 'Gaddafi Wants EU Cash to Stop African Migrants', *BBC News* website, 31 August 2010, available at: https://www.bbc.co.uk/news/world-europe-11139345

BBC (2016) 'Australian Aboriginal MP Linda Burney Vows to Fight for Change', 31 August 2016.

Beaubien, Jason (2020) 'COVID-19's Global Spread Among The Relatively Rich Has Been Remarkable', *NPR*, 14 March 2020, available at: https://www.npr.org/2020/03/15/815828858/coronavirus-and-the-rich-beaubien (accessed 18 February 2021).

Béguin, Bernard (1959) 'ILO and the Tripartite System', *International Conciliation* 32: iii–448.

Beinart, William and Lotte Hughes (2007) *Environment and Empire*, Oxford University Press.

Belton, Kristy (2015) 'Rooted Displacement: The Paradox of Belonging Among Stateless People', *Citizenship Studies* 19(8): 907 –21.

Belton, Kristy (2017) *Statelessness in the Caribbean: The Paradox of Belonging in a Postnational World*, University of Pennsylvania Press.

Bengali, Shashank, Kate Linthicum and Victoria Kim (2020) 'How Coronavirus – A "rich man's disease" – Infected the Poor', *Los Angeles Times*, 8 May 2020, available at: https://www.latimes.com/world-nation/story/2020-05-08/how-the-coronavirus-began-as-a-disease-of-the-rich

Benli, Ali Emre (2018) 'March of Refugees: An Act of Civil Disobedience', *Journal of Global Ethics* 14(3): 315–31.

Benson, Rodney (2013) 'Why Narrative is Not Enough: Immigration and the Genres of Journalism', in Giovanna dell'Orto and Vicki Birchfield (eds), *Reporting at the Southern Borders: Journalism and Public Debates on Immigration in the EU and US*, London: Routledge, 73–87.

Benswait, Ahmad (2021) 'Language and Statelessness: The Impact of Political Discourses on the Bidoon Community in Kuwait', in Tendayi Bloom and Lindsey Kingston (eds), *Statelessness, Governance, and the Problem of Citizenship*, Manchester University Press.

Berry, Mike, Inaki Garcia-Blanco and Kerry Moore (2015) 'Press Coverage of the Refugee and Migrant Crisis in the EU: A Content Analysis of Five European Countries', Report prepared for the United Nations High Commission for Refugees.

Benswait (Jaber Ahmad), and Miguel Pérez-Milans (2022) 'Pressing Times, Losing Voice: Critique and Transformative Spaces in Higher Education', London Review of Education 20(1): 1–15.

Betts, Alexander (2011) *Global Migration Governance*, Oxford University Press.

Bhabha, Jacqueline (2018) *Can We Solve the Migration Crisis?*, Polity.

Bhagwati, Jagdish (1994) 'The World Trading System', *Journal of International Affairs* 48(1): 279–85.

Bharadwaj, Prashant, Asim Khwaja and Atif Mian (2008) 'The Big March: Migratory Flows after the Partition of India', *Economic and Political Weekly* 43(35): 39–49.

Bharadwaj, Prashant, Asim Ijaz Khwaja and Atif R. Mian (2009) 'The Partition of India: Demographic Consequences', Available from SSRN.

Bhatt, Rakesh M. (2001) 'World Englishes', *Annual Review of Anthropology* 30: 527–50.

Billig, Michael (1995) *Banal Nationalism*, Sage.

Black, Maggie (2008) *The No-Nonsense Guide to the United Nations*, New Internationalist Publications.

Bloom, Tendayi (2014) *Extended Report: Global Migration Governance: A Decade of Change?*, Policy Report No. 02/07, United Nations University Institute on Globalization, Culture and Mobility.

Bloom, Tendayi (2016) 'Privatised Migration Management in the Mediterranean Region and Sub-Saharan Migration Decision-Making', in Belachew Gebrewold and Tendayi Bloom (eds), *Understanding Migrant Decisions: From Sub-Saharan Africa to the Mediterranean Region*, Routledge, 99–119.

Bloom, Tendayi (2018) *Noncitizenism: Recognising Noncitizen Capabilities in a World of Citizens. Noncitizenism*, Routledge.

Bloom, Tendayi (2019) 'When Migration Policy Isn't about Migration: Considerations for Implementation of the Global Compact for Migration', *Ethics and international Affairs* 33(4): 481–97.

Bloom, Tendayi (2021) 'Human Rights are Not Enough: Understanding Noncitizenship and Noncitizens in Their Own Right', in Molly Land, Kathryn Libal and Jillian Chambers (eds), *Beyond Borders: The Human Rights of Non-Citizens at Home and Abroad*, Cambridge University Press.

Bloom, Tendayi (2021) 'The Problem of Citizenship in Global Governance', in Tendayi Bloom and Lindsey Kingston (eds), *Statelessness, Governance, and the Problem of Citizenship*, Manchester University Press.

Bloom, Tendayi (2022) 'Can Citizenship Studies Escape Citizenism?', *Citizenship Studies* 26(4–5): 372–81.

Bloom, Tendayi and Lindsey Kingston (2021) 'Opening a Conversation about Statelessness, Governance, and the Problem of Citizenship', in Tendayi Bloom and Lindsey Kingston (eds), *Statelessness, Governance, and the Problem of Citizenship*, Manchester University Press.

Bloom, Tendayi and Lindsey Kingston (eds) (2021) *Statelessness, Governance, and the Problem of Citizenship*, Manchester University Press.

Bloom, Tendayi and Katherine Tonkiss (2013) 'European Union and Commonwealth Free Movement: A Historical-Comparative Perspective', *Journal of Ethnic and Migration Studies* 39(7): 1067–85.

Bloque Latinoamericano (2017) 'Puntos de partida para un pacto global de migración que beneficie a la población en las migraciones y sus gobiernos', *Migración y desarrollo* 15(21): 137–40.

Blue, Richard, Danielle de García and Kristine Johnstone (2012) 'Study of the Outcomes and Impacts of the Global Forum on Migration and Development Civil Society Days', Social Impact Inc.

Böhning, Roger (1976) 'The ILO and Contemporary International Economic Migration', *The International Migration Review* 10(2): 147–56.

Böhning, Roger (1991) 'The ILO and the New UN Convention on Migrant Workers: The Past and Future', *The International Migration Review* 25(4): 698–709.

Boyer, Pierre C., Thomas Delemotte, Germain Gauthier, Vincent Rollet and Benoît Schmutz (2020) 'Les determinants de la mobilization des Gilets jaumes', *Revue économique* 17(1): 109–38.

Brian, Tara and Frank Laczko (eds) (2015) *Fatal Journeys: Tracking Lives Lost During Migration*, International Organisation for Migration.

Brinham, Natalie (2021) '"We are *Not* Stateless! You can Call us What You Like, But we are Citizens of Myanmar!": Rohingya Resistance and the Stateless Label', in Tendayi Bloom and Lindsey Kingston (eds), *Statelessness, Governance, and the Problem of Citizenship*, Manchester University Press, 342–55.

Brock, Gillian (2020) *Justice for People on the Move: Migration in Challenging Times*, Cambridge University Press.

Brockmeier, Jens (2009) 'Reaching for Meaning: Human Agency and the Narrative Imagination', *Theory and Psychology* 19(2): 213–33.

Brownlee, Kimberley (2004) 'Features of a Paradigm Case of Civil Disobedience', *Res Publica* 10: 337–51.

Bruton, John (2018) 'Peter Sutherland: A Gifted Administrator and Humanitarian', *The Irish Times*, 8 January 2018, available at: https://www.irishtimes.com/news/politics/peter-sutherland-a-gifted-administrator-and-humanitarian-1.3347580 (accessed 31 July 2021).

Buonanno, Laurie (2017) 'The European Migration Crisis', in Desmond Dinan et al. (eds), *The European Union in Crisis*, Palgrave.

Butalia, Urvashi (2000) *The Other Side of Silence: Voices from the Partition of India*, Duke University Press.

Byrnes, Sholto (2010) 'Colonel Gaddafi Warns Europe over "turning black"', *The New Statesman*, 1 December 2010.

Cabrera, Luis (2010) *The Practice of Global Citizenship*, Cambridge University Press.

Cabrera, Luis (2019) 'Free Movement, Sovereignty and Cosmopolitan State Responsibility', in Richard Beardsworth et al. (ed.), *The State and Cosmopolitan Responsibilities*, Oxford University Press.

Calabresi, Guido and Philip Bobbitt (1971) *Tragic Choices*, W.W. Norton and Company, New York.

Calhoun, Craig (2002) 'The Class Consciousness of Frequent Travelers: Toward a Critique of Actually Existing Cosmopolitanism', *South Atlantic Quarterly* 101: 869–97.

Cammaerts, Bart and Nico Carpentier (2006) 'The Unbearable Lightness of Full Participation in a Global Context: WSIS and Civil Society Participation', in Jan Servaes and Nico Carpentier (eds), *Towards a Sustainable Information Society: Deconstructing WSIS*, Intellect Books.

Campbell, Tobias (2019) '"Ours will be a tent": The Meaning and Symbolism of the Early Aboriginal Tent Embassy', *ANU Historical Journal II* (1): 57–71.

Cannon, Cecilia (2017) 'Modes of Knowledge Mobilization by/for International Bureaucracies Throughout International Policy Processes', in Annabelle

Littoz-Monnet (ed.), *The Politics of Expertise in International Organizations*, Routledge, 128–47.

Cannon, Cecilia and Thomas Biersteker (2020) 'The Governance of International Organisations: Structural Components, Internal Mechanisms, and Contemporary Challenges', in Helmut K. Anheier and Theodor Baums (eds), *Advances in Corporate Governance: Comparative Perspectives*, Oxford University Press, 203–29.

Cao, Deborah and Xingmin Zhao (2008) 'Translation at the United Nations as Specialized Translation', *The Journal of Specialised Translation* 9, January 2008.

Cardoso, Fernando Henrique, Sara Regine Hassett and Christine Weydig (2005) 'An Interview with Fernando Henrique Cardoso', *Journal of International Affairs* 58(2): 211–19.

Carens, Joseph (1987) 'Aliens and Citizens: The Case for Open Borders', *The Review of Politics* 49(2): 251–73.

Cass, Deborah (2005) 'The Sutherland Report: The WTO and its Critics', *International Organizations Law Review* 2: 153–66.

Castles, S. M. Arias Cubas, C. Kim and D. Ozkul (2012) 'Irregular Migration: Causes, Patterns, and Strategies', in Irena Omelaniuk (ed.), *Global Perspectives on Migration and Development*, Springer, 117–51.

Catala, Amandine (2022) 'Academic Migration, Linguistic Justice, and Epistemic Injustice', *The Journal of Political Philosophy* 30(2): 324–46..

Celikates, Robin (2018) 'Constituent Power Beyond Exceptionalism: Irregular Migration, Disobedience, and (Re-) Constitution', *Journal of International Political Theory* 15(1): 67–81.

Cerulus, Laurens and Eline Schaart (2019) 'How the UN Migration Pact Got Trolled', *Politico*, 3 January 2019.

Chan, Carol and Maria Montt Strabucchi (2020) 'Many-Faced Orientalism: Racism and Xenophobia in a Time of the Novel Coronavirus in Chile', *Asian Ethnicity* 22(2): 374–94.

Chandhoke, Neera (2005) 'How Global is Global Civil Society?', *Journal of World Systems Research* XI(2): 355–71.

Chandhoke, Neera (2007) 'Global Civil Society and Global Justice', *Economic and Political Weekly*, July 21: 3016–22.

Chang, Robert S. (2018) 'Whitewashing Precedent: From the Chinese Exclusion Case to Korematsu to the Muslim Travel Ban Cases', *Case Western Reserve Law Review* 68(4): 1183–222.

Charles, Matthew (2020) '"Disease of the rich, killer of the poor" How Covid-19 brought Latin America to Its Knees', *The Telegraph*, available at: https://www.telegraph.co.uk/global-health/science-and-disease/coronavirus-in-latin-america/

Chatterji, Joya (2010) 'Migration Myths and the Mechanics of Assimilation: Two Community Histories from Bengal', *Studies in Humanities and Social Sciences* 17(1–2): 139–74.

Chemni, B. S. (1998) 'The Geopolitics of Refugee Studies: A View from the South', *Refugee Studies* 11(4): 350–74.

Chetail, Vincent (2016) 'Is There Blood on my Hands? Deportation as a Crime of International Law', *Leiden Journal of International Law* 29(3): 917–43.

Chetail, Vincent (2020) 'The Global Compact for Safe, Orderly and Regular Migration: A Kaleidoscope of International Law', *International Law in Context* 16(3): 253–68.

Chetail, Vincent (2022) 'The International Organization for Migration and the Duty to Protect Migrants: Revisiting the Law of International Organizations', in Jan Klabbers (ed.), *The Cambridge Companion to International Organizations Law*, Cambridge University Press, 244–64.

Chikezie, Chukwu-Emeka (2012) 'Civil Society, the Common Space, and the GFMD', in Irena Omelaniuk (ed.), *Global Perspectives on Migration and Development: GFMD Puerto Vallarta and Beyond*, Springer.

Chouliaraki, Lilie, Myria Georgiou, Rafal Zaborowski and Wouter Oomen (2016) 'The European 'migration crisis' and the Media: A Cross-European Press Content Analysis', Project Report, London School of Economics and Political Science.

Chowdhury, Md. Arif, Md. Khalid Hasan and Syed Labib Ul Islam (2022) 'Climate Change Adaptation in Bangladesh: Current Practices, Challenges and the Way Forward', *The Journal of Climate Change and Health* 6: 1–8.

Chuvileva, Yulia E., Andrea Rissing and Hilary B. King (2020) 'From Wet Markets to Wal-Marts: Tracing Alimentary Xenophobia in the Time of COVID-19', *Social Anthropology* 28(2): 241–3.

Çidam, Çigdem, William E. Schuerman, Candice Delmas, Erin R. Pineda, Robin Celikates and Alexander Livingston (2020) 'Theorizing the Politics of Protest: Contemporary Debates on Civil Disobedience', *Contemporary Political Theory* 19: 513–46.

Cobb, Jelani (2018) 'When Newsrooms Are Dominated by White People, they Miss Crucial Facts', *The Guardian Opinion*, available at: https://www.theguardian.com/world/commentisfree/2018/nov/05/newsroom-diversity-media-race-journalism (accessed 19 November 2020).

Cole, Phillip (2017) 'Insider Theory and the Construction of Statelessness', in Tendayi Bloom, Katherine Tonkiss and Phillip Cole (eds), *Understanding Statelessness*, Routledge, 255–67.

Conklin, William (2014) *Statelessness: The Enigma in the International System*, Hart.

Conrad, Maximilian (2021) 'Post-Truth Politics, Digital Media, and the Politicization of the Global Compact for Mgiration', *Politics and Governance* 9(3): 301–11.

Cook, Maria Lorena (2010) 'The Advocate's Dilemma: Framing Migrant Rights in National Settings', *Studies in Social Justice* 4(2): 145–64.

Craggs, Ruth (2018) 'The 2018 Commonwealth Heads of Government Meeting, the Windrush Scandal and the Legacies of Empire', *Round Table* 107(3): 361–2.

Crawley, Heaven, Franck Düvell, Katharine Jones, Simon McMahon and Nando Sigona (2018) *Unravelling Europe's 'Migration Crisis': Journeys over Land and Sea*, Policy Press.

Crawley, Heaven, Simon McMahon and Katharine Jones (2016) *Victims and Villains: Migrant Voices in the British Media*, Coventry: Centre for Trust, Peace and Social Relations, Coventry University.

Crawley, Heaven and Dimitris Skleparis (2018) 'Refugees, Migrants, neither, Both: Categorical Fetishism and the Politics of Bounding in Europe's "migration crisis"', *Journal of Ethnic and Migration Studies* 44(1): 48–64.

Crépeau, François (2016) 'La mobilité et la diversité, défis des sociétés contemporaines', presentation to Organisation internationale de la Francophonie, Conseil constitutionnel de France, Paris, les 31 mai et 1 juin 2016.

Crépeau, François and Idil Atak (2016) 'Global Migration Governance: Avoiding Commitments on Human Rights, Yet Tracing a Course for Cooperation', *Netherlands Quarterly of Human Rights* 34(2): 113–46.

Crépeau, François and Bethany Hastie (2015) 'The Case for "Firewall" Protections for Irregular Migrants', *European Journal of Migration and Law* 17(2–3): 157–83.

Cronin, Michael (2013) *Translation in the Digital Age*, Routledge.

Crouch, Colin (2008) 'Change in European Societies since the 1970s', *West European Politics* 31(1–2): 14–39.

Cuttitta, Paolo (2014) 'From the *Cap Anamur* to *Mare Nostrum*: Humanitarianism and Migraiton Controls at the EU's Maritime Borders', in Claudio Matera and Amanda Taylor (eds), *The Common European Asylum System and Human Rights: Enhancing Protection in Times of Emergencies*, Asser Institute.

Darach, Amanda (2018) 'It's Getting more Difficult for Foreign Journalists to Work in the US', *Columbia Journalism Review*, 12 September 2018.

Darwich, May (2019) *Threats and Alliances in the Middle East: Saudi and Syrian Policies in a Turbulent Region*, Cambridge University Press.

Darwich, May and Tamirace Fakhoury (2016) 'Casting the Other as an Existential Threat: The Securitization of Sectarianism in the International Relations of the Syria Crisis', *Global Discourse* 6(4): 712–32.

Das, Glorene (2018) 'Migrant Estate Workers Toil in Tough Conditions', *New Straits Times*, 28 September 2018, available at: https://www.nst.com.my/opinion/letters/2018/09/415872/migrant-estate-workers-toil-tough-conditions (accessed 1 September 2022).

Dauvergne, Catherine (2004) 'Sovereignty, Migration and the Rule of Law in Global Times', *Modern Law Review* 67(4): 588–615.

Dauvergne, Catherine (2008) *Making People Illegal: What Globalization Means for Migration and the Law*, Cambridge University Press.

Davey, Jacob and Julia Ebner (2017) 'The Fringe Insurgency: Connectivity, Convergence and Mainstreaming of the Extreme Right', Institute for Strategic Dialogue Report.

Davis, Emmalon (2016) 'Typecasts, Tokens, and Spokespersons: A Case for Credibility as Testimonial Injustice', *Hypatia* 31(3): 485–501.

De Genova, Nicholas (2013) '"We are of the connections": Migration, Methodological Nationalism, and "militant research"', *Postcolonial Studies* 16(3): 250–8.

De Genova, Nicholas (2015) 'Extremities and Regularities: Regularity Regimes and the Spectacle of Immigration Enforcement', in Yolande Jansen, Robin Celikates and Joost de Bloois (eds), *The Irregularities of Migration in Contemporary Europe: Detention, Deportation, Drowning*, Rowman and Littlefield.

De Genova, Nicholas (2018) 'The "migrant crisis" as Racial Crisis: Do *Black Lives Matter* in Europe?', *Ethnic and Racial Studies* 41(10): 1765–82.

de Haas, Hein (2007) 'North African Migration Systems: Evolution, Transformations and Development Linkages', International Migration Institute, James Martin 21st Century School, University of Oxford Working Paper 6.

de Haas, Hein, Mathias Czaika, Marie-Laurence Flahaux, Edo Mahendra, Katharina Natter, Simona Vezzoli and María Villares-Varela (2018) 'International Migration: Trrends, Determinants and Policy Effects', DEMIG paper 33IMIn Working Paper Series No. 142.

de Haas, Hein, Mathias Czaika, Marie-Laurence Flahaux, Edo Mahendra, Katharine Natter, Simona Vezzoli and María Villares-Varela (2019) 'International Migration: Trends, Determinants, and Policy Effects', *Population and Development Review* 45(4): 885–922.

de Haas, Hein, Katharina Natter and Simona Vezzoli (2016) 'Growing Restrictiveness or Changing Selection? The Nature and Evolution of Migration Policies', *International Migration Review*, Early View, 1–44.

de Noronha, Luke (2019) 'Deportation, Racism and Multi-status Britain: Immigration Control and the Production of Race in the Present', *Ethnic and Racial Studies* 42(14): 2413–30.

de Noronha, Luke (2022) 'Hierarchies of Membership and the Management of Global Population: Reflections on Citizenship and Racial Ordering', *Citizenship Studies* 26(4–5): 426–35.

Debandi, Natalia and Joanna Cecilia Sander (2020) 'Proceso de adopción del Pacto Mundial sobre Migración: Actores, tramas y repercusiones en Sudamérica', *Diarios del Teruño* 10(julio-diciembre 2020): 58–87.

Dedijer, Steven (1964) 'Migration of Scientists: A World-Wide Phenomenon and Problem', *Nature* 201: 964–7.

Delgado, Manuel (2016) *Ciudadanismo: La reforma ética y estética del capitalismo*, Catarata.

Delgado Wise, Raúl (2018) 'The Global Compact in Relation to the Migration-Development Nexus Debate', *Global Social Policy* 18(3): 328–31.

Delgado Wise, Raúl (2018) 'Is there a Space for Counterhegemonic Participation?', *Globalizations* 15(6): 746–61.

Deloison, Guillaume (2018) 'Critique de la Democratie', on his blog . . . https://guillaumedeloison.wordpress.com/2018/07/02/critique-de-la-democratie/

Deshingkar, Priya, C. R. Abrar, Mirza Taslima Sultana, Kazi Nurmohammad Hossainul Haque and Md Selim Reza (2018) 'Producing Ideal Bangladeshi Migrants for Precarious Construction Work in Qatar', *Journal of Ethnic and Migration Studies* 45(14): 2723–38.

Desmet, Ellen, Ine Lietaert, Jeffrey Goegiers and Rosella Marino (2020) 'Belgium and the Global Compact for Migration: Taking Stock after Two Years', Centre for the Social Study of Migration and Refugees, Ghent University, Belgium.

Devrim Gürsel, Zeynep (2010) '*U.S. Newsworld*: The Rule of Text and Everyday Practices of Editing the World', in S. Elizabeth Bird (ed.), *The Anthropology of News and Journalism: Global Perspectives*, Indiana University Press.

Díaz, Junot (2008) *Drown*, Faber.

Diouf, Sylviane A. (ed.) (2003) *Fighting the Slave Trade: West African Strategies*, Ohio University Press.

Dreier, Peter (2006) 'Rosa Parks: Angry, Not Tired', *Dissent* 53(1): 88–92.

Dummett, Ann and Andrew G. Nicol (1990) *Subjects, Citizens, Aliens and Others: Nationality and Immigration Law*, Weidenfeld and Nicolson.

Dunai, Marton (2019) 'Four Jailed for Life over Death of 71 Migrants in Hungarian Truck', *Reuters*, 20 June 2019, available at: https://www.reuters .com/article/us-europe-migrants-hungary-trial-idUSKCN1TL0LX

E, Ekaterina (2020) 'A Stateless Person's Take on "Stateless"', *European Network on Statelessness blog*, 10 September 2020, available at: https://www .statelessness.eu/updates/blog/stateless-persons-take-stateless (accessed 1 September 2022).

E, Ekaterina (2021) 'United Stateless in the United States: Reflections from an Activist', in Tendayi Bloom and Lindsey Kingston (eds), *Statelessness, Governance, and the Problem of Citizenship*, Manchester University Press, 356–64.

Ehdeed, Sukaina (2019) 'The Impact of Visa Denial in Academia', *LSE Blogs*, available at: https://blogs.lse.ac.uk/mec/2019/08/27/the-impact-of-visa -denial-in-academia/ (accessed 27 November 2020).

Elden, Stuart (2007) 'There is a Politics of Space because Space is Political: Henri Lefebvre and the Production of Space', *Radical Philosophy Review* 10(2): 101–16.

Elias, Amanuel, Jehonathan Ben, Fethi Mansouri and Yin Paradies (2020) 'Racism and Nationalism during and beyond the COVID-19 Pandemic', *Ethnic and Racial Studies* 44(5): 783–93.

Elsahar, Hady (2018) 'Highlighting Visa Issues in Scientific Conferences', *Medium*, 9 June 2018.

Eltis, David and David Richardson (2008) 'A New Assessment of the Transatlantic Slave Trade', in David Eltis and David Richardson (eds), *Essays on the New Transatlantic Slave Trade Database*, Yale University Press.

ENS (2017) 'Protecting Stateless Persons from Arbitrary Detention', European Network on Statelessness.

Estevens, Joao (2018) 'Migration Crisis in the EU: Developing a Framework for Analysis of National Security and Defence Strategies', *Comparative Migration Studies* 6: 1–24.

Eze, Chielozona (2014) 'Rethinking African Culture and Identity: The Afropolitan Model', *Journal of African Cultural Studies* 26(2): 234–47.

Fakhoury, Tamirace (2016) 'Securitising Migration: The European Union in the Context of the Post-2011 Arab Upheavals', *The International Spectator: Italian Journal of International Affairs* 51(4): 67–79.

Falk, Richard A. (1999) 'Kosovo, World Order, and the Future of International Law', *American Journal of International Law* 93(4): 847–57.

Fanon, Frantz (1986) *Black Skin White Masks*, Pluto Press (trans. Charles Lam Markmann).

Fassin, Éric (2011) '"Immigration et Délinqunce": La construction d'un problème entre politique, journalism et sociologie', *Cités* 2(46): 69–85.

Fasulo, Linda (2015) *An Insider's Guide to the UN*, Third Edition, Yale University Press.

Fazila-Yacoobali Zamindar, Vazira (2007) *The Long Partition and the Making of Modern South Asia*, Columbia University Press.

Fehrenbach, Heide and Davide Rodogno (2015) '"A Horrific Photo of a Drowned Syrian Child": Humanitarian Photography and NGO Media Strategies in Historical Perspective', *International Review of the Red Cross* 97(900): 1121–55.

Fehrenbach, Heide and Davide Rodogno (eds) (2015) *Humanitarian Photography: A History*, Cambridge University Press.

Feller, Erika (2005) 'Refugees are not Migrants', *Refugee Survey Quarterly* 24(4): 27–35.

Ferris, Elizabeth G. and Katharine M. Donato (2020) *Refugees, Migration and Global Governance*, Routledge.

Festman, Carla (2019) 'Using Criminal Law to Restrict the Work of NGOs Supporting Refugees and Other Migrants in Council of Europe Member States', Expert Council on NGO Law, December 2019, CONF/EXP(2019)I.

Flores, Nelson and Jonathan Rosa (2015) 'Undoing Appropriateness: Raciolinguistic Ideologies and Language Diversity in Education', *Harvard Educational Review* 85(2): 149–71.

Foot, Paul (1969) *The Rise of Enoch Powell*, Penguin.

Frank-Vitale, Amelia and Margarita Núñez Chaim (2020) '"Lady Frijoles": Las caravanas centroamericanas y el poder de la hípervisibilidad de la migración indocumentada', *EntreDiversidades Revista de ciencias sociales y humanidades* 7(1): 37–61.

Fransen, Sonja and Hein de Haas (2021) 'Trends and Patterns of Global Refugee Migration', *Population and Development Review* 48(1): 97–128.

Frelick, Bill, Ian M. Kysel and Jennifer Podkul (2016) 'The Impact of Externalization of Migration Controls on the Rights of Asylum Seekers and Other Migrants', *Journal on Migration and Human Security* 4(4): 190–220.

Fricker, Miranda (2006) 'Powerlessness and Social Interpretation', *Episteme* 3(1–2): 96–108.

Fricker, Miranda (2007) *Epistemic Justice: Power and the Ethics of Knowing*, Oxford University Press.

Fricker, Miranda (2017) 'Evolving Concepts of Epistemic Injustice', in Ian James Kidd, José Medina and Gaile Pohlhaus (eds), *Routledge Handbook of Epistemic Injustice*, Routledge, 53–60.

Frye, Marilyn (1983) 'Oppression', in Marilyn Frye, *The Politics of Reality: Essays in Feminist Theory*, Crossing Press, Berkeley, 1–16.

Gabrielli, Lorenzo (2011) 'European Immigration Policies Outside the Union: An Impact Analysis on Migration Dynamics in Northern African Transit Areas', in Jocelyne Streiff-Fénart and Aurélia Segatti (eds), *The Challenge of the Threshold: Border Closures and Migration Movements in Africa*, Lexington Books.

Gallagher, Peter (2005) *The First Ten Years of the WTO 1995–2005*, Cambridge University Press.

Gammeltoft-Hansen, Thomas (2011) *Access to Asylum*, Cambridge University Press.

Gammeltoft-Hansen, Thomas, Elspeth Guild, Violeta Morena-Lax, Marion Panizzon and Isobel Roele (2017) 'What is a Compact? Migrants' Rights and State Responsibilities Regarding the Design of the UN Global Compact for Safe, Orderly and Regular Migration', Raoul Wallenberg Institute of Human Rights and Humanitarian Law.

Gammeltoft-Hansen, Thomas and Ninna Nybert Sorensen (2013) *The Migration Industry and the Commercialisation of International Migration*, Routledge.

Gardiner Barber, Pauline and Catherine Bryan (2018) 'International Organization for Migration in the Field: "walking the talk" of Global Migration Management in Manila', *Journal of Ethnic and Migration Studies* 44(1): 1725–42.

Garelli, Glenda and Martina Tazzioli (2017) 'Choucha beyond the Camp: Challenging the Border of Migration Studies', in Nicholas De Genova (ed.), *The Borders of "Europe": Autonomy of Migration, Tactics of Belonging*, Duke University Press.

Gaspari, Federico and John Hutchins (2007) 'Online and Free? Ten Years of Online Machine Translation: Origins, Developments, Current Use and Future Prospects', *Proceedings of Machine Translation Summit* XI: Papers.

Gebrewold, Belachew (2007) 'Migration as a Transcontinental Challenge', in Belachew Gebrewold (ed.), *Africa and Fortress Europe: Threats and Opportunities*, Routledge.

Gebrewold, Belachew and Tendayi Bloom (2015) *Understanding Migration Decisions*, Routledge.

Geisser, Vincent (2020) 'L'hygiéno-nationalisme, remède miracle à la pandémie? Populismes, racismes et complotismes autor du Covid-19', *Migrations Soicété* 2020/2(180): 3–18.

Genier, Yves (2020) 'Une maladie de l'élite', *Pour La Tête*, 7 April 2020, available at: https://bonpourlatete.com/analyses/une-maladie-de-l-elite (accessed 18 February 2021).

Gentleman, Amelia (2017) '"I can't eat or sleep": The Woman Threatened with Deportation after 50 years in Britain', *The Guardian*, 28 November 2017.

Gentleman, Amelia (2019) *The Windrush Betrayal*, Faber and Faber.

Gentleman, Amelia (2020) 'Wolverhampton Marks Life of Windrush Campaigner Paulette Wilson', *The Guardian*, 4 September 2020, available at:

https://www.theguardian.com/uk-news/2020/sep/04/wolverhampton-marks
-life-of-windrush-campaigner-paulette-wilson (accessed 11 January 2021).

Gerbaudo, Paul (2017) *The Mask and the Flag: Populism, Citizenism and Global Protest*, Oxford University Press.

Gewin, Virginia (2019) 'What Scientists should know about Visa Hurdles', *Nature* 569: 297–9.

Gibney, Matthew (2013) 'Is Deportation a Form of Forced Migration?', *Refugee Survey Quarterly* 32(2): 116–29.

Glerum, David R. (2021) 'Tainted Heroes: The Emergence of Dirty Work during Pandemics', *Industrial and Organizational Psychology* 14: 41–4.

Global Passport Index, 2019 iteration.

Gnes, Davide (2013) 'Maghnia: Crossing the Uncrossable Border', Mission report on vulnerability of Sub-Saharan migrants and refugees at the Algerian-Moroccan border, Euro-Mediterranean Human Rights Network, Copenhagen.

Goastellec, Gaële (2016) 'La mobilité international: Une qualité des carriers et des marchés académiques en Europe?', *Journal of International Mobility* 2016/1(4): 171–88.

Gois, William and Karen Campbell (2013) 'Stranded Migrants: A Call to Rethink the Current Labour Migration Paradaigm', *Migration and Development* 2(2): 157–72.

Goldenziel, Jill I (2017) 'Displaced: A Proposal for an International Agreement to Protect Refugees, Migrants, and States', *Berkeley Journal of International Law* 35(1): 47–89.

Goodin, Robert (1992) 'If People Were Money . . ', in Brian Barry and Robert E. Goodin (eds), *Free Movement*, Harvester Weatsheaf, 6–22.

Goodsell, Charles T. (2003) 'The Concept of Public Space and Its Democratic Manifestations', *American Review of Public Administration* 33(4): 361–83.

Griggs, Brandon (2015) 'Photographer Describes "scream" of Migrant Boy's "silent body"', *CNN Online*, 3 September 2015.

Grugel, Jean and Nicola Piper (2011) 'Global Governance, Economic Migration and the Difficulties of Social Activism', *International Sociology* 26(4): 435–54.

Guadagno, Lorenzo (2020) 'Migrants and the COVID-19 Pandemic: An Initial Analysis', International Organisation for Migration.

Guerrero Nova, Edwin (2018) 'Censura en Colombia: ¿Se están negando visas a periodistas extranjeros?' *Latin American Post*, 7 September 2018.

Guhl, Jakob (2019) 'Too Little, Too Late', interview with Jakob Guhl, Friedrich Ebert Stiftung website, 7 February 2019.

Guild, Elspeth, Stefanie Grant and Kees Groenendijk (2020) 'Unfinished Business: The IOM and Migrants' Human Rights', in Martin Geiger and Antoine Pécoud (eds), *The Internatinoal Organization for Migration: The New 'UN Migration Agency' in Critical Perspective*, Palgrave Macmillan.

Hambye, Philippe (2019) 'La minorisation linguistique, entre discrimination et domination symbolique. Différences et enjeux de deux lectures des inégalités', *Minorités linguistiques et société* 12: 15–30.

Hamel, Rainer Enrique (2013) 'L'anglais, langue unique pour les Sciences? Le rôle des modèles plurilingües dans la recherche, la communication scientifique et l'enseignement supérieur', *Synergies Europe* 8: 53–66.

Hathaway, James (1984) 'The Evolution of Refugee Status in International Law: 1920–1950', *International Comparative Law Quarterly* 33(2): 348–80.

Heimans, Jeremy and Henry Timms (2019) *#newpower: Why Outsiders Are Winning, Institutions Are Failing, and How the Rest of us can Keep up in the Age of Mass Participation*, Pan Macmillan.

Hennebry, Jenna and Nicola Piper (2021) 'Global Migration Governance and Migrant Rights Advocacy: The Flexibilization of Multi-stakeholder Negotiations', in Catherine Dauvergne (ed.), *Research Handbook on the Law and Politics of Migration*, Edward Elger.

Henry, Janet and James Pomeroy (2018) 'The World in 2030: Our Long-Term Projections for 75 Countries', Economics Global September 2018, HSBC Global Research.

Herliky-Mera, Jeffrey (2015) 'Visa Restrictions Limit Academic Freedom', *University World News*, 17 July 2015.

Hershkovitz, Linda (1993) 'Tiananmen Square and the Politics of Place', *Political Geography* 12(5): 395–420.

Hewitt, Guy and Kevin M. Isaac (2018) 'Windrush: The Perfect Storm', *Social and Economic Studies* 67(2/3): 293–302.

Hill, K., W. Seltzer, J. Leaning, S. J. Malik and S. S. Russell (2008) 'The Demographic Impact of Partition in the Punjab in 1947', *Population Studies* 62(2): 155–70.

Hilpold, Peter (2021) 'Opening up a New Chapter of Law-Making in International Law: The Global Compacts on Migration and for Refugees of 2018', *European Law Journal* 26(3–4): 226–44.

Hindess, Barry (2003) 'Responsibility for Others in the Modern System of States', *Journal of Sociology* 39(1): 23–30.

Hobolth, Mogens (2014) 'Researching Mobility Barriers: The European visa Database', *Journal of Ethnic and Migration Studies* 40(3): 424–35.

Holliday, Adrian (2015) 'Native-Speakerism: Taking the Concept Forward and Achieving Cultural Belief', in Anne Swann, Pamela Aboshiha and Adrian Holliday (eds), *(En)Countering Nativespeakerism*, Palgrave Macmillan.

Hough, J. R. (1988) 'Social Policy and the Birthrate', *International Journal of Sociology and Social Policy* 8(5): 35–50.

Houghton, Stephanie Ann, Damian J. Rivers and Kayoko Hashimoto (eds) (2018) *Beyond Native-Speakerism: Current Explorations and Future Visions*, Routledge.

Howell, Edwina (2014) 'Black Power – By any Means Necessary', in Gary Foley, Andrew Schaap and Edwina Howell (eds), *The Aboriginal Tent Embassy*, Routledge.

Howell, Edwina and Andrew Schaap (2014) 'The Aboriginal Tent Embassy and Australian citizenship', in Engin F. Isin and Peter Nyers (eds), *Routledge Handbook of Global Citizenship Studies*, Routledge, 568–80.

Human Development Index (2019) Revision UNDP.

Human Rights Watch (2019) 'Trading in Suffering: Detention, Exploitation and Abuse in Libya', *Human Rights Watch*, 23 December 2019.

Human Rights Watch (2020) 'China: Covid-19 Discrimination Against Africans: Forced Quarantines, Evictions, Refused Services in Guangzhou', *Human Rights Watch News*, 5 May 2020, available at: https://www.hrw.org/news /2020/05/05/china-covid-19-discrimination-against-africans (accessed 10 September 2021).

Hume, Tim (2020) 'Corona Virus Is Giving Europe's Far Right The Perfect Excuse to Scapegoat Refugees', *Vice News*, 19 March 2020.

Ibrahim, Yasmin (2018) 'The Unsacred and the Spectacularized: Alan Kurdi and the Migrant Body', *Social Media + Society*, October–December 2018.

ICMC (2018) 'Peter Sutherland, In Memoriam', *ICMC website*, 8 January 2018, available at: https://www.icmc.net/2018/01/08/peter-sutherland-in -memoriam/# (accessed 31 July 2021).

ILO (n.d.) 'Reinforcing Ties: Enhancing Contributions from Bangladeshi Diaspora Members', International Labour Organisation and Government of Bangladesh.

ILO (1919) R002 – Reciprocity of Treatment Recommendation, 1919 (No.2), available at Information System on International Labour Standards: https:// www.ilo.org/dyn/normlex/en/f?p=1000:12100:1889755223957::NO::P12100 _SHOW_TEXT:Y (accessed 1 August 2021).

ILO (1956) 'Report of the Committee on the Extent of the Freedom of Employers' and Workers' Organisations', *International Labour Office Official Bulletin* xxxix: 9.

Inikori, Joseph E. (2003) 'The Struggle against the Transatlantic Slave Trade: The Role of the State', in Sylviane A. Diouf (ed.), *Fighting the Slave Trade: West African Strategies*, Ohio University Press.

International Organization for Migration (2010) Bangladesh Household Remittance Survey 2009.

IOM (2013) *World Migration Report 2013: Migrant Well-Being and Development*, IOM.

Isalska, Anita (2015) 'How to Plan a Trip to Malaysia's Cameron Highlands', *Lonely Planet online*, 18 December 2015.

Isin, Engin (2008) 'Theorizing Acts of Citizenship', in E. Isin and G. Nielsen (eds), *Acts of Citizenship*, Zed Books, 15–43.

Jalal, Ayesha (1985) *The Sole Spokesman: Jinnah, The Muslim League and the Demand for Pakistan*, Cambridge University Press.

Johnson, Heather L. (2015) 'These Fine Lines: Locting Noncitizenship in Polititical Protest in Europe', *Citizenship Studies* 19(8): 951–65.

Kaldor, Mary (2002) 'The Ideas of 1989: The Origins of the Concept of Global Civil Society', in Richard Falk, R. B. J. Walker and Lester Ruiz (eds), *Reframing the International: Law, Culture, Politics*, Routledge, 70–82.

Kaldor, Mary (2003) 'Civil Society and Accountability', *Journal of Human Development* 4(1): 5–27.

Kaldor, Mary (2003) 'The Idea of Global Civil Society', *International Affairs* 79(3): 583–93.

Kasozi, Keneth Iceland et al. (2020) 'Misconceptions on COVID-19 Risk Among Ugandan Men: Results From a Rapid Exploratory Survey, April 2020', *Frontiers in Public Health* 8(416): 1–10.

Kaur, Amarjit (2012) 'Labour Brokers in Migration: Understanding Historical and Contemporary Transnational Migraiton Regimes in Malaya/Mayalsia', *IRSH* 57: 225–52.

Kawashima, Tomoyuki (2021) 'English use by the Heads of State at the United Nations General Assembly', *English Today* 37(2): 92–114.

Keane, David (2004) 'The Environmental Causes and Consequences of Migration: A Search for the Meaning of "Environmental Refugees"', *Georgetown International Environmental Law Review* 16(2): 209–24.

Kerwin, Donald (2020) 'International Migration and Work: Charting an Ethical Approach to the Future', *Journal on Migration and Human Security* 8(2): 111–33.

Kerwin, Donald, Daniela Alulema, Michael Nicholson and Robert Warren (2020) *Statelessness in the United States: A Study to Estimate and Profile the US Stateless Population*, CMS Report, January, Center for Migration Studies, New York.

Khan, Adnan R. (2015) 'Alan Kurdi's Father on His Family Tragedy: "I should have died with them"', *The Guardian*, 22 December 2015.

Khan, Izhar (2007) 'Academic Apartheid by the Back Door', *The Lancet* 369(9560): 463.

Khan, Yasmin (2007) *The Great Partition: The Making of India and Pakistan*, Yale University Press.

Khosravi, Shahram (2010) *'Illegal' Traveller: An Auto-Ethnography of Borders*, Palgrave.

Kihato, Caroline Wanjiku (2018) 'The "Containment Compact": The EU Migration "Crisis" and African Complicity in Migration Management', South African Institute of International Affairs Occassional Paper 288, September 2018.

Kim, Terri (2011) 'Globalization and Higher Education in South Korea – Towards Ethnocentric Internationalization or Global Commercialization of Higher Education?' in R. King, S. Marginson and R. Naidoo (eds), *Handbook of Globalization and Higher Education*, Edward Elgar Publishing Ltd., 286–305.

Kim, Terri (2017) 'Academic Mobility, Transnational Identity Capital, and Stratification under Conditions of Academic Capitalism', *Higher Education* 73: 981–97.

Kingston, Lindsey (2013) '"A Forgotten Human Rights Crisis": Statelessness and Issue Emergence', *Human Rights Review* 14(2): 73–87.

Kingston, Lindsey (2019) 'Conceptualizing Statelessness as a Human Rights Challenge: Framing, Visual Representation, and (Partial) Issue Emergence', *Journal of Human Rights Practice* 11(1): 52–72.

Kingston, Lindsey (2019) *Fully Human: Personhood, Citizenship, and Rights*, Oxford University Press.

Klabbers, Jan (2019) 'Notes on the Ideology of International Organizations Law: The International Organization for Migration, State-Making, and the Market for Migration', *Leiden Journal of International Law* 32: 383–400.

Klausser, Nicolas (2016) 'Les associations de défense du droit des étrangers, des lanceurs d'alerte?', *La Revue des droits de l'homme* 10: 1–10.

Klein Solomon, Michele and Suzanne Sheldon (2018) 'The Global Compact for Migration: From the Sustainable Development Goals to a Comprehensive Agreement on Safe, Orderly and Regular Migration', *International Journal of Refugee Law* 30(4): 584–90.

Koch, Susanne (2020) '"The Local Consultant Will Not Be Credible": How Epistemic Injustice is Experienced and Practised in Development Aid', *Social Epistemology* 34(5): 478–89.

Kocka, Jürgen (2004) 'Civil Society from a Historical Perspective', *European Review* 12(1): 65–79.

Kockelman, Paul (2007) 'Agency: The Relation between Meaning, Power, and Knowledge', *Current Anthropology* 48(3): 375–401.

Koslowski, Rey (2000) *Migrants and Citizens*, Cornell University Press.

Kunz, Rahel, Sandra Lavenex and Marion Panizzon (eds) (2012) *Multilayered Migration Governance: The Promise of Partnership*, Routledge.

Kushner, A. R. (1999) 'Kosovo and the Refugee Crisis, 1999: The Search for Patterns Amidst the Prejudice', *Patterns of Prejudice* 33(3): 73–86.

Kyris, George (2022) 'State Recognition and Dynamic Sovereignty', *European Journal of International Relations* 28(2): 287–311.

Lancaster, James (2019) 'Access Denied: Focus on Delegate Visa Issues', *AMI Magazine*, available at: https://amimagazine.global/features/delegate-visa-issues-access-denied/ (accessed 27 November 2020).

Landis Mackellar, F. (2020) 'COVID-19: Demography, Economics, Migration and the Way Forward', *Migration Policy Practice* 10(2): 8–14.

Landler, Mark and Rick Gladstone (2014) 'U.S. Says Iran's Pick for U.N. Envoy Won't Get a Visa', *New York Times*, 11 April 2014.

Lantos, Tom (2002) 'The Durban Debacle: An Insider's View of the UN World Conference Against Racism', *The Fletcher Forum on World Affairs* 26(1): 31–52.

Laurens, Sylvain (2008) '<<1974>> et la fermeture des frontièrs: Analyse critique d'une décision érigée en turning-point', *Politix* 2008/2(82): 69–94.

Lavenex, Sandra and Nicola Piper (2022) 'Regions in Global Migration Governance', *Journal of Ethnic and Migration Studies* 48(12): 2837–54.

Le Breton, Jean-Marie (2004) 'Réflexions Anglophiles Sur La Géopolitique De L'Anglais', *La Découverte: Hérodote* 115: 11–23.

Lebon-Mcgregor, Elaine and Nicholas R. Micinski (2021) 'The Changing Landscape of Multilateral Financing and Global Migration Governance', in Tesseltje de Lange, Willem Maas and Annette Schrauwen (eds), *Money Matters in Migration: Policy, Participation, and Citizenship*, Cambridge University Press, 19–37.

Lee, Christina (2018) 'Why Visa Privilege is a Press Freedom Issue', *Hostwriter*, 30 October 2018.

Lee, Harper (2010) *To Kill a Mockingbird*, Arrow Books.

Lee, Jean N., Mahreen Mahmud, Jonathan Morduch, Saravana Ravindran and Abu S. Shonchoy (2021) 'Migration, Externalities, and the Diffusion of COVID-19 in South Asia', *Journal of Public Economics* 193: 104312.

Lefebvre, Henri (1991) *The Production of Space*, Blackwell (trans. Donald Nicholson-Smith).

Lem, Winnie (2020) 'Notes on Militant Populism in Contemporary France: Contextualizing the Gilets Jaunes', *Dialectical Anthropology* 44: 397–413.

Lemay, Marie-Pier (2020) 'Erreur de diagnostic: Préférences adaptives et impérialisme', *Philosophiques* 47(1): 139–64.

Lepp, Annalee (2016) 'Eni Lestari in Conversation with Annalee Lepp', *Migration, Mobility, and Displacement* 2(1): 55–66.

Lewis, Becca (2020) 'All of YouTube, Not Just the Algorithm, is a Far-Right Propaganda Machine', *Medium*, 8 January 2020.

Libal, Kathryn, Scott Harding, Marciana Popescu, S. Megan Berthold and Grace Felten (2021) 'Human Rights of Forced Migrants During the COVID-19 Pandemic: An Opportunity for Moblization and Solidarity', *Journal of Human Rights and Social Work* 6: 148–60.

'Locksley Hall' by Alfred, Lord Tennyson and published in 1842.

Long, Katy (2013) 'When Refugees Stopped being Migrants: Movement, Labour and Humanitarian Protection', *Migration Studies* 1(1): 4–26.

Lu, Catherine (2011) 'Colonialism as Structural Injustice: Historical Responsibility and Contemporary Redress', *The Journal of Political Philosophy* 19(3): 261–81.

Lu, Catherine (2017) *Justice and Reconciliation in World Politics*, Cambridge University Press.

Lynch, Colum (2011) 'TurtleLeaks: No Visa, No Entry! How the U.S. Bars Diplos from the U.N.', *Foreign Policy*, 4 May 2011.

Maâ, Anissa (2020) 'Manufacturing Collaboration in the Deportation Field: Intermediation and the Institutionalization of the International Organisation for Migration's "voluntary return" Programmes in Morocco', *The Journal of North African Studies* 26(5): 932–53.

MacDougald, Park and Jason Willick (2017) 'The Man Who Invented Identity Politics for the New Right', *New York Magazine*, 30 April 2017, available at: https://nymag.com/intelligencer/2017/04/steve-sailer-invented-identity -politics-for-the-alt-right.html (accessed 11 January 2022).

Mafu, Lucas (2019) 'The Libyan/Trans-Mediterranean Slave Trade, the African Union, and the Failure of Human Morality', *Sage Open*, January–March 2019, 1–10.

Mahmood, Saba (2005) *Politics of Piety: The Islamic Revival and the Feminist Subject*, Princeton University Press.

Mahmud, Tayyab (1997) 'Migration, Identity and the Colonial Encounter', *Oregon Law Review* 73: 633–90.

Mainwaring, Cetta (2016) 'Migrant Agency: Negotiating Borders and Migration Controls', *Migration Studies* 4(3): 289–308.

Maiyegun, Olawale (2019) 'Role of Regional Consultative Processes in the Lead Up to the Negotiations of Global Compact on Migration: The Case of Africa', *International Migration* 57(6): 258–72.

Maja-Pearce, Adewale (2020) 'Rich Man's Disease', *London Review of Books Blog*, 31 March 2020, available at: https://www.lrb.co.uk/blog/2020/march/rich-man-s-disease (accessed 23 June 2020).

Malkki, Liisa H. (1996) 'Speechless Emissaries: Refugees, Humanitarianism, and Dehistoricisation', *Cultural Anthropology* 11(3): 377–404.

Maly, Ico (2019) 'Algorithmic Populism and Algorithmic Activism', *Diggit Magazine*, 26 November 2019.

Mann, Itamar (2016) *Humanity at Sea: Maritime Migration and the Foundations of International Law*, Cambridge University Press.

Manto, Saadat Hasan (2008) 'Shyam: Krishna's Flute', in Khalid Hasan (ed. and trans.) *Bitter Fruit: The Very Best of Saadat Hasan Manto'*, Penguin, 485–502.

Martin, Philip and Manolo Abella (2009) 'Migration and Development: The Elusive Link at the GFMD', *The International Migration Review* 43(2): 431–9.

Martin, Susan and Rola Abimourched (2009) 'Migrant Rights: International Law and National Action', *International Migration* 47(5): 115–38.

Matloff-Nieves, Susan, Dana Fusco, Joy Connolly and Monami Maulik (2015) 'Democratizing Urban Spaces A Social Justice Approach to Youth Work', in Michael Heathfield and Dana Fusco (eds), *Youth and Inequality in Education: Global Actions in Youth Work*, Routledge.

Mau, Steffen, Heike Brabandt, Lena Laube and Christof Roos (2012) *Liberal States and the Freedom of Movement: Selective Borders, Unequal Mobility*, Palgrave.

Mau, Steffen, Fabian Gülzau, Lena Laube and Natascha Zaun (2015) 'The Global Mobility Divide: How Visa Policies Have Evolved over Time', *Journal of Ethnic and Migration Studies* 41(8): 1192–213.

Maulik, Monami (2011) 'Our Moment Is for the Long Haul: Ten Years of DRUM's Community Organizing by Working-Class South Asian Migrants', *Race/Ethnicity: Multidisciplinary Global Contexts* 4(3): 455–67.

Mazrui, Alamin (1993) 'Language and the Quest for Liberation in Africa: The Legacy of Frantz Fanon', *Third World Quarterly* 14(2): 351–63.

McEntee-Atalianis, Lisa J. (2017) '"Leave no one behind": Linguistic and Digital Barriers to the Dissemination and Implementation of the United Nations Sustainable Development Agenda', *Language Problems and Language Planning* 41(3): 217–44.

McGregor, Elaine (2017) 'Movement: A Global Civil Society Report on Progress and Impact on Migrants' Rights and Development: through Year 3 of Civil Society's 5-year 8-point Plan of Action', International Catholic Migration Commission Europe.

McGregor-Lebon, Elaine (2020) *International Organizations and Global Migration Governance*, Doctoral Thesis, Maastricht University.

McLaughlin, Carly (2017) '"They don't look like children": Child Asylum-Seekers, the Dubs Amendment and the Politics of Childhood', *Journal of Ethnic and Migration Studies* 44(11): 1757–73.

McNevin, Anne (2011) *Contesting Citizenship: Irregular Migrants and the New Frontiers of the Political*, Columbia University Press.

Médecins Sans Frontièrs (2021) 'Constructing Crisis at Europe's Borders', MSF.

Medina, José (2011) 'The Relevance of Credibility Excess in a Proportional View of Epistemic Injustice: Differential Epistemic Authority and the Social Imaginary', *Social Epistemology* 25(1): 15–35.

Meixler, Eli (2018) 'Journalism Is Under Threat.' Inside a Bangladeshi Journalist's Dangerous Journey From Photographer to Prisoner', *Time*, 11 December 2018, available at: https://time.com/5475494/shahidul-alam-bangladesh-journalist-person-of-the-year-2018/ (accessed 8 August 2022).

Migrant Forum in Asia (2009) 'Mobilizing Migrant Community and Civil Society Voices for the Second Global Forum on Migration and Development (GFMD): The Migrant Forum in Asia Experience'. Migrant Forum in Asia Report.

Miller, Vincent (2015) 'Phatic Culture and the Status Quo: Reconsidering the Purpose of Social Media Activism', *Convergence: The International Journal of Research into New Media Technologies* 23(3): 251–69.

Mills, Charles (2015) 'Unwriting and Unwhitening the World', in Alexander Anievas, Nivi Manchanda and Robbie Shilliam (eds), *Race and Racism in International Relations: Confronting the Global Colour Line*, Routledge, 202–14.

MIO (2019) 'Africa's Youth: Jobs or Migration?', Mo Ibrahim Foundation Report.

Miranda, Lin-Manuel (2015) 'The Room Where It Happens', song from *Hamilton*.

Mlambo, Victor H (2020) 'Consolidating Rgional Integration Through a Free Movement Protocol: The Quest for Collective Development in the SADC', *African Journal of Governance and Development* 9(2): 455–71.

Mohammed, Marwan (2015) 'La transfersalité politique de l'islamophobie: Analyse de quelques ressorts historiques et idéologiques', *Confluences Méditerranée* 2015/4(95): 131–42.

Moore, Will H. and Stephen M. Shellman (2006) 'Refugee or Internally Displaced Person?: To Where Should One Flee?', *Comparative Political Studies* 39(5): 599–622.

Morley, Louise, Nafsika Alexiadou, Stela Garaz, José González-Monteagudo and Marius Taba (2018) 'Internationalisation and Migrant Academics: The Hidden Narratives of Mobility', *Higher Education* 76: 537–54.

Mouthaan, Melissa (2021) 'Old Wine in New Bottles? The European Union's Organizational Response to Reforming the EU-African Migration Cooperation', *Journal of Common Market Studies* 59(5): 1177–84.

Movsisyan, Ani, Jacob Burns, Renke Biallas, Michaela Coenen, Karin Geffert, Olaf Horstick, Irma Klerings, Lisa Maria Pfadenhauer, Peter von Philipsborn,

Kerstin Sell, Brigitte Strahwald, Jan M. Stratil, Stephan Voss and Eva Rehfuess (2021) 'Travel-Related Control Measures to Contain the COVID-19 Pandemic: An Evidence Map', *British Medical Journal Open* 11: e041619.

Mowbray, Jacqueline (2010) 'Language in the UN and EU: Linguistic Diversity as a Challenge for Multilateralism', *New Zealand Journal of Public and International Law* 8(1): 91–116.

Mowbray, Jacqueline (2012) *Linguistic Justice: International Law and Policy*, Oxford University Press.

Muhammad, Patricia M. (2004) 'The Trans-Atlantic Slave Trade: A Forgotten Crime Against Humanity as Defined by International Law', *American University International Law Review* 19: 883–948.

Mukharji, Projit Bihari (2015) 'Technospatial Imaginaries: Masud Rana and the Vernacularization of Popular Cold War Geopolitics in East Pakistan, 1966–1971', *History and Technology* 31(3): 324–40.

Munger, Kevin and Joseph Phillips (2022) 'Right-Wing YouTube: A Supply and Demand Perspective', *The International Journal of Press/Politics* 27(1): 186–219.

Muray, Philippe (2000) 'Citoyen: De la citoyennophilie', *Le Débat* 2000/5(112): 53–7.

Mwaura, Waihiga (2020) 'Letter from Africa: The Spread of Coronavirus Prejudice in Kenya', *BBC News*, 9 March 2020.

Myers, Norman (1997) 'Environmental Refugees', *Population and Environment* 19(2): 167–82.

Nafziger, James and Barry Bartel (1991) 'The Migrant Workers Convention: Its Place in Human Rights Law', *International Migration Review* 25(4): 771–99.

Ndovulu, Finex (2015) 'Ignored Lingualism: Another Resource for Overcoming the Monlingual Mindest in Language Education', *Australian Journal of Linguistics* 35(4): 398–414.

Ndhlovu, Finex and Leketi Makalela (2021) *Decolonising Multilingualism in Africa: Recentering Silenced Voices from the Global South*, Multilingual Matters.

Neumayer, Eric (2006) 'Unequal Access to Foreign Spaces: How states Use Visa Restrictions to Regulate Mobility in a Globalized World', *The Transactions of the Institute of British Geographers* 31(1): 72–84.

Newkirk, Pamela (2002) *Within the Veil: Black Journalists, White Media*, New York University Press.

Newland, Kathleen (2005) *The Governance of International Migration: Mechanisms, Processes and Institutions*, Paper prepared for the Policy Analysis and Research programme of the Global Commission on International Migration, September 2005.

Newland, Kathleen (2010) 'The Governance of International Migration: Mechanisms, Processes, and Institutions', *Global Governance* 16(3): 331–43.

Newland, Kathleen (2018) 'The Global Compact for Safe, Orderly and Regular Migration: An Unlikely Achievement', *International Journal of Refugee Law* 30(4): 657–60.

Newland, Kathleen (2018) 'An Overheated Narrative Unanswered: How the Global Compact for Migration Became Controversial', *Migration Policy Institute blog*, December 2018, available at: https://www.migrationpolicy .org/news/overheated-narrative-unanswered-how-global-compact-became -controversial (accessed 19 September 2022).

Newland, Kathleen (2020) 'Will International Migration Governance Survive the COVID-19 Pandemic?', *Policy Brief*, Migration Policy Institute.

Norris, James J. (1958) 'The International Catholic Migration Commission', *Catholic Lawyer* 4(Spring): 118–22.

Nuti, Alasia (2019) *Injustice and the Reproduction of History: Structural Inequalities, Gender and Redress*, Cambridge University Press.

O'Connell, Rachel (2013) 'Migrant Life: An Interview with Colin Rajah', *The Politic,* 12 July 2013.

O'Connell Davidson, Julia (2012) 'Absolving the State: The Trafficking-Slavery Metaphor', *Global Dialogue* 14(2): 31–41.

Ogu, Patricia Ihuoma (2016) 'Africa's Irregular Migration to Europe: A Re-enactment of the Transatlantic Slave Trade', *Journal of Global Research in Education and Social Science* 10(2): 49–69.

Okunade, Samuel Kehinde and Olusola Ogunnubi (2019) 'The African Union Protocol on Free Movement: A Panacea to End Border Porosity?', *Journal of African Union Studies* 8(1): 73–91.

Okunade, Samuel Kehinde and Olusola Ogunnubi (2021?) 'A "Schengen" Agreement in Africa? African Agency and the ECOWAS Protocol on Free Movement', *Journal of Borderlands Studies* 36(1): 119–37.

Olusegun Ikuteyijo, Lanre (2020) 'Irregular Migration as Survival Strategy: Narratives from Youth in Urban Nigeria', in Mora L. McLean (ed.), *West African Youth Challenges and Opportunity Pathways*, Palgrave Macmillan, 53–77.

Oqubay, Ankebe (2020) 'UK Visa System for African Visitors Requires Urgent Reform', *New African*, 12 February 2020.

Oryem, Robin (2020) 'Xenophobia and Behavioural Responses to COVID-19 in Uganda', *London School of Economics blog*, 1 May 2020, available at: https:// blogs.lse.ac.uk/africaatlse/2020/05/01/xenophobia-racism-ebola-behavioural -change-covid19-uganda/

Ostoyich, Kevin (2009) 'Emigration, Nationalism and Church Identity in Europe: The Legacy of the German St Raphael Society in International Catholic Migration Assistance', *International Journal for the Study of the Christian Church* 9(3): 240–54.

Osuagwu, Uchechukwu L., Chundung A. Minder, Dipesh Bhattarai, Khathutshelo Percy Mashige, Richard Oloruntoba, Emmanuel Kwasi Abu, Bernadine Ekpenyong, Timothy G, Chikasirimobi, Piwuna Christopher Goson, Godwin O. Ovenseri-Ogbomo, Raymond Langsi, Deborah Donald Charwe, Tanko Ishaya, Obinna Nwaeze and Kingsley Emwinyore Agho (2020) 'Misinformation About COVID-19 in Sub-Saharan Africa: Evidence from a Cross-Sectional Survey', *Health Security* 19: 1.

Oustinoff, Michaël (2008) 'Le tout-à-l'anglais est-il inévitable?', *HERMÈS, La Revue* 51: 79–84.

Pai, Hsiao-Hung (2018) *Bordered Lives: How Europe Fails Refugees and Migrants*, New Internationalist.

Patrick, Donna (2010) 'Language Dominance and Minorization', in Jürgen Jaspers, Jan-Ola Östman and Jef Verschueren (eds), *Society and Language Use*, John Benjamins Publishing Company.

Pécoud, Antoine (2018) 'What do we know about the International Organization for Migration?' *Journal of Ethnic and Migration Studies* 44(10): 1621–38.

Pécoud, Antoine and Paul de Guchteneire (2006) 'Migration, Human Rights and the United Nations: An Investigation into the Obstacles to the UN Convention on Migrant Workers' Rights', *Windsor Yearbook of Access to Justice* 24: 241–66.

Pennycook, Alastair (1994) *Cultural Politics of English as an International Language*, Longman.

Pérez Firmat, Gustavo (1995) *Bilingual Blues*, Bilingual Press.

Pérez Quiles, Julián Javier (2018) 'La Agencia Europea de Fronteras y Guardacostas, Frontex', *Revista Jurídica Región de Murcia* 52: 143–56.

Perl, Gerhild and Sabine Strasser (2018) 'Transnational Moralities: The Politics of Ir/Responsibility of and against the EU Border Regime', *Identities* 25(5): 507–23.

Pew Research Center (2018) 'At Least a Million Sub-Saharan Africans Moved to Europe Since 2010', available at: https://www.pewresearch.org/global/2018 /03/22/at-least-a-million-sub-saharan-africans-moved-to-europe-since -2010/

Pheng Pha, Kong (2020) 'Two Hate Notes: Deportations, COVID-19, and Xenophobia against Hmong Americans in the Midwest', *Journal of Asian American Studies* 23(3): 335–9.

Phillipson, Robert (1992) *Linguistic Imperialism*, Oxford University Press.

Phillipson, Robert (1999) 'International Languages and International Human Rights', in Miklós Kontra, Robert Phillipson, Tove Skuntnabb-Kangas and Tibor Várdy (eds), *Language: A Right and a Resource*, Central European University Press, Budapest.

Phillipson, Robert and Tove Skutnabb-Kangas (1996) 'English Only Worldwide or Language Ecology?', *TESOL Quarterly* 30(3): 429–53.

Pike, Lisa L. (1990) 'The Arafat visa Denial: Successful Diplomatic Persuasion, but a Violation of the Headquarters Agreement Treaty', *Suffolk Transnational Law Journal* 13: 634–55.

Piper, Nicola (2015) 'Democratising Migration from the Bottom Up: The Rise of the Global Migrant Rights Movement', *Globalizations* 12(5): 788–802.

Piper, Nicola and Stefan Rother (2012) 'Let's Argue about Migration: Advancing a Right(s) Discourse via Communicative Opportunities', *Third World Quarterly* 33(9): 1735–50.

Quijano, Aníbal (1992) 'Colonialidad y Modernidad/Racionalidad', *Perú Indígena* 13(29): 11–20.

Quijano, Aníbal (2000) 'Coloniality of Power and Eurocentrism in Latin America', *International Sociology* 15(2): 215–32.

Quijano, Aníbal (2007) 'Coloniality and Modernity/Rationality', *Cultural Studies* 21(2–3): 168–78 (trans. Sonia Therborn).

Rabbani, M. M. Golam, Matthew Cotton and Richard Friend (2022) 'Climate Change and Non-migration – Exploring the Role of Place Relations in Rural and Coastal Bangladesh', *Population and Environment* 44: 99–122.

Rahman, Jyoti (2019) 'A Bangladeshi Superhero', *Dhaka Tribune*, 21 January 2019, available at: https://www.dhakatribune.com/opinion/op-ed/2019/01/21/a-bangladeshi-superhero (accessed 23 July 2021).

Rahman, Mahmud (2008) 'Pulp Fiction in Bangladesh', *World Literature Today* 82(3): 39–42.

Rajan, S. Irudaya (2020) 'Migrants at a Crossroads: COVID-19 and Challenges to Migration', *Migration and Development* 9(3): 323–30.

Rajan, S. Irudaya, P. Sivakumar and Aditya Srinivasan (2020) 'The COVID-19 Pandemic and Internal Labour Migration in India: A "Crisis of Mobility"', *The Indian Journal of Labour Economics* 63: 1021–39.

Raley, Rita (2003) 'Machine Translation and Global English', *The Yale Journal of Criticism* 16(2): 291–313.

Ramati, Ido and Amit Pinchevski (2018) 'Uniform Multilingualism: A Media Genealogy of Google Translate', *New Media & Society* 20(7): 2550–65.

Ramsland, John (2004) 'Bringing up Harry Penrith: Injustice and Becoming Burnum Burnum: The Formative Years of a Child of the StolenGeneration', *Education Research and Perspectives* 31(2): 94–106.

Rasche, Andreas (2009) '"A Necessary Supplement": What the United Nations Global Compact Is and Is Not', *Business and Society* 48(4): 511–537.

Rasche, Andreas and Georg Kell (2010) (eds) *The United Nations Global Compact: Achievements, Trends and Challenges*, Cambridge University Press.

Redden, Elizabeth (2019) 'Conference Visa Woes . . . in Canada', *Inside Higher Ed*, available at: https://www.insidehighered.com/news/2019/03/28/scholars-complain-visa-problems-ahead-international-conference-canada (accessed 27 November 2020).

Reichert, Elisabeth (1996) '"Keep on Moving Forward": NGO Forum on Women, Beijing, China', *Social Development Issues* 18(1): 89–97.

Reid, Andrew (2019) 'Buses and Breaking Point: Freedom of Expression and the "Brexit" Campaign', *Ethical Theory and Moral Practice* 22: 623–37.

Reid, Andrew (2019) 'What Facts Should be Treated as "Fixed" in Public Justification?', *Social Epistemology* 33(6): 491–502.

Reidy, Eric (2020) 'The COVID-19 Excuse? How Migration Policies are Hardening around the Globe', *The New Humanitarian*, 17 April 2020.

Rejai, Mostafa and Cynthia H. Enloe (1969) 'Nation-States and State-Nations', *International Studies Quarterly* 13(2): 140–58.

Reny, Tyler T. and Matt A. Barreto (2022) 'Xenophobia in the Time of Pandemic: Othering, Anti-Asian Attitudes, and COVID-19', *Politics, Groups, and Identities* 10(2): 209–32.

Riaz, Ali (2016) *Bangladesh: A Political History Since Independence*, I. B. Tauris.

Rickford, John and Sharese King (2016) 'Language and Linguistics on Trial: Hearing Rachel Jeantel (and other Vernacular Speakers) in the Court Room and Beyond', *Language* 92(4): 948–88.

Ridde, Valéry (2008) 'Defying Boundaries: Globalization, Bureaucracy and Academic Exchange', *Promotion and Education* 15(1): 3–4.

Robinson, Sean (1994) 'The Aboriginal Embassy: An Account of the Protests of 1972', *Aboriginal History* 18(1): 49–63.

Rone, Julia (2020) 'Far Right Alternative News Media as "indignation mobilization mechanisms": How the Far Right Opposed the Global Compact for Migration', *Information, Communication and Society* 25(9): 1333–50.

Roose, Kevin (2019) 'The Making of a YouTube Radical', *New York Times*, 8 June 2019.

Rosenfeld, Esther (1995) 'Fatal Lessons: United States Immigration Law during the Holocaust', *University of California Davis Journal of International Law and Policy* 1(2): 249–66.

Rother, Stefan (2009) '"Inside-Outside" or "Outsiders by choice"? Civil Society Strategies towards the 2nd Global Forum on Migration and Development (GFMD) in Manila', *ASIEN* 111: 95–107.

Rother, Stefan (2013) 'Civil Society and Competing Visions of Global Migration Governance from Below', in Martin Geiger and Antoine Pécoud (eds), *Disciplining the Transnational Mobility of People*. Palgrave Macmillan.

Rother, Stefan (2017) 'Indonesian Migrant Domestic Workers in Transnational Political Spaces: Agency, Gender Roles and Social Class Formation', *Journal of Ethnic and Migration Studies* 43(6): 956–73.

Rother, Stefan (2018) 'Angry Birds of Passage – Migrant Rights Networks and Counter-Hegemonic Resistance to Global Migration Discourses', *Globalizations* 15(6): 854–69.

Rother, Stefan (2019) 'The Global Forum on Migration and Development as a Venue of State Socialisation: Stepping Stone for Multi-level Migration Governance?', *Journal of Ethnic and Migration Studies* 45(8): 1258–74.

Rother, Stefan (2022) *Global Migration Governance from Below: Actors, Spaces, Discourses*, Palgrave.

Rother, Stefan (2022) 'Global Migration Governance from below in Times of COVID-19 and "Zoomification": Civil Society in "invited" and "invented" spaces', *Comparative Migration Studies* 10(1): 1–21.

Rother, Stefan and Elias Steinhilper (2019) 'Tokens or Stakeholders in Global Migration Governance? The Role of Affected Communities and Civil Society in the Global compacts on Migration and Refugees', *International Migration* 57(6): 243–57.

Rowlands, Lyndal (2017) 'Travel Restrictions Cast Shadow on UN Women's Meeting', *Inter Press Service News Agency*, 16 March 2017.

Ryan, Hannah and Katie Tonkiss (2022) 'Loners, Criminals, Mothers: The Gendered Misrecognition of Refugees in the British Tabloid News Media', *Sociological Research*, Online Early View.

Said, Edward W. (2003) *Orientalism*, Penguin Random House (first published 1978).

Sailer, Steve (2006) 'Americans First', *The American Conservative*, 13 February 2006, available at: https://www.theamericanconservative.com/articles/americans-first/ (accessed 22 July 2021).

Sailer, Steve (2009) *America's Half-Blood Prince: Obama's "Story of Race and Inheritance"*, VDare Foundation.

Sajjad, Tazreena (2018) 'What's in a Name? "Refugees", "Migrants" and the Politics of Labelling', *Race and Class* 60(2): 40–62.

Sartre, Jean-Paul (1970) *L'existentialisme est un humanisme*, Les Éditions Nagel (first published 1946).

Scheuerman, William E (2018) *Civil Disobedience*, Polity.

Schierup, Carl-Ulrik, Branka Likic-Brboric, Raúl Delgado Wise and Gülay Toksöz (eds) (2019) *Migration, Civil Society and Global Governance*, Routledge.

Scholte, Jan Aart (2004) 'Civil Society and Democratically Accountable Global Governance', *Government and Opposition* 39(2): 211–33.

Schultz, James (2003) 'Sluggish Visa Approval Process Hamstrings Scientific Conferences', *Journal of the National Cancer Institute* 95(8): 579–80.

Seligman, Adam B. traces the re-emergence of the terminology of civil society particularly in the US: Adam B. Seligman (1995) *The Idea of Civil Society*, Princeton University Press.

Sen, Amartya (1977) 'Rational Fools: A Critique of the Behavioral Foundations of Economic Theory', *Philosophy and Public Affairs* 6(4): 317–44.

Sen, Amartya (2006) *Identity and Violence: The Illusion of Destiny*, Penguin.

Shachar, Ayelet (2009) *Birthright Lottery: Citizenship and Global Inequality*, Harvard University Press.

Shotwell, Lynn Frendt (1999) 'Temporary Worker Visa Policy: Meeting the Needs of the 21st Century', *Defense of the Alien* 22: 55–8.

Sigona, Nando (2012) '"I Have Too Much Baggage": The Impacts of Legal Status on the Social Worlds of Irregular Migrants', *Social Anthropology* 20(1): 50–65.

Sigona, Nando (2014) 'The Politics of Refugee Voices: Representations, Narratives, and Memories', in Elena Fiddian-Qasmiyeh, Gil Loescher, Katy Long and Nando Sigona (eds), *The Oxford Handbook of Refugee and Forced Migration Studies*, Oxford, 369–82.

Simon, Jonathan (2007) *Governing Through Crime: How the War on Crime Transformed American Democracy and Created a Culture of Fear*, Oxford University Press.

Simpson, Ruth and Rachel Morgan (2020) '"Gendering" Contamination: Physical, Social and Moral Taint in the Context of COVID-19', *Gender in Management* 35(7/8): 685–91.

Sinclaire, Kristine (2016) 'The Dead Boy and the Aftermath', Centre for Mellemøst Studies, Syddansk Universitet.

Singer, Peter (2009) *The Life You Can Save*, Penguin.

Singh, S. K., Vibhuti Patel, Aditi Chaudhary and Nandlal Mishra (2020) 'Reverse Migration of Labourers Amidst COVID-19', *Economic and Political Weekly* LV(32): 25–30.

Sivapriyan, E. T. B. (2020) 'COVID-19 is a Rich Man's Disease: Tamil Nadu CM', *Deccan Herald*, 16 April 2020, available at: https://www.deccanherald.com /national/covid-19-is-a-rich-man-s-disease-tamil-nadu-cm-826123.html (accessed 23 June 2020).

Slovic, Paul, Daniel Västfjäll, Arvid Erlandsson and Robin Gregory (2017) 'Iconic Photographs and the Ebb and Flow of Empathetic Response to Humanitarian Disasters', *Proceedings of the National Academy of Sciences of the United States of America* 114(4): 640–4.

Smith, Evan and Marinella Marmo (2014) 'The Myth of Sovereignty: British Immigration Control in Policy and Practice in the Nineteen-Seventies', *Historical Research* 87: 344–69.

Sohlberg, Jacob, Peter Esaiasson and Johan Martinsson (2019) 'The Changing Political Impact of Compassion - Evoking Pictures: The Case of the Drowned Toddler Alan Kurdi', *Journal of Ethnic and Migration Studies* 45(13): 2275–88.

Solé, Robert (1988) 'Le journalisme et l'immigration (Entretien avec Jacqeline Costa-Lascoux)', *Revue Européenne des Migrations internationals* 1988: 157–66.

Somers, Harold (2003) 'Introduction', in Harold Somers (ed.), *Computers and Translation: A Translator's Guide*, John Benjamins Publishing Company.

Sontag, Susan (2003) *Regarding the Pain of Others*, Penguin.

Spanu, Maja (2020) 'The Hierarchical Society: The Politics of Self Determination and the Constitution of New States after 1919', *European Journal of International Relations* 26(2): 372–92.

Spini, Debora (2010) 'Civil Society and the Democratization of Global Public Space', in David Armstrong, Valeria Bello, Julie Gilson and Debora Spini (eds), *Civil Society and International Governance: The Role of Non-state Actors in Global and Regional Regulatory Frameworks*, Routledge.

Squire, Vicki (2017) 'Unauthorised Migration beyond Structure/Agency? Acts, Interventions, Effects', *Politics* 37(3): 254–72.

Squire, Vicki (2019) 'A Milestone Missed: The Global Compact on Migration and the Limits of Solidarity', *Global Affairs* 5(2): 155–62.

Squire, Vicki, A. Dimitriadi, N. Perkowski, M. Pisani, D. Stevens and N. Vaughan-Williams (2017) *Crossing the Mediterranean Sea by Boat: Mapping and Documenting Migratory Journeys and Experiences*, Final Project Report, University of Warwick, www.warwick.ac.uk/crossingthemed

St. John, Paige and Joel Rubin (2018) 'ICE held an American Man in Custody for 1,273 Days: He's not the Only One Who had to Prove His Citizenship', *Los Angeles Times*, 27 April 2018.

Staples, Kelly (2012) 'Statelessness and the Politics of Misrecognition', *Res Publica* 18: 93–106.

Staples, Kelly (2019) "'The Problem with Refugees": International Protection and the Limits to Solidarity', *International Politics* 56: 158–74.

Stoler, Ann Laura (2016) *Duress: Imperial Durabilities in Our Times*, Duke University Press.

Su, Zhaohui, Dean McDonnell, Junaid Ahmad, Ali Cheshmehzangi, Xiaoshan Li, Kylie Meyer, Yuyang Cai, Ling Yang and Yu-Tao Xiang (2020) 'Time to Stop the Use of "Wuhan Virus", "China Virus", or "Chinese Virus" Across the Scientific Community', *British Medical Journal Global Health* 5(9): 1–3.

Sutherland, Peter (2010) 'The Age of Mobility: Can We Make Migration Work for All?', *Global Policy*, February 2010.

Sutherland, Peter D. (2013) 'The International Migrants Bill of Rights: Why it Matters', *Georgetown Immigration Law Journal* 28: 269–71.

Teichler, Ulrich (2015) 'Academic Mobility and Migration: What We Know and What We Do Not Know', *European Review* 23: S6–S37.

Tharoor, Shashi (2016) *Inglorious Empire: What the British Did to India*, Penguin.

Theroux, Louis (1998) "Weird Christmas", Season 1, Episode 5, *Louis Theroux's Weird Weekends*, produced by BBC Bristol and the Independent Film Channel for the British Broadcasting Corporation BBC released 23 December 1998.

Thompson, Alvin O. (1976) 'Race and Colour Prejudices and the Origin of the Trans-Atlantic Slave Trade', *Caribbean Studies* 16(3/4): 29–59.

Tiktin, Miriam (2017) 'A World without Innocence', *American Ethnologist* 44(4): 577–90.

Tinker, Hugh (1977) *Race, Conflict and International Order: From Empire to United Nations*, MacMillan.

Tondo, Lorenzo (2020) 'Salvini Attacks Italy PM over Coronavirus and Links to Rescue Ship', *The Guardian*, 24 February 2020, available at: https://www.theguardian.com/world/2020/feb/24/salvini-attacks-italy-pm-over-coronavirus-and-links-to-rescue-ship (accessed 10 September 2021).

Tonkiss, Katherine (2018) 'The Narrative Assemblage of Civil Society Interventions into Refugee and Asylum Policy Debates in the UK', *Voluntary Sector Review* 9(2): 119–35.

Tonkiss, Katie and Luis Cabrera (2022) "'I Felt Like a Bird Without Wings": Incorporating the Study of Emotions into Grounded Normative Theory', *Contemporary Political Theory*, Early View, 1–22.

Traut, Carol Ann (1997) 'China and the 1995 United Nations Conference on Women', *Journal of Contemporary China* 6(16): 581–9.

Traynor, Ian (2010) 'EU Keen to Strike Deal with Muammar Gaddafi on Immiration', *The Guardian*, 1 September 2010.

Tshimba, David N. (2021) 'The Ghost of Racism in the Contemporary Global Compact on Refugees', *Journal of Refugee Studies*, feab103.

Tsourapas, Gerasimos (2017) 'Migration Diplomacy in the Global South: Cooperation, Coercion and Issue Linkage in Gaddafi's Libya', *Third World Quarterly* 10: 2367–85.

Tsuda, Yukio (1998) 'Critical Studies on the Dominance of English and the Implications for International Communication', *Japan Review* 10: 219–36.

Tunaboylu, Sevda and Jill Alpes (2017) 'The EU-Turkey Deal: What Happens to People Who Return to Turkey?', *Forced Migration Review* 54: 84–7.

Ul Haq, Mahbub (1976) *The Poverty Curtain.*

Ullah, AKM Ahsan (2013) 'Irregular Migrants, Human Rights and Securitization in Malaysia: An Analysis from a Policy Perspective', in Claudia Tazreiter and Siew Yean Tham (eds), *Globalization and Social Transformation in the Asia-Pacific*, Palgrave Macmillan, 178–88.

UN News, 'COVID-19: Agencies Temporarily Suspend Refugee Resettlement Travel', 17 March 2020.

UNDESA (2015) *Trends in International Migrant Stock: The 2015 Revision*, UNDESA, New York.

UNDP (n.d.) 'Comprehensive Disaster Management Programme Phase II', Project Factsheet United Nations Development Program Bangladesh.

UNDP (2020) 'The Next Frontier: Human Development and the Anthropocene: Briefing note for countries on the 2020 Human Development Report: Bangladesh', UNDP.

UNFPA (2004) *Meeting the Challenges of Migration: Progress since the ICPD*, UNFPA.

UNGA (2000) 'United Nations Millennium Declaration', General Assembly Resolution 55/2, 8 September 2000.

UNGA (2002) 'Strengthening of the United Nations: An Agenda for Further Change, Report of the Secretary-General', United Nations General Assembly Fifty-seventh session Item 53 on the provisional agenda, A/57/387.

UNHCR (2019) *Global Trends: Forced Displacement in 2018*, UNHCR.

UNHCR (2020) 'Beware Long-Term Damage to Human Rights and Refugee Rights from the Corona Virus Pandemic', *Press Release*, 22 April 2020.

United Nations General Assembly (2004) 'We the Peoples: Civil Society, the United Nations and Global Governance, Report of the Panel of Eminent Persons on United Nations-Civil Society Relations', A/58/817.

Valentino Bryant, Lauren (2020) 'The YouTube Algorithm and the Alt-Right Filter Bubble', *Open Information Science* 4(1): 85–90.

Valor Miró, Juan Daniel, Pau Baquero-Arnal, Jorge Civera, Carlos Turró and Alfons Juan (2016) 'Multilingual Videos for MOOCs and OER', *Educational Technology & Society* 21(2): 1–12.

van Seem, Joanne (2020) 'A Pandemic-Fueled Approach to Immigration in the United States and the Neighboring Region', *Migration Policy Practice* 10(2): 40–47.

Van Waas, Laura (2009) *Nationality Matters*, Intersentia Publishers.

Vega Macías, Daniel (2021) 'La pandemia del COVID-19 en el discurso antimigratorio y xenófobo en Europa y Estados Unidos', *Estudios fronterizos* 22: 1–22.

Vollmer, Maarja (2021) 'Being Excluded or Excluding Yourself?: Citizenship Choices Among the Stateless Youth in Estonia', in Tendayi Bloom and

Lindsey Kingston (eds), *Statelessness, Governance, and the Problem of Citizenship*, Manchester University Press, 181–94.

Vosyliūtė, Lina and Carmine Conte (2019) 'Crackdown on NGOs and Volunteers Helping Refugees and Other Migrants', Final Synthetic Report June 2019, Research Social Platform on Migration and Asylum.

wa Thiong'o, Ngũgĩ (1986) *Decolonising the Mind: The Politics of Language in African Literature*, Heinemann.

wa Thiong'o, Ngũgĩ (2005) *Decolonising the Mind: The Politics of Language in African Literature*, East African Educational Publishers Ltd, Nairobi (first published 1986).

Wahab, Andika (2020) 'The Outbreak of Covid-19 in Malaysia: Pushing Migrant Workers at the Margin', *Social Sciences and Humanities Open* 2: 100073.

Wari, Iddrisu (2016) '"You make a decision and you start your journey": Reflections of a Ghanaian Economic Migrant and Founder of the NGO, CEHDA', in Belachew Gebrewold and Tendayi Bloom (eds), *Understanding Migrant Decisions: From Sub-Saharan Africa to the Mediterranean Region*, Routledge, 194–218.

Waugh, David (1982) 'The ILO and Human Rights', *Comparative Labor Law* 5(2): 186–96.

Weaver, Matthew (2018) 'WHO Voices Alarm as Academics Denied Visas to Visit UK Conference', *The Guardian*, 9 October 2018.

Webber, Frances (2011) 'How Voluntary are Voluntary Returns?', *Race and Class* 53(4): 98–107.

Webber, Frances (2019) 'The Embedding of State Hostility: A Background Paper on the Windrush Scandal', Institute of Race Relations Briefing Paper No. 11.

Wee, Kellynn, Kudakwashe P. Vanyoro and Zaheera Jinnah (2018) 'Repoliticizing International Migration Narratives? Critical Reflections on the Civil Society Days of the Global Forum on Migration and Development', *Globalizations* 15(6): 785–808.

Weebers, Robert C. M. (2017) 'Tanah Rata and the Development of the Cameron Highlands, 1925–2030', *Journal of the Malaysian Branch of the Royal Asiatic Society* 90(312): 101–112.

Weissbrodt, David (2009) *The Human Rights of Non-Citizens*, Oxford University Press.

Wheeler, Nicholas J. (2001) 'Humanitarian Intervention After Kosovo: Emergent Norm, Moral Duty or the Coming Anarchy?', *International Affairs* 77(1): 113–28.

Whipple, Amy (2009) 'Revisiting the "Rivers of Blood" Controversy: Letters to Enoch Powell', *Journal of British Studies* 48(3): 717–35.

Whitman, Jim (2000) 'The Kosovo Refugee Crisis: NATO's Humanitarianism versus Human Rights', *The International Journal of Human Rights* 4(3–4): 164–83.

Whittaker, Elvi (1994) 'Public Discourse on Sacredness: The Transfer of Ayers Rock to Aboriginal Ownership', *American Ethnologist* 21(2): 310–34.

Wihtol de Wenden, Catherine (2002) 'Ouverture et fermeture de la France aux étrangers: Un siècle d'évolution', *Vingtième Siécle Revue d'Histoire* 1(73): 27–38.

Wilmer, Franke (1993) *The Indigenous Voice in World Politics*, Sage.

Wolff, Sarah (2014) 'The Politics of Negotiating EU Readmission Agreements: Insights from Morocco and Turkey', *European Journal of Migration and Law* 16(1): 69–95.

Wooding, Bridget (2021) 'Supra-National Jurisprudence: Necessary but Sufficient to Contest Statelessness in the Dominican Republic', in Tendayi Bloom and Lindsey Kingston (eds), *Statelessness, Governance, and the Problem of Citizenship*, Manchester University Press, 292–305.

World Health Organisation (2020) 'ApartTogether Survey: Preliminary Overview of Refugees and Migrants Self-Reported Impact of Covid-19', World Health Organisation.

Wright, Lindsay (2019) 'Giving a Voice to Migrant Workers in Malaysia', *Ethical Trading Initiative*, 17 July 2019, available at: https://www.ethicaltrade.org/blog/giving-voice-to-migrant-workers-malaysia

Yei-Mokuwa, Esther, Carolin Dieterle and Elizabeth Storer (2019) 'The UK's Self-Harming Scandal of Visa Rejections for Visiting Academics', *London School of Economics Africa at LSE blog*, 21 May 2019.

Yeo, Colin (2018) 'Briefing: What is the Hostile Environment, Where does it Come from, Who Does it Affect?', *Freemovement Briefing*, 1 May 2018.

Young, Ian (2018) 'Special Report: How Canadian Immigration Fraud Saw 860 rich Chinese Blacklisted', *South China Morning Post*, 1 September 2018.

Young, Iris Marion (1990) *Justice and the Politics of Difference*, Princeton University Press, Princeton.

Young, Iris Marion (2001) 'Equality of Whom? Social Groups and Judgements of Injustice', *The Journal of Political Philosophy* 9(1): 1–18.

Young, Iris Marion (2011) *Responsibility for Justice*, Oxford University Press, Oxford.

Young, Ros (1986) 'Report from Nairobi: The UN Decade for Women Forum', *Race and Class* 27(2): 67–71.

Zetter, Roger (2015) *Protection in Crisis: Forced Migration in a Global Era*, Migration Policy Institute, Transatlantic Council on Migration.

Zimmer, Katarina (2019) 'As Visa Difficulties Persist, Scientists Push for Change', *The Scientists*, available at: https://www.the-scientist.com/news-opinion/as-visa-difficulties-persist--scientists-push-for-change-66114.

# Index